# Robert E. Park

## ON SOCIAL CONTROL

## AND COLLECTIVE BEHAVIOR

# THE HERITAGE OF SOCIOLOGY

*A Series Edited by* Morris Janowitz

# Robert E. Park

# ON SOCIAL CONTROL AND

# COLLECTIVE BEHAVIOR

## Selected Papers

*Edited and with an Introduction by*

RALPH H. TURNER

PHOENIX BOOKS

THE UNIVERSITY OF CHICAGO PRESS

CHICAGO AND LONDON

*This book is also available in a clothbound edition from*
THE UNIVERSITY OF CHICAGO PRESS

THE UNIVERSITY OF CHICAGO PRESS, CHICAGO & LONDON
The University of Toronto Press, Toronto 5, Canada

## Acknowledgments

THE EDITOR owes a considerable debt to Herbert Blumer, Emory S. Bogardus, G. Franklin Edwards, Morris Janowitz, and Pauline V. Young, each of whom read an early version of the introductory essay and offered valuable suggestions. Each would still disagree with the editor's interpretations in certain respects. The late Ernest W. Burgess graciously answered questions about his collaboration with Robert Park.

The entire task of preparing this volume was facilitated by the prior work of Everett C. Hughes, Charles S. Johnson, Jutsuichi Masuoka, Robert Redfield, and Louis Wirth in assembling the comprehensive three volumes: *The Collected Papers of Robert Ezra Park,* published by the Free Press in 1950, 1952, and 1955.

# Contents

## IV. PERSON IN SOCIAL PROCESS

## V. COLLECTIVE BEHAVIOR

# *Introduction*

PROBABLY no other man has so deeply influenced the direction taken by American empirical sociology as Robert Ezra Park. His students, inspired by his teaching and impressed with the serious task of finding out what actually went on about them, carried out much of the early empirical research in sociology and established a pattern for the work of others. Perhaps it is because of Park's intense personal impact on his students that rather less attention has been devoted to the system of sociology that is conveyed in his own writings. In this brief essay we hope to recall attention to some of Park's own major ideas, selecting especially those which have applicability to current sociological preoccupations.

Like any seminal thinker, Park put forth some incompletely digested ideas, revised his thinking in the course of his intellectual career, and suffered from some of the limitations of the era in which he worked. To call attention to these features of his thought is not to detract from his stature. His was "an exceedingly vigorous, searching mind. His thought was continually roving around, ever on the alert to new leads and ever searching for new insights and perspectives."[1] Many of his characteristically dynamic ideas were rendered static in the hands of his followers. Renewed attention to Park's own writings may help to restore some of the lost vitality.

The only comprehensive account we have of Park's view of

[1]    Herbert Blumer, in personal communication.

sociology is to be found in the *Introduction to the Science of Sociology*,[2] a collaborative work. Although Burgess was admittedly a junior author, and Park himself wrote the chapter on the nature of sociology and either wrote or outlined the content of the initial essays in the remaining chapters, the collaboration was lively.

## The Nature and Tasks of Sociology

In the *Introduction,* Park traces the development of the idea of sociology since Comte's initial statement, stressing the distinctions from history, from the special social sciences, and from the applied sciences. The pivotal idea is Simmel's distinction between the concrete, factual character of history, and the abstract, generalizing nature of sociology. Education and social service apply principles which sociology and psychology deal with explicitly.

That Park today is best known for his contributions to such concrete areas as urban sociology and race relations seems to belie this formal conception of an abstract science. But the impression is not altogether just. The tendency to generalize to process rather than structure—to be remarked at greater length—turned his attention toward a different kind of generalization than came to dominate a subsequent generation of sociologists. A reading of his papers shows a characteristic approach in which he moves from the close examination of some restricted datum to explore parallels in a wide range of phenomena. His overarching concern with abstraction and generalization becomes clear as the reader discovers that a very few facts about the press are used again and again to support a constant search for the general conditions affecting consensus in society, and that a relatively small amount of objectifiable information about race relations serves to launch Park into broad exploration of the accommodations among groups or the relationship between individual and society.

Park's definition of sociology as "the science of collective be-

2    *Introduction to the Science of Sociology,* with Ernest W. Burgess (Chicago: University of Chicago Press, 1921; 2d ed. 1924). Hereafter referred to as *Introduction.* All citations refer to the second edition.

havior"[3] suggests at once the study of a fluid congeries rather than a stable structure. The import of the definition can best be grasped by considering the tasks which are assigned to the discipline. In tracing the historical conceptions of sociology, Park takes up the "social organism" issue, the reality of society apart from the individuals who make it up. He concludes that society is more than a body of like-minded individuals "because of the existence (1) of a social process and (2) of a body of tradition and opinion—the products of this process—which has a relatively objective character and imposes itself upon the individual as a form of control, social control."[4] Accordingly, social control becomes the "central fact and the central problem of society."[5]

Society is everywhere a control organization. Its function is to organize, integrate, and direct the energies resident in the individuals of which it is composed.[6]

*Social control as the central problem.* Social control has had several meanings in sociological usage. It has commonly meant the constraint or organization of human impulses by some system of mores, folkways, laws, collective representations, culture—that is, the imposition of impersonal patterns on individual behavior. Students divide into those who, like Sumner, assume a simple opposition between individual impulse and culture, and those who, like Durkheim, see culture as supplying avenues for the crystallization and productive expression of impulse. On another axis, students divide between those who see a relatively fixed pattern that is acquired by internalization or habituation and those who see control as situational—as the constantly changing requirements for collaboration within sets of relationships. Park's views are clearly stated, and fall closer to the second alternative in each case, although he occasionally lapses into an opposite stance.

From Herbert Spencer, Park takes the question, "How does a

3 *Ibid.*, p. 42.
4 *Ibid.*, p. 39.
5 *Ibid.*, p. 42.
6 "Human Ecology," *American Journal of Sociology*, 42 (July, 1936): 14.

mere collection of individuals succeed in acting in a corporate and consistent way?"[7] Giddings' "like-mindedness" and Tarde's "imitation" supply one kind of answer: "men act together because they act alike."[8] Durkheim on the other hand answers that a *common purpose* "imposes itself upon the individual members of a society at the same time as an ideal, a wish and an obligation."[9] After acknowledging some virtue in both sides of the Giddings-Tarde versus Durkheim controversy, he opts for the latter, saying, "the thing that distinguishes a mere collection of individuals from a society is not like-mindedness, but corporate action."[10]

Differences are often as necessary as likenesses for society to operate. Accordingly, sociology is "a point of view and method for investigating the processes by which individuals are inducted into and induced to cooperate in some sort of permanent corporate existence we call society."[11] The imposition of fixed behavior patterns is but one phase of the larger problem of human collaboration, which Park identifies as social control.

This view of social control is underlined by the close identification Park makes between social control and collective behavior. The two terms apply to the same phenomena, except that social control refers to *mechanism* and collective behavior to *process*. Since collective behavior describes the forming and reforming of society, social control concerns not only the mechanisms underlying traditional continuity but also the means through which the coordination involved in change is achieved. The most elementary form of control is the rapport among crowd members, entirely without tradition; but even such highly rationalized forms of control as law and public opinion arise out of efforts to compromise conflict. Although the force of the mores is acknowledged, they are merely the residuals of earlier public opinion, with the issues forgotten. In the formal discussion of social control, Park even leaves

7    *Introduction*, p. 27.
8    *Ibid.*, p. 33.
9    *Ibid.*
10   *Ibid.*, p. 42.
11   *Ibid.*

the impression that an aroused public opinion might readily overwhelm the mores.

Likewise, as Park deals with social control in the abstract, he finds little occasion to stress opposition between human impulses and societal demands. Public opinion and the mores are collective responses to changing situations and are based on fundamental human nature. They are "forms of behavior which spring directly and spontaneously out of the innate and instinctive responses of the individual to a social situation."[12] At one point Park seems to presage that type of social psychological functionalism which sees human impulse as fully harnessed to the requirements of society. Thus, "as members of society, men act as they do elsewhere from motives they do not fully comprehend, in order to fulfill aims of which they are only dimly or not at all conscious."[13]

But as Park leaves the abstract treatment of social control to examine concrete problems, his words are occasionally different. The family is singled out as a vestige from an earlier "authoritative and sacred society in which everyone has duties and no one has rights,"[14] and in which personal interests are invariably subject to communal authority. At a still earlier date, in connection with his one brief foray into the problem of juvenile delinquency, Park had written bitterly of a much more ubiquitous opposition.

So ill-adapted is the natural, undomesticated man to the social order into which he is born, so out of harmony are all the native impulses of the ordinary healthy human with the demands which society imposes, that it is hardly an exaggeration to say that if his childhood is spent mainly in learning what he must not do, his youth will be devoted mainly to rebellion. As to the remainder of his life, his recreations will very likely turn out to be some sort of vacation and escape from this same social order to which he has finally learned to accommodate, but not wholly reconcile, himself. . . .

One reason why human beings, in contrast with the lower animals, seem to be so ill-adapted to the world in which they are born is that

12    *Ibid.*, p. 787.
13    *Ibid.*, p. 30.
14    "Personality and Cultural Conflict," *Publications of the American Sociological Society*, 25 (May, 1931): 101.

the environment in which human beings live is so largely made up of the experience and memories and the acquired habits of the people who have preceded them.[15]

In spite of these early jeremiads, Park never supported an anarchistic fantasy of society, nor did he ever incline toward a utopia in which the oppositions might be engineered away. Perhaps his closest approach to utopianism is found in an observation that the best integrated society is one in which there are the fewest enacted laws—an assumption which is contradicted by a large body of his thinking regarding *civilization* as contrasted with *culture*. His last writings contain frequent assertions of the necessity for a universe of discourse, including shared and understandable personal loyalties. In a mood which contrasts sharply with his earlier protest, Park at one point argues even that a system of magical belief is essential to social order. But the balanced view, that social control involves the creation of enthusiasms as well as negative restraints, is perhaps best exemplified in the culminating chapter of the *Introduction*, where progress is interpreted as a vital myth.

The conception that man's fate lies somehow in his own hands, if it gains general acceptance, will still be, so far as it inspires men to work and strive, an article of faith, and the image in which he pictures the future of mankind, toward which he directs his efforts, will still have the character of myth. That is the function of myths. It is this that lends an interest to those ideal states in which men at different times have sought to visualize the world of their hopes and dreams.[16]

Selection of social control, and the problem of the relationship of the individual to the group, as a central concern for sociology, suggests an approach that is social psychological in emphasis. The impression is reinforced in a chapter dealing with the "social forces" in the *Introduction*. The unexpected obstacles to social reform which can be traced to influential persons and powerful groups suggest that community life should be conceived as a *con-*

[15]    "Community Organization and Juvenile Delinquency," in *The City*, by Park, Ernest W. Burgess, and R. D. McKenzie (Chicago: University of Chicago Press, 1925; reissued 1966), pp. 99–100.
[16]    *Introduction*, p. 692.

*stellation of social forces.* But instead of offering a discussion of the distribution and exercise of power, Park carries the reader by steps back to a sort of social atom, which is the individual attitude, and is in turn constituted from the four wishes of W. I. Thomas. The task of resolving attitudes into finer elements Park assigns to psychology, but the sociologist locates the dynamic element shaping the accommodations of society in the individual attitude. In a subsequent chapter of the book we read that "It is with social forces and human nature that sociology is mainly concerned."[17]

Although social control is the central problem of sociology, there is a sharp contrast to the thoroughly socio-psychological concern of E. A. Ross and others with the dynamics of particular control mechanisms. The materials deal rather with the historical and situational evolution and use of the various means of control. If control mechanisms intervene between society and the individual, Park is less interested in the link between mechanism and individual than he is in the link between society and mechanism.

Park did indeed have a deep concern for human nature, and his conception of society seldom moves far from the patterned collaboration and accommodation among persons. His most important contributions include *social role,* the *self conception,* and the *marginal man*—all concepts dealing with the relationship between individual and society. But seldom did his attention turn to the psychological makeup of the individual, or even to microsociology. Although he did not describe "structures" in the sense in which sociologists have come to use the term, the patterns of interaction he describes generally take place on a large scale, or in organized community and institutional settings, or between groups rather than individuals. Park's reference to the social forces can perhaps be dismissed as a concession to completeness which he never followed up in his own work. His emphasis upon social control directs more attention to the individual than approaches that center on institutions, culture, or organization structures, but he uses a conception of the individual that depends very little upon the discipline of psychology. It is not then a psychological bias but his

[17]    *Ibid.,* p. 785.

conception of a fluid social order that requires constant attention to individual attitudes as phases of societal process.

*Uses of sociology.* Although Park adopted an abstract formal conception of sociology from Simmel, he nevertheless saw sociology as ultimately useful and practical. Social problems are the natural focus for sociological research, and the pursuit of sociology appears to be inseparable from the point of view of Graham Wallas' "Great Society" and the liberal tradition. It is largely, but not exclusively, this orientation that leads Park to concern himself disproportionately with what some call the pathologies of society. But Park is satisfied to take for granted that the inequities of race relations, the corruption of political machines, criminality, and vice are problems, and proceed directly to their examination without stopping to moralize in the fashion so common during his era. Park endorses W. I. Thomas' repudiation of "ordering-forbidding" as an approach to social reform, and explicitly defers the practical contribution until the problem area has been studied in breadth and depth. Burgess points out how Park dealt with students who were predisposed to fight for Negro rights.

Park told them flatly that the world was full of crusaders. Their role instead was to be that of the calm, detached scientist who investigates race relations with the same objectivity and detachment with which the zoologist dissects the potato bug.[18]

Park acknowledges that administrative problems offer a legitimate focus for sociological research but passes quickly to the more fundamental problems of policy, which have to do with the character of social institutions and of human nature. Applied sociology is not concerned with uncovering mechanisms and devices for reform, but with exposing the broad setting of social organization and human nature which policy-makers must take into account. Park's few attempts to offer specific advice to social workers, educators, and others must have been disappointing to the practitioners, for this very reason.

[18]   Ernest W. Burgess, "Social Planning and Race Relations," in *Race Relations: Problems and Theory: Essays in Honor of Robert E. Park*, ed. Jitsuiki Masuoka and Preston Valien (Chapel Hill: University of North Carolina Press, 1961), p. 17.

Foremost among the guiding values for his approach to applied sociology is the counterpart to his theoretical emphasis upon social control: a concern with reconciling or balancing the requirements of human collaboration against the goal of individual freedom. Coupled with this concern is the goal of rationality in human society, but not so much in the individual as in the collective sense. Park plainly approved of the historical shift from a society in which men are governed by sentiment to a society which takes account, through public opinion, of the divergent interests intrinsic to a heterogeneous social structure.

For all of his concern with race relations, it is striking that the achievement of social and economic equality never emerges as a dominant goal in Park's thought. He toyed with ideas of racial temperament, and never wholly rejected the idea of a biological basis for racial inequality. The problems he examined are not those that would have preoccupied an investigator convinced that reduction of inequalities was the most urgent agendum. Perhaps it is for this reason that Park took no substantial steps toward developing a theory of stratification.

## The Method of Sociology

Park continued the work of W. I. Thomas in turning the attention of sociologists away from speculation over vast evolutionary fictions, away from moralization, and toward the development of a body of knowledge firmly based upon those phenomena that were close enough and concrete enough to be examined reliably. But he also came to be identified popularly with an atheoretical and undisciplined empirical approach, personifying a stereotype of the dominant trend in American sociology during the interwar period. His reluctance to engage in formalization, his avoidance of the language of deductive inquiry or hypothesis-testing, his tendency to generalize from anecdotes, all suggest a wholly inductive approach, guided by intuition rather than systematic concerns. But a fuller account of Park's methodological concerns will show the popular version to be a badly distorted picture.

*Scientific sociology.* In spite of strong views regarding the essentially empirical character of sociology and the importance of working with facts rather than suppositions, Park concerned himself very little with details of data collection and analysis. An essay entitled "The Sociological Methods of William Graham Sumner, and of William I. Thomas and Florian Znaniecki"[19] turns out to be an exposition of their conceptual apparatus, without serious consideration of the means employed in data gathering and data analysis. The exposition contains the justification for this emphasis. The chief contribution of the *Polish Peasant*, we are told, "is not a body of fact, but a system of concepts." Sumner started with an interest rather than a problem, and then defined the problem only after he had learned a good deal about his subject. Only after problem formulation is it appropriate to speak of methods. Concepts and frame of reference are the most important part of method, but are usually the by-products of research, rather than antecedent to it.

Without formalizing it, Park adumbrates a sophisticated conception in which the method of social science supplies a frame of reference through which it is possible to observe significant regularities. Without a conceptual apparatus, useful observation is impossible; with such an apparatus, the specific data-gathering procedures are of lesser moment. But not *any* conceptual apparatus will do, for what one can see is dependent upon the concepts employed. Hence there must be a continuous interplay between observation and conceptualization. He repudiates the practice by which an investigator takes a full-blown theory into the field with him, and seeks to confirm or refute it. In one of his most bitter attacks upon quantification, Park stresses the deficiency of "a purely scholastic exercise in which the answers to all the questions are already implicit in the conceptions and assumptions with which the inquiry started."[20] At the same time, Park could not have commended Lundberg's "social bookkeeping." His method was deeply committed to theory and intertwined with theory.

19    *Methods in Social Science: A Case Book*, ed. Stuart A. Rice (Chicago: University of Chicago Press, 1931), pp. 154–75.
20    "The City as a Natural Phenomenon," in *Human Communities* (Glencoe, Ill.: Free Press, 1952), p. 125.

Although all of Park's own work follows the same pattern, seeking creative conceptualizations that will informally illumine empirical observation and then using the concepts to shed light on a wider range of observations, his early writings advocate enhanced methodological rigor. "Facts have not been collected to check social theories. Social problems have been defined in terms of common sense . . ."[21] "Sociology seems now, however, in a way to become, in some fashion or other, an experimental science."[22] Although his conception of an experiment was perhaps closer to common sense than to current scientific usage, the student was being encouraged explicitly to follow the lead of experimental psychology and medicine.

Park gave impetus to quantification through his formulation of the idea of *social distance* and of the *ecological* approach to community study. The concept of social distance does two things to the ideas of prejudice and antagonism. It directs attention beneath the overt manifestations of intergroup relations to the stable terms of their accommodation, and it formulates the latter as a readily quantifiable phenomenon. "The point is that we are clearly conscious, in all our personal relationships, of degree of intimacy. A is closer to B than C and the degree of this intimacy measures the influence which each has over the other."[23] E. S. Bogardus credits Park with the suggestion that he develop a generally applicable device for the measurement of social distance—a suggestion which resulted in the widely used social distance scale.[24]

One aspect of the ecological approach in sociology was the use of the more tangible and hence measurable phenomena as indexes for the more strictly social processes. Land values are prime indicators of social forces. Social metabolism, measured through such indexes as mobility rates, indicates in quantitative terms the intensity of the social process. "In so far as social structure can be de-

---

21    *Introduction*, p. 44.

22    *Ibid.*, p. 45.

23    "The Concept of Social Distance: As Applied to the Study of Racial Attitudes and Racial Relations," *Journal of Applied Sociology*, 8 (July, 1924): 339.

24    E. S. Bogardus, *Social Distance* (Los Angeles: 1959), p. 5.

fined in terms of position, social changes may be defined in terms
of movement; and society exhibits, in one of its aspects, characters
that can be measured and described in mathematical formulas."[25]

Perhaps it is unfair to employ a paper that Park never chose
to publish to exemplify his later thoughts. Yet Thorndike's
attempt to measure the "goodness of life" in American cities
brought forth pungent comments on the misuse of quantification.
After berating Thorndike for reducing a complex set of processes
to oversimplified perspective, and overlooking the difference
among communities in the relationship of the incorporated city to
the daily round of life among its inhabitants, Park speaks in more
general terms. "The manipulation of statistical data by which such
scales are contrived and applied has always impressed me a good
deal like parlor magic. One is frequently startled by the results but
is mainly interested to discover by what sleight of hand the trick
was turned."[26] Although Park did not actively repudiate his earlier
views, he did not employ the newer quantitative procedures, and
made less and less use of quantitative materials of any sort in his
later writings.

More characteristic, then, than Park's advocacy of a rigorously
scientific approach to sociology are his endorsement of the
"methods of anthropologists" and his insistence on the crucial place
of history. After his review of devices for quantifying the objects
of study, Park asserts that "History alone can, it would seem, make
these different meanings intelligible to us. . . . Just because it has
been a *record of events* rather than a *description of things*, history
has given sociology much, if not most, of its subject matter."[27]
Park's own most serious excursion into empirical research, reported
in *The Immigrant Press and its Control*,[28]  is fundamentally like
the work of a historian who writes topically rather than chronologi-

[25]    "The Urban Community as a Spatial Pattern and a Moral Order,"
in *The Urban Community*, ed. Ernest W. Burgess (Chicago: University of
Chicago Press, 1926), p. 4.
[26]    "The City as a Natural Phenomenon" (1952), pp. 123–24.
[27]    "Sociology," in *Research in the Social Sciences*, ed. Wilson Gee
(New York: Macmillan, 1929), p. 38.
[28]    Chicago: University of Chicago Press, 1922.

cally. The methodological problems are chiefly those of ferreting out the many obscure records, and employing letters and similar documents as a guide to commonsense interpretations of the record.

*Meaning and process.* A scholar's choice of methods depends upon the character of findings and conclusions that he finds most useful or intuitively most satisfying. The crucial emphasis upon history, the reliance on life histories and the procedures of participant observation, and the reaction against trends in quantification are understandable in light of the two prime objectives that governed Park's work. His conclusions were characteristically the description of a *process* and the specification of the *meaning* of an individual or collective action.

Park insisted that we search for causes rather than correlations, and that we concern ourselves with the meanings of acts, rather than with behavior in a limited sense. Park sometimes used William James' essay, "A Certain Blindness in Human Beings,"[29] as the springboard for exposition of the preferred method in sociology. Before one can begin to make sociological sense of any group, the investigator must overcome the normal "blindness to the feelings of creatures and people other than ourselves." If anything customary seems shocking or quaint, it is because the custom is not quite intelligible to the observer. The difficulties in sociological investigation do not lie in describing external forms, but in discovering the meaning and function of usages and institutions. The investigator must involve himself until he uncovers the basis of the zest for life in a particular culture. "This zest for life is just that personal and vital secret which, for each one of us, gives meaning and significance not merely to the life of the individual but of the society, of whatever sort it be, of which he is a member and a part."[30]

The influence of W. I. Thomas upon Park—or the similarity of their outlooks—is clearest in this respect. Human documents are the foremost media for achieving sympathetic identification.

[29]    William James, *Talks to Teachers on Psychology; and to Students on Some of Life's Ideals* (New York: Henry Holt, 1901).
[30]    Introduction to *Shadow of the Plantation* by Charles S. Johnson (Chicago: University of Chicago Press, 1934; reissued 1966), p. xvi.

Not only the ability to predict the course of action, but the investigator's intuitive sense of being at home in the culture, feeling the depression and elation of a member of the society, is the criterion of successful investigation. Thus while Park is on the side of *verstehen* sociology as opposed to positivistic approaches, his goals are not to be confused with the primarily cognitive and formalistic typologies of action which come out of the work of Max Weber.

If the central concern with affective meanings, approached through sympathetic identification, limits the usefulness of most objective procedures to supplying quite indirect indexes of sociology's main concerns, the emphasis upon process renders the easy formalizations and the simple correlational models so characteristic of structural analysis of equally limited value. Society is in constant flux, and Park is more interested in the past and future of events than he is in their momentary interrelationships.

Contemporary debate concerns the usefulness of equilibrium models of society. Park's view might be labeled a dynamic disequilibrium model. Implicit in his formulations are potential states of equilibrium—the end points of his idealized natural histories—and the constant pull in the direction of these states keeps the system changing. An idealized state of assimilation stands at the end of conflict; institutionalization is the end product of collective behavior; public opinion process rigidifies into the mores. But either these states are never reached or the approach to one equilibrium creates another disequilibrium that starts a second sequence before the first is finished.

Unlike equilibrium theorists, Park tells us little about the hypothetical states of equilibrium. He seems to be little interested in the characteristics of states of assimilation and institutionalization, and when he does take time to describe them, his characterizations are contradictory and sound more like states of disequilibrium. These states merely serve as points of reference, and his preoccupation is with the movements, the sequences, that take place. But his concern with patterned sequences of change likewise distinguishes him from the most articulate opponents of equilibrium theory in sociology today.

Nowhere more than in ecology did Park develop the idea of process. While Burgess elaborated his concept of natural areas into zones, Park dwelt more on the processes of invasion and succession—the sequence of events through which natural areas were constantly being transformed. The principal tool, and probably the most important concept in Park's methodology, is the natural history. The natural history is typically described as a series of stages that are set in motion by some disequilibrating event and lead toward the hypothetical state of equilibrium. Under Park's influence Lyford Edwards uncovered a set of stages that applied equally to several revolutions in history. Bogardus developed an informative "race relations cyle" based on West Coast experience, expressing the tendency for both conflict and accommodation in the economic sphere to precede and bring about changes in the social area. Stonequist applied the approach to identifying the crucial process through which an individual becomes a marginal man.

At different places Park reveals what he regards as essential elements in a natural history, although he offers neither formal definition nor careful prescription. A natural history is, first, a typical or collective account, the sequence leading to establishmnet of a form rather than a specific instance. "What is needed, however, is not so much a history as a natural history of the press—not a record of the fortunes of individual newspapers, but an account of the evolution of the newspaper as a social institution."[31] Second, a natural history is a cycle produced by natural forces, rather than by human planning.

> The newspaper has a history; but it has, likewise, a natural history. The press, as it exists, is not, as our moralists sometimes seem to assume, the willful product of any little group of living men. On the contrary, it is the outcome of an historic process in which many individuals participated without foreseeing what the ultimate product of their labors was to be.[32]

Third, in the natural history each stage inevitably triggers the next. And finally, the natural history is not foreign to the natural order but is part and mechanism in the functioning of a social order.

---

[31]    "The American Newspaper," *American Journal of Sociology,* 32 (March, 1927) : 806.

[32]    "The Natural History of the Newspaper," *American Journal of Sociology,* 29 (November, 1923) : 273.

Race relations . . . can best be interpreted if what they seem to be at any time and place is regarded merely as a phase in a cycle of change which, once initiated, inevitably continues until it terminates in some predestined racial configuration and one consistent with an established order of which it is a part.[33]

The natural history approach fell into gradual disrepute in sociology after the initial period of vital use, chiefly because neither Park nor its other adherents elaborated it from common sense into a sophisticated method. Inevitable stages were seldom inevitable; the statistically typical series had little meaning in Park's own frame of reference; the prediction that cycles should ultimately be measurable temporally came to naught; stages were often—like Hiller's—no more than logical dissections of a definition; what to do with the stages after they were identified other than to classify phenomena was often unclear; and frequently the natural history became, instead of a phase of inevitable disequilibrium, a series of steps toward a utopian equilibrium. Even Park fell into the latter error, contributing to the paradisiacal fantasy about Hawaii with his observation that "Race relations in Hawaii today seem to be approaching the terminus of such a cycle as here described."[34] But a refined natural history approach, allowing for branching, and specifying the different contingencies which determine progression between each pair of stages, may still be a vital alternative to static, relational formulations.

*City as laboratory.* One final feature of Park's methodology deserves to be stressed. All of Park's interests found their focus in the city, a world which he often romanticized, and which he urged on other sociologists as a "laboratory" for the study of human society. One of his earliest papers was a lengthy catalog of suggestions for investigating human behavior in the urban environment, and Park's name has come to be identified with the monographic studies of city life, such as *The Gold Coast and the Slum, The Ghetto, The Gang*, conducted by his students. Although there is nothing in the logic of Park's ecological theory which restricts its applica-

33    Introduction to *Interracial Marriage in Hawaii* by Romanzo Adams (New York: Macmillan, 1937), p. xiv.
34    *Ibid.*

tions to cities, the ideas have taken concrete form almost exclusively with reference to the metropolis.

It is characteristic of Park's generalizing propensity that he was not satisfied to concentrate on the city merely because he found it interesting, but that he should justify his work as shedding light on issues that transcended the city. The city is a convenient locus for investigation because every human impulse finds expression somewhere in a relatively small area, and because institutions grow more rapidly there. It is also a more relevant environment than small towns and primitive societies because the city is par excellence the world that man has made for himself.

But there is a very special sense in which Park sees the city as a microcosm in which are exposed and magnified, as under a microscope, the processes taking place in the larger society.

Our political system is founded upon the conviction that people who live in the same locality have common interests, and that they can therefore be relied upon to act together for the common welfare. This assumption, as it turns out, is not valid for large cities. The difficulty of maintaining in the city intimate contacts which in the small town insured the existence of a common purpose and made concerted action possible is certainly very great.[35]

The processes of establishing concerted action are in continuous operation everywhere. But just because they function smoothly, it is difficult to detect their operation in the small town. When the processes are blocked, their operation is exposed to public view. In this special sense the city is a laboratory in which the investigator can see what he may only infer elsewhere. Here as elsewhere it is Park's interest in process rather than factual description or static relationship that turns him toward purposive observation rather than representative sampling.

## Symbiosis and Socialization

Because it gave rise to a "school," Park's most conspicuous contribution to sociology was the distinction between two orders,

35    Introduction to *The Gold Coast and the Slum* by Harvey W. Zorbaugh (Chicago: University of Chicago Press, 1929), p. ix.

governed by somewhat different principles, yet constantly interacting upon one another. Park adumbrated the distinction in
his earliest writings, and continued to rework the fomulation until
his death. In the *Introduction to the Science of Sociology* they are
not yet presented as separate orders, but the idea is implicit in the
separate treatment of competition and conflict processes. The orders are best known as the ecological and the social, and the distinction gave rise to the distinctively American sociological specialty
known as ecology. But Park also spoke of community and society,
of the biotic and the moral orders, and later of two contrasting
processes, symbiosis and socialization. A distinction between civilization and culture seems to be related to these distinctions,
although it does not carry the same implications.

*The ecological order.* There were at least two stages in the
development of Park's formulation of ecology. In the first stage
the specification of separate orders had not yet appeared or did
not receive primary emphasis. Park was still concerned with making sociology scientific, although he was convinced that the social
phenomena in which he was most interested were not directly
measurable. The social tends to be projected into a spatial realm,
social groups finding their habitats in natural areas, and social
change being reflected in spatial mobility. The distribution and
movement of populations in space can be precisely quantified, and
thus they supply useful indexes for the social realm. At this stage,
Park did not stress an autonomous ecological order, nor did he
suggest the study of spatial patterns as a field of investigation in
its own right. Some of the misunderstanding of Park's sociology
stems from the fact that many investigators have used these early
formulations without taking account of the subsequent probing
efforts to develop a more vital and fundamental set of ideas.

The formulation of a distinctive ecological order appears in
the second phase. "Symbiosis" and "socialization" come closest to
capturing the main impetus of Park's repeated discussions. If Park
first discovered the spatial order by approaching sociology from
geography, his more characteristic and enduring outlook derived
from the biological or organismic approach. The organismic
approach had been brought from Europe and given its fullest de-

velopment in American sociology by Lester F. Ward, who extended the biological idea of symbiosis into a universal principle of *synergy*, "the systematic and organic working together of the anti-thetical forces of nature."[36]

The recognition of a biological and a social order in human life was not uncommon, but followers of the organismic school often simply derived the categories and principles for analysis of the social order from the biological. Park recognized that the two orders were governed by different principles but interacted. The clue to the symbiotic (or ecological) order was to be found in the imper-sonal struggle for existence among animals and plants, and its imperfect analogy in economic competition among men. A differ-ent set of principles was required, however, to deal with man's capacity to create a *moral* order and to engage in communication. Park contrasts Spencer's view of society, founded upon the division of labor, to Comte's idea of society as consensus.

Now, it is an indubitable fact that societies do have this double aspect. They are composed of individuals who act independently of one another, who compete and struggle with one another for mere existence, and treat one another, as far as possible, as utilities. On the other hand, it is quite as true that men and women are bound together by affections and common purposes; they do cherish traditions, am-bitions, and ideals that are not all their own, and they maintain, in spite of natural impulses to the contrary, a discipline and a moral order that enables them to transcend what we ordinarily call nature, and through their collective action, recreate the world in the image of their collective aspirations and their common will.[37]

If the central problem of sociology is social control, the most important difference lies in the mechanism through which the two orders are regulated. Competition governs the ecological order, not merely as a divisive and selective principle, but as a bonding pro-cess through the interdependencies it produces. The social order is governed by communication, directed by the conceptions of *self*

[36]    Lester F. Ward, *Pure Sociology*, 2d ed. (New York: Macmillan, 1908), p. 171.
[37]    "Sociology" (1929), p. 6.

and *other* which the members develop as social beings. The peculiar significance of communication is that it makes *collective* action possible. There is no collective action in the ecological order: individuals constitute a mass, and their actions are patterned because similar interests respond similarly to similar situations. Demographic methods are best suited for the study of parallel individual behavior but not for the distinctively collective behavior in society.

Some of the confusion regarding the essential nature of ecology emerges from Park's effort to integrate his earlier concern with a spatial realm into an order in which the assignment of position and change depend upon the operation of the impersonal process of competition. Park effects the integration by locating these processes in the *community*, which is

(1) a population, territorially organized, (2) more or less completely rooted in the soil it occupies, (3) its individual units living in a relationship of mutual interdependence that is symbiotic rather than societal, in the sense in which that term applies to human beings.[38]

The division of labor, which reflects specialized competence and competitive advantage, sorts people into *natural areas*. Certain of these areas exhibit dominance, meaning that they are most responsive to external influence, and they control the competitive struggle in other areas. There is a tendency toward equilibrium, in which competition is regularized and its intensity reduced to a moderate level. When the equilibrium is disturbed by an external event which alters the "balance of nature," competition is intensified, setting in motion a process of *succession* in which the division of labor and the distribution in space are readjusted until once more a less intense competition serves merely to maintain the existing patterns of dominance and dispersion.

Nowhere else are the dynamic interrelations between the ecological order and the social (or moral) order systematically described, but they are mentioned in scattered contexts. Occasionally Park followed the earlier organismic theorists who derived social processes from the biotic, when he attempted to describe dominance and succession as processes manifested at every level. Typi-

[38]    "Human Ecology" (1936), p. 4.

cally, however, he saw the social order as restricting the intensity and softening the impact of the struggle for existence, by the operation of custom and sentiment. On the other hand, through technological innovation, the social order might disrupt the biotic equilibrium and intensify competition. Influence from the biotic to the social order is simpler, as social definitions tend to arise to express and reinforce the interpersonal order which has been produced by competition. Competition tends to become conflict, and such vital social facts as racial prejudice are ultimately social expressions of an impersonal division of labor. On those frequent occasions when the biotic order is grossly disrupted, competition is greatly intensified and society (in the narrow sense) ceases to function until biotic equilibrium has been approached closely enough so that competition subsides to a normal pace. There is also a more complex kind of influence, as when high density of population brings about individuation, partly through the necessarily more complex division of labor and partly because the absence of natural barriers to social intercourse forces the individual to erect social walls.

It is unfortunate that the study of urban spatial patterns is sometimes identified as ecology. The effect of spatial distribution on social life is one among many problems for ecological analysis, and propinquity in mate selection and de facto segregation in race relations are elementary ecological concerns. But Park's ecology refers to a set of processes that cannot be observed except in conjunction with social processes. Spatial patterns may be a direct indication of the biotic order among animals and plants, but among humans they reflect the joint operation of the two orders. Empirically the ecological order is an inference that supplies the explanation for many failures in control at the social level, and for innovations and deviations from the patterns of human collaboration embodied in the strictly social order. If the system of values and norms that men erect is conservatizing, the ecological order is like the unconscious realm in the individual, constantly unsettling the stable order and precipitating change.

Because of the emphasis on competition there is sometimes a mistaken tendency to identify the ecological order with economic processes and to equate Park's thought with a type of economic determinism. But Park reminds us that commercial bargaining is a highly evolved social transaction, and thus different in kind from the biotic competition that underlies social life. Nevertheless, when Park sought to specify just what constitutes the ecological order among human beings, he sometimes referred to impersonal and utilitarian dealings as contrasted to relationships governed by positive sentiment and obligation. Furthermore, the emergence of Marxian class consciousness through a group's discovery of their true interests supplies an excellent instance of the translation of ecological competition into social conflict. Here, as elsewhere, Park suggests an approach rather than developing a scheme in sufficient detail to yield researchable hypotheses. But in light of the constant failure of our expressed ideals to shape the functioning social order about us, renewed attention might profitably be devoted to the idea of a biotic order constantly interacting with the moral, the political, and the economic orders.

*Civilization.* Oddly, the idea of civilization, so inextricably linked to the metropolis and formulated from many of the same ideas that directed Park's thinking about the ecological order, is broached chiefly in another context. It is when Park seeks to account for race relations that he resorts to the idea of civilization, as a recent principle of social organization vaster than those that characterize the less developed world.

The focal point of a civilization is the marketplace. Its boundaries are the limits of the market, and the key to the growth of civilization has been expansion of the market. People come together in the market, not because of shared sentiments or any desire to participate in a common life, but because they are useful to each other. People of diverse races and cultures come together. Although tradition and sentiment develop, the sense of solidarity characteristic of simpler societies is lacking. On the other hand, trading requires a special skill—to know both one's own and the other's mind at a single instant.

Civilization has distinctive organizational characteristics. There is an inherent opposition between the unity of the whole and the closed sentiments of we-groups. Like W. I. Thomas, Park

sometimes sees primary groups and the family in particular as in-
congruous survivals of an earlier era, although one senses that the
struggle between we-groups and civilization will not soon end. The
once autonomous territorial societies are brought under common
domination, and superordination-subordination replaces territori-
ality as a principle of organization. Nationalistic movements are
the natural reaction to the new principle. But people move about,
territorial integrity is diluted, and race becomes temporarily a major criterion for stratification, only to be replaced eventually by
caste and class. Class consciousness replaces ethnic and racial consciousness, since it expresses more faithfully the pattern of relationships to the market.

Once again Park owes much to German scholars, such as
Simmel, Tonnies, and Oswald Spengler. But the relation of this
idea, which is especially prominent in his later writings, to the
ecological and social orders is not made explicit. Certain features
of civilization suggest the interpretation that intensified ecological
competition undermines the strictly social order and reinstates an
order resembling the plant and animal world in the minimal effectiveness of social norms and primary group sentiments. But social
contact and communication are of central importance, civilization
is plainly not territorial and precultural but multicultural, and the
capability for collective behavior is high. Thus the distinction
between culture and civilization refers to the social and ecological
systems together and does not rely upon the one or the other.

It is illuminating to contrast civilization to ecology as a basis for
understanding the distinctive features of cities. The ecological approach as developed by Park's students stressed demographic
criteria in defining the urban community. But this view has been
called into question because of evidence that the way of life in
cities outside the Western world often fails to fit theories derived
from the study of American communities. But Park's conception
of civilization distinguishes modern cities, which grew up about the
international marketplaces, from the older cities, which grew up as
fortresses. Not simply density of population and similar demographic considerations give the modern city its characteristic tendencies (such as weakening kinship ties), but the fact that people

with diverse cultures are permanently brought together to carry
on a distinctive type of social relationship. Here Park's wide knowledge of history led him to a more viable conception of urbanism
than was possible for students who knew only the modern Western city.

## The Social Order as Accommodation

If there is one aspect of Park's work that was ahead of its
time, it is the conception of the social order as a pattern maintained by accommodation. If the central problem of sociology is
to account for human collaboration, Park describes this collaboration as the continual accommodation necessary to carry on
a collective life in the presence of competition and conflict. The
formal treatment of conflict in the *Introduction* and the central
place it occupies in his thought are notable reflections of his studies
under Georg Simmel. But sociologists were unready to make constructive use of such an approach, and so for two decades the followers dutifully mentioned competition, conflict, accommodation, and
assimilation in their introductory courses, without going much beyond taxonomy and illustration. After World War II equilibrium
theory found little need for these concepts, and it was only as a
reaction set in that scholars began to ask why there was no American sociology of conflict and to urge a conflict model of society
as a corrective to equilibrium theory.

The "natural" state of society is not one of peace derived from
unanimity, but a working adjustment to differences.

Every society represents an organization of elements more or less
antagonistic to each other but united for the moment, at least, by an
arrangement which defines the reciprocal relations and respective
spheres of action of each. This accommodation, this *modus vivendi*,
may be relatively permanent as in a society constituted by castes, or
quite transitory as in societies made up of open classes.[39]

Conflict remains latent although antagonisms are regulated. Any
change in the situation may upset the accommodation and nullify

[39]    *Introduction*, p. 665.

control over the antagonistic forces. Although tradition, the mores, and collective representations constitute consensus, this very consensus represents a set of social accommodations.

If accommodation is the normal state of society, it is reached through a series of stages that Park described first in completely general form and later rediscovered in the natural history of race relations in Hawaii. *Competition* comes first, as "interaction without contact," meaning that the individual is unaware of his competitors or is impersonal in his relations with them. Competition is universal and continuous, and normally proceeds unobserved. But in a crisis, when the circumstances of competition are altered, it is converted into conflict. *Conflict* is intermittent, is personal and conscious, and aims at control. If competition dictates the division of labor, conflict fixes the individual's place in society. *Accommodation* is a cessation of overt conflict, an agreement to disagree, which comes about when the systems of superordination-subordination and control which have developed in conflict become fixed and established in custom and the mores. Once an accommodation is reached, the slower process of *assimilation* sets in. The absorption of a cultural heritage and a thoroughgoing transformation of personality take place under the influence of intimate and concrete contacts.

The concept of assimilation is one of the more difficult of Park's terms to define precisely. Writers who like neat schemes often identify it as a process of losing separate group identity by adopting the host culture. One might then interpret the natural history as movement to a quiescent state founded on unanimity. But Park explicitly repudiates the view that assimilation means becoming alike. In national groups, likeness is superficial, and individual differences are considerable. But the superficial similarity is important because it nullifies the taboos against free movement and enables the individual to move into strange groups. It is in spite of individual differences that a unity of experience and of orientation permits development of a "community of purpose and action."

The nature of assimilation as the ultimate resolution of conflict relates to another large problem, the basis for solidarity in society.

Giddings' *consciousness of kind* had considerable currency as an explanation for intergroup prejudices, and as a positive principle relating bondedness to likeness. Park rejected the concept in no uncertain terms while making clear what he regarded as the nature of social ties.

Likeness is, after all, a purely formal concept which of itself cannot hold anything together.

In the last analysis social solidarity is based on sentiment and habit. It is the sentiment of loyalty and the habit of what Sumner calls "concurrent action" that gives substance and insures unity to the state, as to every other type of social group. This sentiment of loyalty has its basis in a *modus vivendi*, a working relation and mutual understanding, of the members of the group. Social institutions are not founded in similarities any more than they are founded in differences, but in relations, and in the mutual interdependence of parts. When these relations have the sanction of custom and are fixed in individual habit, so that the activities of the group are running smoothly, personal attitudes and sentiments, which are the only forms in which individual minds collide and clash with one another, easily accommodate themselves to the existing situation.[40]

The immigrant does not become assimilated simply by adopting American ways. He first forms an immigrant group, which helps him find a place and make his way in American society. By arousing nationalistic feelings and a concern for the reputation of his first country among Americans, he breaks down the provincial loyties he brought with him.

Although Park looked at race relations over the long run in terms of assimilation in this untidy sense, his chief preoccupation lay in the movements between accommodation and conflict. He saw a stable accommodation under slavery, made possible by the intimate relations between master and slave and the observance of well-understood patterns of social distance. Reduction of interracial intimacy led to mobilization of the racial minority, increasing contact within the race, and the development of common interest and sense of solidarity among Negroes. The result was

[40]    "Racial Assimilation in Secondary Groups: With Particular Reference to the Negro," *American Journal of Sociology*, 19 (March, 1914): 609.

movement toward a new basis for accommodation, a biracial organization of society with parallel class structures. In the simplest of terms, accommodation prevails when social distances are known and every man is in his place; conflict breaks out when the distances are ill defined or people abandon their assigned stations. Racial conflict is not so much the relationship among individuals as it is among persons conscious of their racial identities. The upshot of racial conflict is readjustment in the distribution of status and power between the races, which is translated into accommodation temporarily by devices such as accepting an "etiquette" of race relations.

## The Person in Society

In spite of the social psychological tenor of his approach and his explicit concern with human nature, Park is seldom singled out for his contributions to this area. He was indeed overshadowed at Chicago by Thomas, Mead, and Faris, and in much that he wrote he was merely an able disciple of Thomas. But his concentration upon the person coping with the dynamic features of urban civilization, as the focus of the conflict and accommodation between races led him to certain profound and influential formulations. These have principally to do with race prejudice, self-conception and role, and the marginal man.

*Race prejudice.* Park was concerned with the dynamics of race prejudice throughout his career. At least three features of his approach were unchanged during this time. First, he approached prejudice as he did everything else, as merely a special case of a universal phenomenon. Men are practical creatures, and their attitudes and their knowledge are relative to their purposes. Race prejudice is no different from any other attitude in this respect. Second, race prejudice is an aspect of an intergroup process rather than a product of personal peculiarities. "Prejudice, in this broad conception of the term, seems to be an incident of group consciousness just as reserve seems to be an incident of self-consciousness."[41]

41    "The Concept of Social Distance: As Applied to the Study of Racial Attitudes and Race Relations" (1924), p. 343.

Races and ethnic groups meet as strangers, and as strangers people see a type rather than an individual.

Third, it is only when relationships are established on a personal rather than group basis that prejudices are undermined. But Park did not seem, here, to be referring to the reduction of prejudice in occasional individuals. His discussion and examples refer to the system of relations between the groups. Park often noted that nothing like the personal relationship of master and slave had arisen to take its place, and that the Negro's position as a stranger in the North made his position there, though more egalitarian, especially precarious. It is not that personal relations destroy the attitudes that foster an established system of racial superordination-subordination; these are changed only as the actual relations between groups change. But the attitudes of compassion and acceptance of the other as human develop in these settings.

Park's treatment of race prejudice evolved in his successive writings. In 1917 he laid the foundation, with a thoroughly economic interpretation. Prejudice is not dispelled by knowledge or acquaintanceship. Rather, we hate because we fear. We fear because of economic competition, and especially because the competitor has the advantage of a lower standard of living.

In 1924 the conception that forms the basis for his chief contribution to the understanding of race prejudice took form when he advanced the idea of social distance. Social distance does not imply ill feeling, antagonism, or conflict, but merely a degree of intimacy. "Everyone, it seems, is capable of getting on with everyone else, providing each preserves his proper distances."[42] To explain the rise of prejudice, we look at the analogy of individual self-consciousness, which develops from personal conflict. Prejudice, then, is manifested when social status is threatened.

Prejudice and race prejudice are by no means to be identified by social distance, but arise when our personal and racial reserves are, or seem to be, invaded. Prejudice is not on the whole an aggressive but a conservative force; a sort of spontaneous conservation which

[42]   *Ibid.*, p. 341.

tends to preserve the social order and the social distances upon which that order rests."[43]

Later, Park altered the terms by which he referred to these phenomena. Prejudice came to be equated more nearly with social distance, and contrasted with racial antagonism. Antagonisms are found where there is conflict between the races. "There is probably less racial prejudice in America than elsewhere, but there is more racial conflict and more racial antagonism. There is more conflict because there is more change, more progress."[44] Prejudice and antagonism must be clearly separated in the student's thinking. Both are group phenomena. The former refers merely to the normal process of categorizing individuals according to the positions they are assigned in the traditional order. Race antagonism is often a sign that the traditional order is weakening, that the customary accommodations are no longer effective, and thus may be taken as an encouraging sign of change.

In his later writing Park further extended his thinking to observe that a fundamental cause of prejudice is the insecurity of relations with a stranger. Thus he recognized predictability as an essential condition to human interaction. As the sense of insecurity becomes an attitude, the racial mark becomes a symbol of that insecurity, and the intitial relationship of stranger is kept in effect. The explanation of prejudice is a historical event whose initial character is perpetuated in time through embedding a symbol and its associated sentiments into an ideology. Thus, while emergence of race prejudice as a phase in intergroup process is a constant throughout Park's thought, he progressed from identifying a rather direct response to economic competition to describing a complex attitude preserved through ideology and conservative of the social structure.

*Role and self.* A constant theme in Park's treatment of human nature is self-consciousness, developed in a manner which probably owes most to William James. Self-consciousness is rooted in the

[43]    *Ibid.*, p. 344.
[44]    "The Bases of Race Prejudice," *Annals of the American Academy of Political and Social Science,* 140 (November, 1928): 13.

moral order rather than the ecological. In Park's efforts to deal with the continuous dialectic between the two orders, an idea such as the self, which can view itself as an object, becomes a crucial link in the social process. Unlike social psychologists who based their theories of human nature on the primary group, Park's treatment was centered in civilization, marked by the constant challenge to tradition through the medium of collective behavior, and by the pervasive clash of divergent cultures. Mead's self-process was formulated in complete generality, Cooley insisted upon the key place of primary groups even in the most secular society, and Thomas leaned toward a frustration theory. But Park saw more clearly a self-consciousness specifically charged with coming to terms with civilization.

As compared with animals, man lives in a world with a temporal dimension. "The fact that men can look back with regret to their past, and forward with lively expectation to their future, suggests that there is, ordinarily, in the lives of human beings, an amount of tension and sustained suspense which tends to break up established habits and to hold those habits not yet established in solution."[45] Because our actions cover a long period and many objects, man's life is a series of episodes and adventures. "These episodes in so far as they are integrated in some general scheme or life program, represent a career. It is characteristic of man that he has a career."[46] The career, like the life history, is one of the foundation concepts in Park's analysis of human nature.

A crucial feature of the social order for the individual is the division of labor. Each part in the division of labor is a role. The social order exists only insofar as there is a capacity for concerted action, which in turn depends upon the division of labor. This capacity becomes less fragile only as roles are fixed in habit and regularized in custom and tradition. But habit is not sufficient to insure a functioning social order, and we must look toward social control. Human control revolves about the capacity of individuals for conscious participation in a common purpose, and the tend-

[45]   "Human Nature, Attitudes, and the Mores," in *Social Attitudes*, ed. Kimball Young (New York: Henry Holt, 1931), p. 25.
[46]   *Ibid.*, p. 27.

ency of every action to become a gesture that is observed by one's fellows as an indication of one's intentions. The word "person" in its first meaning is "mask." "Everyone is always and everywhere, more or less consciously, playing a role. . . . It is in these roles that we know each other; it is in these roles that we know ourselves."[47] It is this conception of social role, subsequently expanded by Ralph Linton, upon which the modern burgeoning of role theory was built.

It was but a step from this conception of role to formulation of the crucial idea of *self-conception*. As early as 1921 Park and Burgess had used the title, "The Self as the Individual's Conception of his Role," to designate a selection from Alfred Binet dealing with transformations in personality under the influence of suggestion in hypnosis.[48] Thomas and Znaniecki had spoken of "life organization" as bringing unity into the individual's perspective. Park borrowed their concept, but renamed it to reflect more fully the process which was involved. Man forms a conception of self, through which he gets and maintains control over his impulses. But the self-conception is rooted in the division of labor.

The conceptions which men form of themselves seem to depend upon their vocations, and in general upon the role that they seek to play in the communities and social groups in which they live, as well as upon the recognition and status which society accords them in these roles.[49]

In this way the perspectives of Thomas and Znaniecki were united with those of Mead and Cooley to produce a concept which is perhaps especially applicable to civilization, in which conflict and change of cultures make habit alone an ineffective basis for social control.

*Marginal Man.* The idea of the marginal man is in one sense the application of role and self-conception to the situation of unusually intense culture clash. Certain groups of people, such as

47    "Behind Our Masks," *Survey Graphic*, May 1, 1926, p. 137.
48    *Introduction*, pp. 116–20.
49    "Human Nature, Attitudes, and the Mores" (1931), p. 37.

the American mulattoes, European Jews, Asiatic mixed bloods, and the Chinese traders of southeast Asia, have become deeply enough involved in two distinct societies that they cannot wholly accept the one, or be wholly accepted into the other. Confronted with the necessity to strive toward an internally consistent self-conception, these people develop distinctive personal characteristics. Building upon Simmel's analysis of the stranger, Park observes that it is not his mixed blood but the fact that he "lives in two worlds, in both of which he is more or less of a stranger,"[50] which accounts for the marginal man's distinctive characteristics.

That the marginal man experiences stress, uncertain self-conception, depression, and other symptoms was not the most important part of Park's observation. "Inevitably he becomes, relatively to his cultural milieu, the individual with the wider horizon, the keener intelligence, the more detached and rational viewpoint. The marginal man is always relatively the more civilized human being."[51] As compared with other Negroes, the mulatto is more enterprising, restless, aggressive, and ambitious. "He is more intelligent because, for one thing, he is more stimulated, and, for another, takes himself more seriously."[52]

Aside from the continuing intrinsic utility of the concept of marginal man, two aspects of the idea have grown in importance since Park wrote. The idea that a man's attitudes reflect the group with which he identifies, and that this need not be the group in which he has recognized membership and active participation, underlies the modern concept of reference group behavior. And although Park's influence was neither first nor greatest, the wide circulation given his comments on the social determination of intelligence undoubtedly contributed to the more sophisticated understanding of the nature of intelligence which is now general.

[50]   "Human Migration and the Marginal Man," *American Journal of Sociology*, 33 (May, 1928) : 893.
[51]   Introduction to *The Marginal Man* by Everett V. Stonequist (New York: Charles Scribner's Sons, 1937), p. xviii.
[52]   "Mentality of Racial Hybrids," *American Journal of Sociology*, 36 (January, 1931) : 545.

## Collective Behavior

Park named the field of study and identified the major forms and processes of collective behavior in much the fashion that prevails today. Although he accepted the substance of LeBon's description of crowd behavior, he appraised its relation to social order differently. The crowd, to Park, was merely the most intense example of social control, upon which social order depends, and a special form of the recurrent collaborative efforts to bring about change in society. Dramatic forms of collective behavior develop because custom and the mores (that is, society) impede continuous adjustments in social structure, and the natural end product of collective behavior is a new or modified institution.

It is characteristic of Park that he presented collective behavior more as an approach to the study of social order than as a distinctive field of investigation. Although he focused on distinctive phenomena such as social unrest and social movements, which have become staples of the field, collective behavior was identified as the group in action. A formal definition of collective behavior has broad applicability; "Collective behavior, then, is the behavior of individuals under the influence of an impulse that is common and collective, an impulse, in other words, that is the result of social interaction."[53] Although he advanced the principle of *circular interaction*, which Blumer then refined as the central concept in crowd analysis, he found it equally characteristic of both crowds and publics and went further to offer it as a generally applicable historical principle.

In firmly identifying collective behavior as a normal operation of society, Park was in tune with trends which developed much later. His cautious observation that the students of crowd behavior had failed to distinguish clearly between the psychological crowd and other similar types of social groups was echoed more loudly four decades later than it was when he wrote it. Of many continui-

[53] *Introduction*, p. 865.

ties in Park's writing about collective behavior, three will serve to illustrate the social order in process.

*Process of societal change.* It is well to recall the special meaning Park gave to "society" as the traditional and rigidified patterns of collaboration. The central problem of collective behavior is to identify the processes by which society is formed and reformed. Park's most general answer was a three-stage sequence or "natural history," beginning with social unrest, leading to mass movements, and ending in the formation or modification of institutions. Social unrest "represents at once a breaking up of the established routine and a preparation for new collective action."[54] It often develops from discovery that an individual or family problem requires modification of the social order. Riots—an intense form of social unrest —stem from desperation over the group's declining capacity for collective action, in the face of rapid social change.

Under appropriate circumstances the crowd excitment and rapport supply the basis for collaboration of a different sort. "The crowd has no tradition. . . . It has therefore neither symbols, ceremonies, rites, nor ritual; it imposes no obligations and creates no loyalties."[55] Individual unrest becomes social unrest when it is transmitted through milling. "The effect of this circular form of interaction is to increase the tensions in the group and, by creating a state of expectancy, to mobilize its members for collective action."[56] Religious sects and social movements have their origins in this crowd excitement.

Park noted that scholars had generally concentrated on the characteristics of crowds as if they were transitory disruptions in the social order. He urged that more attention be given to the manner and course of change from ephemeral actions to permanent organization. The strike, for example, is not to be viewed as an isolated incident, but as part of a social movement of which the members are only dimly conscious. The enduring effects of social unrest depend upon the imposition of stable control over its vital energies. Because the crowd lacks tradition and the movement re-

54     *Ibid.*, p. 866.
55     *Ibid.*, p. 790.
56     *Ibid.*, p. 789.

pudiates tradition, leaders must develop techniques for exercising discipline over the membership. When tradition as the basis for human collaboration is weakened, its place is necessarily taken by authority if the group is still to act. This general principle took on further significance in Park's later writing. During World War II, without direct reference to totalitarianisms of the right or the left, Park pointed to a danger from too rapid social change. Through the effects of collective behavior in undermining tradition, reformers might inadvertantly deliver the community into the hands of irresponsible and intractable authority during the period when needed reforms were being consolidated.[57]

The sect was singled out for special attention, although Park seemed undecided whether it was a deviant terminus to the collective behavior sequence, an alternative line of development to more active movements, or a stage in the mobilization and discipline of members for extreme action. The sect develops out of a crowd: Park endorses Sighele's view that a sect is a chronic sort of crowd, with established membership. The thoroughly intransigent posture of the sect and its demand for absolute unanimity distinguish the sect from other groups. Every thoroughgoing revolution has its origin in a sect, for the internal ferment and fervor of the sect is necessary for new and daring ideas to be made articulate. Why some sects turn outward to political action and others turn inward as religious communities is unanswered, except that they have their origins respectively in acting and expressive crowds. Additionally, in order to explain the otherwise incomprehensible behavior in religious sects we must recognize that they have at some time been individually or collectively frustrated in their efforts to act.

The view that from expressive crowd to religious sect is an altogether separate line of development is compromised when Park examines nationalistic movements. He did not have the advantage of the more recent studies that have shown the interrelationship and sequence between millennial and political movements in underdeveloped areas of the world; yet he seemed aware that nation-

---

[57]    "Social Planning and Human Nature," *Publications of the American Sociological Society* (August, 1935), pp. 19–28.

alistic movements have at successive stages the attributes of religious sect and of political movements. Like a religious sect, a nationalistic movement arises in response to culture conflict, to save the individual from personal disorganization. But the sectarian life then arouses a lively sense of common purpose and the inspiration of a common cause, which may permit the group to develop a political aim and become a power to be reckoned with.

*Public and the News.* In the *Introduction*, the public receives only the briefest attention but appears as a repeated and central concern in Park's essays dealing with news and the workings of democratic society. Unlike the crowd, interaction in the public "takes the form of discussion. Individuals tend to act upon one another critically; issues are raised and parties form. Opinions clash and thus modify and moderate one another."[58] Park takes the crucial importance of the public as the mechanism for democratic decision-making and its function of facilitating change without disruption so entirely for granted that he does not deal with these matters explicitly.

It is perhaps obvious that the public thrives in a free society and that the people must have access to knowledge of what is going on. But the essential mechanism of the public is discussion that centers on the news. And here we find requirements both of uniformity and of diversity. It is only because the news is capable of more than one interpretation that we discuss it. Yet, "there can be no such thing as news, in so far as concerns politics, except in a community in which there is a body of tradition and common understanding in terms of which events are ordinarily interpreted."[59] For news to circulate there must be both a degree of rapport in the community and a degree of inner tension.

The impact of the press in this process drew Park's special attention. He frequently observed that it was the historic shift from the journal filled primarily with editorial views to the paper dispensing news that gave the press its mass appeal. Editorial views in an earlier era had considerable influence because each locality

[58]    *Introduction*, p. 869.
[59]    "News and the Power of the Press," *American Journal of Sociology*, 47 (July, 1941): 1–11.

and occupation had its intellectual leaders who read the journals and relayed the opinions. While thus adumbrating the theory of a two-step communication flow, Park deemphasized its application to modern mass communication. Perhaps in retrospect he overstressed the rapidity with which happenings cease to be news and attention shifts. His discussions likewise give us no basis for anticipating the vital place of syndicated columnists and other media commentators in recent years.

Park explicitly denied that it was the function of the news to shape public opinion. It is the role of the press to facilitate the emergence of a collective will *after* a sequence of agitation and unrest. By dispersing and distracting attention, news decreases tension, and by keeping people in touch with a larger world than the immediate publics, encourages them to break out of these limited circles and act on their own. Although he addressed himself to the problem of propaganda on one occasion, one may feel that he never threw off his identity as a reporter sufficiently to distinguish consistently between the news as it ought to be and the news as it is.

In spite of his devotion to the public, Park did not share the utopian conception of consensus through discussion. He noted that at certain times excitement rises, and when this happens interest narrows and discussion ceases and the demand for immediate action strengthens the hands of the dominant community leaders. But more particularly, the product of discussion of public issues is not agreement but heightened dissension. The superficial consensus grounded in tradition gives the impression of an agreement, which sanctions the acts of officials. But through discussion people penetrate this surface consensus, lay bare hidden disagreements, and find the reconciliation of their views more difficult than heretofore. The result, therefore, is not to facilitate change and bring about constructive solutions to problems. Most reform measures are placed on the books when the public is at a low ebb. It is not the function of publics to make peace, and war is often the natural continuation of discussion. His observation concerning the exposure and magnification of latent disagreement through discussion deserves greater attention than it has received. It is consistent with

Park's views in another area that the relinquishment of disagreement in discussion is more a matter of accommodation than of the discovery of similar values and viewpoints.

*Morale.*  Unlike writers who have treated morale as a sort of personal attribute and attitude, Park viewed it plainly as an aspect of collective behavior. Although Park concerned himself explicitly about morale only when World War II brought it to the forefront of attention, the idea of a quality related to the ability of a society (in the more common sense) to maintain tension over time and carry an enterprise to completion appears often in his writing. When individuals are in sufficient rapport, "a diffuse social excitement tends to envelop, like an atmosphere, all participants in the common life and to give direction and tendency to their interests and attitudes."[60] In intimate groups morale is esprit de corps; in religious sects it is founded on dogma. The idea of morale is inapplicable to the crowd, because its actions are unpremeditated. In the larger unit morale is itself the product of involvement in collective action. "There is probably no other social process, no form of interaction, by which the individual components of a society are so effectively or so completely integrated, if not fused, as they are by participation in some form of collective action."[61] The will to carry a collective action to completion is developed in the course of that very collective action. Like his mentor, Simmel, Park observes that conflict with another nation, or a minority group's identification of a supposed oppressor, is often the most effective way to morale.

[60]    "News as a Form of Knowledge," *American Journal of Sociology,* 45 (March, 1940): 683.
[61]    "Morale and the News," *American Journal of Sociology,* 47 (November, 1941): 361–62.

# I. Sociological Method

**1**

# THE CITY AS A SOCIAL LABORATORY

## I. *Human Nature and the City*

THE CITY has been described as the natural habitat of civilized man. It is in the city that man developed philosophy and science, and became not merely a rational but a sophisticated animal. This means, for one thing, that it is in the urban environment —in a world which man himself has made—that mankind first achieved an intellectual life and acquired those characteristics which most distinguish him from the lower animals and from primitive man. For the city and the urban environment represent man's most consistent and, on the whole, his most successful attempt to remake the world he lives in more after his heart's desire. But if the city is the world which man created, it is the world in which he is henceforth condemned to live. Thus, indirectly, and without any clear sense of the nature of his task, in making the city man has remade himself.

It is in some such sense and in some such connection as this that we think of the city as a social laboratory.

As a matter of fact civilization and social progress have assumed in our modern cities something of the character of a controlled experiment. Progress tends to assume that character, for example, wherever fact-finding precedes legislation and reforms are conducted by experts rather than by amateurs. Social sur-

---

Reprinted from *Chicago: An Experiment in Social Science Research*, ed. T. V. Smith and Leonard D. White (Chicago: University of Chicago Press, 1929), pp. 1–19.

*3*

veys and bureaus of municipal research are evidences of a form of politics that has become empirical rather than doctrinaire.

The social problem is fundamentally a city problem. It is the problem of achieving in the freedom of the city a social order and a social control equivalent to that which grew up naturally in the family, the clan, and the tribe.

Civilized man is, so to speak, a late arrival. Viewed in the long perspective of history the appearance of the city and of city life are recent events. Man grew up and acquired most of his native and inheritable traits in an environment in which he lived much as the lower animals live, in direct dependence upon the natural world. In the turmoil of changes which has come with the evolution of city and civil life he has not been able to adapt himself fundamentally and biologically to his new environment.

As long as man lived within the limits of the tribe, custom and tradition provided for all the ordinary exigencies of life and the authority of natural leaders was sufficient to meet the recurrent crises of a relatively stable existence. But the possibilities of human life widened with the rise of the urban community. With the new freedom and the broader division of labor, which the new social order introduced, the city became the center and the focus of social changes that have steadily grown in extent and complexity until every metropolitan city is now a local center of a world-economy, and of a civilization in which local and tribal cultures now in process of fusion will presently disappear altogether.

In a city where custom has been superseded by public opinion and positive law, man has been compelled to live by his wits rather than by his instinct or tradition. The result is the emergence of the individual man as a unit of thought and action.

The peasant who comes to the city to work and live is, to be sure, emancipated from the control of ancestral custom, but at the same time he is no longer backed by the collective wisdom of the peasant community. He is on his own. The case of the peasant is typical. Everyone is more or less on his own in a city. The consequence is that man, translated to the city, has become a problem to himself and to society in a way and to an extent that he never was before.

The older order, based as it was on custom and tradition, was absolute and sacred. It had, besides, something of the character of nature itself; it had grown up, and men took it as they found it, like the climate and the weather, as part of the natural order of things. The new social order, on the other hand, is more or less of an artificial creation, an artifact. It is neither absolute nor sacred, but pragmatic and experimental. Under the influence of a pragmatic point of view education has ceased to be a form of social ritual merely; politics has become empirical; religion is now a quest rather than a tradition, something to be sought rather than to be transmitted.

Natural science came into existence in an effort of man to obtain control over external and physical nature. Social science is now seeking, by the same methods of disinterested observation and research, to give man control over himself. As it is in the city that the political problem, that is, the problem of social control, has arisen, so it is in the city that the problem must be studied.

## II. *The First Local Studies*

It is the detailed and local studies of man in his habitat and under the conditions in which he actually lives, that have contributed most to give the social sciences that realistic and objective character which they have assumed in recent years.

The first of these local studies were, as might be expected, practical rather than theoretic. They were the studies of health and housing; studies of poverty and crime. They became the basis for a whole series of reforms: model tenements, playgrounds, vital statistics. They created a new and romantic interest in the slum. A new literature grew up, telling us how the other half lived, giving us at the same time a new sense of the fact that poor people and immigrants were human like ourselves.

Social settlements, established about near the close of the nineteenth century in England and America, became outposts for observation and for intimate studies of social conditions in regions of the city that up to that time had remained *terra incognita*, except for those pioneer students of urban sociology—politicians and the

police. *Hull House Maps and Papers*, published by Jane Addams
and her associates, in Chicago, 1895, and *The City Wilderness*, and
*Americans in Process*, by Robert Woods, of the South End House,
Boston, a few years later, were in the nature of an exploration and
recognizance, laying the ground for the more systematic and detailed studies which followed. Notable among these were the series
of inquiries into housing conditions in Chicago under the direction
of Sophonisba P. Breckinridge and Edith Abbott begun in 1908
at the request of the chief sanitary inspector of Chicago and under
the auspices of the department of social investigation (Russell Sage
Foundation) of the Chicago School of Civics and Philanthropy.
Early studies included the housing of non-family groups of men;
families in furnished rooms; the Twenty-ninth Ward back of the
yards; the West Side revisited; South Chicago at the gates of the
steel mills; the problem of the Negro; two Italian districts; among
the Slovaks in the Twentieth Ward; Lithuanians in the Fourth
Ward; Greeks and Italians in the neighborhood of Hull House.[1]

Meanwhile Charles Booth had begun, some time about 1888,
his epoch-making study of life and labor in London,[2] followed
in 1901 by Rountree's more minute study of poverty in New York.[3]
These were case studies on a grand scale. The thing that characterized them was a determined and, as it seemed, somewhat pedantic
effort to reduce the descriptive and impressionistic statements of
investigators and observers to the more precise and general formulations of a statistical statement. Booth said:

No one can go, as I have done, over the description of the inhabitants
of street after street in this huge district (East London), taken house
by house and family by family—full as it is of picturesque details
noted down from the lips of the visitor to whose mind they have been
recalled by the open pages of their schedules—and doubt the genuine
character of the information and its truth. Of the wealth of my ma-

[1]    Series of articles on Chicago housing conditions in the *American
Journal of Sociology*, XVI (1910–11), 145–70; 298–308; 433–68; XVII
(1911–12), 1–34; 145–76; XVIII (1912–13), 241–57; 509–42; XX (1914–
15), 145–69, 289–312; XXI (1915–16), 285–316.
[2]    Charles Booth, *Life and Labor of the People of London* (9 vols.)
(London, 1892), p. 97.
[3]    B. Seebohm Rountree, *Poverty: A Study of Town Life* (London,
1901).

terial I have no doubt. I am indeed embarrassed by its mass and by my resolution to make use of no fact that I cannot give a quantitative value. The materials for sensational stories lie plentifully in every book of our notes; but, even if I had the skill to use my material in this way —that gift of the imagination which is called "realistic"—I should not wish to use it here. There is struggling poverty, there is destitution, there is hunger, drunkenness, brutality and crime; no one doubts that it is so. My object has been to attempt to show the numerical relation which poverty, misery and depravity bear to regular earnings and comparative comfort, and to describe the general conditions under which each class lives.[4]

It was not, however, Booth's statistics, but his realistic descriptions of the actual life of the occupational classes—the conditions under which they lived and labored, their passions, pastimes, domestic tragedies, and the life-philosophies with which each class met the crises peculiar to it—which made these studies a memorable and a permanent contribution to our knowledge of human nature and of society. What we have then, finally, in these volumes, is a minute and painstaking account of the phase of modern civilization at the end of the nineteenth century, as manifested in the life of the London laborer. These volumes were a sociological study; they have become a historical document.

The thing which gave the greatest impetus to local studies in the United States was the establishment of the Sage Foundation in 1906, and the publication in the period from 1909 to 1914 of the findings of the Pittsburgh Survey. Pittsburgh was chosen by Paul U. Kellogg and his collaborators for investigation because it was regarded as a particularly flagrant illustration of the working out of forces and tendencies that had their origin in the rapidly expanding industrial life of America. Pittsburgh was conspicuously and exclusively an industrial city. America was in process of industrial transformation. Pittsburgh offered itself as clinical material for a study of American civilization. It seemed possible to exhibit, in a single city, just how the industrial organization of that time affected the personal and cultural life of a people. This was the purpose for which the Survey was undertaken.

The Pittsburgh Survey was timely. It appeared at a moment

[4]    Booth, *op. cit.*, I, 5–6.

when, in every part of the United States, thoughtful people were seeking light upon problems that no longer yielded to the traditional technique embodied in the forms and traditions of party politics. It was a time when reformers were seeking to keep reforms out of politics, that is, out of party politics. The Pittsburgh Survey offered a new method for political education and collective action in local affairs, a method that did not raise party issues and did not involve anything so revolutionary as a change in the control of local government.

Social surveys now came into vogue, and local studies of a sort were undertaken in every part of the country. The wide range of interests with which they thought to deal is indicated by the subject matter of some of the more important of them. *The Springfield Survey*, which undertook to cover the whole field of social politics: public health, education, social service in all its various aspects;[5] the *Survey of Criminal Justice in Cleveland*, published in 1922, and the study of race relations in Chicago after the race riot, published in the same year under the title of *The Negro in Chicago*, are examples.

These surveys have, as regional studies invariably do, the characteristics of local and contemporary history. They emphasize what is unique and individual in the situations investigated. But they are at the same time case studies. Conditions in one city are described in terms that make them comparable to conditions in other cities. They do not yield generalizations of wide or general validity, but they have furnished a body of materials that raise issues and suggest hypotheses which can eventually be investigated statistically and stated in quantitative terms.

## III. *The Urban Community*

In all, or most, of these investigations there is implicit the notion that the urban community, in its growth and organization, represents a complex of tendencies and events that can be described

---

5    *The Springfield Survey: A Study of Social Conditions in an American City*, directed by Shelby M. Harrison; 3 vols. (New York: Russell Sage Foundation, 1918–20).

conceptually, and made the object of independent study. There is implicit in all these studies the notion that the city is a thing with a characteristic organization and a typical life-history, and that individual cities are enough alike so that what one learns about one city may, within limits, be assumed to be true of others.

This notion has been the central theme of a series of special studies of the Chicago Urban Community, some of which have already been published, others of which are still in progress.[6] Among these, three, *The Hobo*, by Nels Anderson, *The Ghetto*, by Louis Wirth, and *The Gold Coast and the Slum*, by Harvey W. Zorbaugh, deal each with one of the so-called natural areas of the city. *The Hobo: A Study of the Homeless Man* is unique in so far as it investigates the casual laborer in his habitat, that is to say in the region of the city where the interests and habits of the casual laborer have been, so to speak, institutionalized. *The Ghetto*, on the other hand, is a study of the Jewish quarter, but it is at the same time the natural history of an instituion of Jewish life, an institution that grew up and flourished in the Middle Ages but has persisted in some fashion down to the present day. It has persisted, however, because it performed a social function, making it possible for two unassimilated peoples to live together, participating in a single economy, but preserving, at the same time, each its own racial and cultural integrity. *The Gold Coast and the Slum*, finally, is a study of the Lower North Side, which is not so much a natural area, as a congeries of natural areas, including, as it does, "Little Sicily," "The Gold Coast," and an extensive region of rooming-houses between.

A region is called "a natural area" because it comes into existence without design, and performs a function, though the function, as in the case of the slum, may be contrary to anybody's desire. It is a natural area because it has a natural history. The existence of these natural areas, each with its characteristic function, is some indication of the sort of thing the city turns out upon analysis to be—not as has been suggested earlier, an artifact merely, but in some sense, and to some degree, an organism.

The city is, in fact, a constellation of natural areas, each with

[6]    Robert E. Park, E. W. Burgess, *et al.*, *The City* (Chicago, 1925).

its own characteristic milieu, and each performing its specific function in the urban economy as a whole. The relation of the different natural areas of the city to one another is typified in the relation of the city and its suburbs. These suburbs are, apparently, mere extensions of the urban community. Every suburb, pushing outward into the open country, tends to have a character which distinguishes it from every other. The metropolis is, it seems, a great sifting and sorting mechanism, which, in ways that are not yet wholly understood, infallibly selects out of the population as a whole the individuals best suited to live in a particular region and a particular melieu. The larger the city, the more numerous and the more completely characterized its suburbs will be. The city grows by expansion, but it gets its character by the selection and segregation of its population, so that every individual finds, eventually, either the place where he can, or the place where he must, live.[7]

Recent studies in Chicago have revealed to what an extraordinary extent this segregation may go. There are regions in Chicago where there are almost no children; regions where half the boys of juvenile-court age are recorded, at least once in the course of a year, as delinquents;[8] other regions where there are no divorces, and still others in which the percentage of divorces and desertions is larger, with one exception, than that of any other political unit in the United States.[9]

The proportion of age and sex groups shows extraordinary variations in different parts of the city, and these variations are dependable indices of other cultural and character differences in the population.

It does not follow, from what has been said, that the populations in the different natural areas of the city can be described as homogeneous. People live together on the whole, not because they are

[7]    See the article by E. W. Burgess, "The Growth of the City," in R. E. Park, *et al.*, *The City*, pp. 47–62.

[8]    See Clifford R. Shaw, *Delinquency and Crime Areas of Chicago* (Chicago, 1929).

[9]    Ernest R. Mowrer, *Family Disorganization*, pp. 116–23.

alike, but because they are useful to one another. This is particularly true of great cities, where social distances are maintained in spite of geographical proximity, and where every community is likely to be composed of people who live together in relations that can best be described as symbiotic rather than social.

On the other hand, every community is to some degree an independent cultural unit, has its own standards, its own conception of what is proper, decent, and worthy of respect. As individuals rise or sink in the struggle for status in the community they invariably move from one region to another; go up to the Gold Coast, or down to the slum, or perhaps occupy a tolerable position somewhere between the two. In any case, they learn to accommodate themselves more or less completely to the conditions and the code of the area into which they move. The case records of social agencies and institutions make it possible to follow the migrations of individuals and families and learn what has happened to them. It is often possible to carry these studies of individuals and families farther and to get information and insight in regard to their subjective experiences, their attitudes and states of mind, outlook on life, and above all their changing conceptions of themselves incident to their movements from one milieu to another. The numerous life-histories of immigrants that have been published in recent years furnish materials of this sort.

The more we understand the attitudes and personal histories of individuals, the more we can know the community in which these individuals live. On the other hand, the more knowledge we have of the milieu in which the individual lives, or has lived, the more intelligible his behavior becomes. This is true, because while temperament is inherited, character and habit are formed under the influence of environment.

As a matter of fact, most of our ordinary behavior problems are actually solved, if solved at all, by transferring the individual from an environment in which he behaves badly to one in which he behaves well. Here, again, social science has achieved something that approaches in character a laboratory experiment. For the purose of these experiments the city, with its natural regions, becomes a "frame of reference," i.e., a device for controlling our observations of social conditions in their relation to human behavior.

## IV. *The Individual*

It is due to the intrinsic nature of society and of social relations that we ordinarily find our social problems embodied in the persons and in the behavior of individuals. It is because social problems so frequently terminate in problems of individual behavior and because social relations are finally and fundamentally personal relations that the attitude and behavior of individuals are the chief sources of our knowledge of society.

The city always has been a prolific source of clinical material for the study of human nature because it has always been the source and center of social change. In a perfectly stable society where man has achieved a complete biological and social equilibrium, social problems are not likely to arise, and the anxieties, mental conflicts, and ambitions which stimulate the energies of civilized man, and incidentally make him a problem to himself and to society, are lacking.

It was with what Simmel calls inner enemies—the poor, the criminal, and the insane—that personality studies seem to have had their origin. It is, however, within comparatively recent years that poverty and delinquency have come to be reckoned along with insanity as personality and behavior problems. At the present time this is so far true that social service has come to be recognized as a branch of medicine, and the so-called psychiatric social worker has come to replace, or at least supplement, the work of the friendly visitor. The probation officer, visiting teacher, and the public playground director have all achieved a new professional status as the notion has gained recognition that social problems are fundamentally behavior problems.

A new impetus was given to the study of personality problems with the organization in 1899 in Chicago of the first juvenile court of the United States. Juvenile courts became at once, as far as was practicable under the circumstances under which they came into existence, behavior clinics. Putting the delinquent on probation was an invitation to him to participate in an experiment, under the direction of a probation officer, that had as its aim his own rehabilitation.

It was through the establishment of the Juvenile Psychopathic Institute[10] in connection with the Juvenile Court of Chicago that Healy began those systematic studies upon which that notable book, *The Individual Delinquent,* published in 1915, was based. It was followed by similar studies, under the Judge Baker Foundation, in Boston, and by the establishment of other institutes for child study and so-called behavior clinics in every part of the country, notably, the Child Welfare Research Station at the University of Iowa, the Institute of Child Welfare at the University of Minnesota, the Institute for Child Welfare Research at Teachers College, New York City, the Institute for Child Guidance, and locally supported child-guidance clinics established through demonstrations of the Commonwealth Fund Program for the Prevention of Delinquency in St. Louis, Dallas, Los Angeles, Minneapolis, St. Paul, Cleveland, and Philadelphia.[11]

The study of juvenile delinquency and of behavior problems in general was established on a firm basis in Chicago with the organization in May, 1926, by Dr. Herman M. Adler of the Behavior Research Fund. Dr. Adler has brought together a notable group of students and experts and has set up an administrative machinery for making accurate scientific records, both psychiatric and social, which as they have accumulated have created a fund of fact and information that is now being subjected to elaborate statistical analyses which are yielding surprising and important results.

Studies of the Institute of Juvenile Research and of the Behavior Research Fund are in certain respects unique. They are at once psychiatric and social studies, i.e., studies not merely of the individual and his behavior but of the environment and of the situation to which the behavior is a response. This realizes, in the form of a definite program, a conception which has been the sub-

---

10     Now the Institute for Juvenile Research.
11     For a review and analysis of the child-study movement see W. I. Thomas and Dorothy S. Thomas, *The Child in America* (New York, 1928).

ject of several conferences between the psychiatrists and representatives of the other social sciences, seeking to define the relation of psychiatric and social studies and to determine the role which psychiatry is likely to play in co-operation with the social sciences in the investigation and solution of social problems.

There is not now, if there ever was, any question that the individual's conception of himself, the role which he plays in any society, and the character which he eventually acquires are very largely determined by the associations which he makes and, in general, by the world in which he lives. The city is a complex of such worlds—worlds which touch but never completely penetrate.

The differences between urban areas in respect to the type and character of the social life which they support is undoubtedly as great as the standards of living that they maintain, or the price of land on which they are situated. One of the important series of local studies which the University of Chicago has undertaken is that which involves a delimitation and characterization of all the important areas of the city. This study is based on the assumption that more complete knowledge of the localities and of the peoples of the city will throw a new light upon the extraordinary variation, in the different areas of the city in the amount and extent of desertion, divorce, delinquency, crime, and other evidences of social disorganization. In doing this it will be of service to every social agency that is seeking to deal directly or indirectly with these problems. But in determining with more definiteness the conditions under which social experiments are actually being carried on, it will make the city in some more real sense than it has been hitherto a social laboratory.

## V. *Institutions*

The city has been made the subject of investigation from many different points of view. There is already a considerable literature on the geography of the city, and there is a vast body of research concerning the city as a physical object, including studies of housing, city planning, and municipal engineering. N. S. B. Gras, in his *Introduction to Economic History*, has made the city the central theme in the history of an economy that has evolved through the stages of village, town, and city to the metropolitan economy of the present day. As a matter of fact economic history assumes a new significance when it is written from the ecological and regional point of view, and when the city, with its market place, is conceived as the focal center of an area of ever widening boundaries over which it is constantly extending and consolidating its dominance and control.

The political and administrative problems of cities have come to occupy a place in political science that has steadily increased in importance as cities have increased in population, in influence, and in complexity.

The urban community is, finally, because it is now as it has always been the melting pot of races and cultures, the region in which new institutions emerge, as earlier ones decline, are modified, and disappear.

The family, in its origin at least, is probably not an institution. It is rather the first and most primitive form of society—a form which has been preserved, although continually modified under all the changing circumstances of man's eventful career. The family has, apparently, formed the basic pattern for every type of civilization except our own. Occidental civilization is based on the city, on the *polis*, as the Greeks called it, and is political rather than familial in origin. It was in the city states of Greece and Rome that society organized on kinship, custom, and the family was superseded by a society based on civil rights and a political organization.

The family is now in process of change and disintegration in every part of the civilized world, including the regions where it has persisted longest in its original form, Japan and China. Changes in the family, however, are taking place more rapidly in cities than elsewhere. Everything that is characteristic of city life, a mobile population, a wide division of labor, and the multiplication of municipal institutions and social conveniences of all sorts have contributed to bring about these changes. Schools, hospitals, and all the numerous agencies for personal service which have taken over, one by one, the functions once performed by the home and in the family have contributed indirectly to undermine that ancient institution and diminish its social importance.

As it is in the urban environment that the older forms of the family have declined, so it is in the city that most of the experiments in new forms of family life are taking place. That is why the institution of the family can be studied to the best advantage in cities rather than elsewhere.

The city and the conditions of life that it imposes have greatly tended to the secularization of all aspects of social life, and this has had profound effect upon the organization of the church. Numerous local studies of city and rural churches have been made in recent years, but as yet no studies have been made to show the extent of changes which involve the structure and function of the church as a social institution.

There is, however, no doubt but that changes are taking place and that as the social sciences develop an interest in and methods for the study of civilized, as they have for primitive, man the changes taking place in contemporary religious institutions will assume an importance that they do not now seem to have.

In recent years, particularly in Chicago, under the inspiration and initiative of Professor Charles E. Merriam, a beginning has been made looking to more realistic studies of the actual workings of the political process as it takes place under the conditions of modern city life.[12]

The political process, broadly conceived, includes much more than the formulation of laws by legislatures and their interpretation by the courts. It includes a whole cycle of events that begins with some sort of general unrest, in which political issues arise, and concludes with the general acceptance into the mores and habits of the community of a new rule of conduct, and—to use an expression which W.I.Thomas has made familiar—a new definition of the situation.

The political process includes public discussion and a definition of issues; the formation and expression of public opinion;

[12]   See Charles E. Merriam, *New Aspects of Politics* (Chicago, 1925) ; *Four American Party Leaders* (New York, 1926) ; *Chicago: A More Intimate View of Urban Politics* (New York, 1929).

the election of legislators; the framing and enactment of legislation; the interpretation and enforcement of the law, and, finally,
the general acceptance of and acquiescence in the enforcement of
the law by the community. In this way the law eventually passes
over into custom and becomes fixed in the habits of the community.
The political process covers all the operations of government; and
since society is essentially an organization for social control, it involves finally every aspect of social life.

The organization in New York City, Chicago, and elsewhere,
of bureaus of municipal research and the more recent studies in
Cleveland and St. Louis of the administration of criminal justice
indicate the direction and progress of research in this field.

The studies of the political science group at the University of
Chicago are indicative not only of the trend toward a more realistic
perception of the political process but of the attempt to introduce
scientific methods into the description and prediction of political
behavior, as in the research projects already published of *Non-
Voting* by Charles E. Merriam and Harold F. Gosnell, *Getting Out
the Vote* by H. F. Gosnell, *The Chicago Primary of 1926: A Study
in Election Methods* by Carroll H. Wooddy, *Carter H. Harrison I:
A Study in Political Leadership* by C. O. Johnson, and *The City
Manager* by Leonard D. White.

Sumner says that there are two kinds of institutions, (1) those
which grow, and (2) those which are enacted. But institutions are
not merely enacted. Rather, they are discovered and invented. The
fact seems to be that institutions always grow, but they grow, ordinarily, by the addition and summation of specific inventions.[13]

One thing that makes the city a peculiarly advantageous place
in which to study institutions and social life generally is the fact
that under the conditions of urban life institutions grow rapidly.
They grow under our very eyes, and the processes by which they
grow are open to observation and so, eventually, to experimentation.

Another thing that makes the city an advantageous place to
study social life and gives it the character of a social laboratory

13    Sumner, *Folkways*, pp. 48–50.

is the fact that in the city every characteristic of human nature is not only visible but is magnified.

In the freedom of the city every individual, no matter how eccentric, finds somewhere an environment in which he can expand and bring what is peculiar in his nature to some sort of expression. A smaller community sometimes tolerates eccentricity, but the city often rewards it. Certainly one of the attractions of a city is that somewhere every type of individual—the criminal and beggar, as well as the man of genius—may find congenial company and the vice or the talent which was suppressed in the more intimate circle of the family or in the narrow limits of a small community, discovers here a moral climate in which it flourishes.

The result is that in the city all the secret ambitions and all the suppressed desires find somewhere an expression. The city magnifies, spreads out, and advertises human nature in all its various manifestations. It is this that makes the city interesting, even fascinating. It is this, however, that makes it of all places the one in which to discover the secrets of human hearts, and to study human nature and society.

# 2

# UNDERSTANDING A

# FOLK CULTURE

SOME TIME during the winter of 1898 and the spring of 1899 William James read to his students in philosophy a notable paper he had then just finished writing, to which he later gave the quaint and intriguing title, "A Certain Blindness in Human Beings."

The "blindness" to which James here refers is a kind of blindness to which we are all subject, by the very limitation of our human nature and of our individual experience, our blindness, namely, "to the feelings of creatures and peoples other than ourselves."

"We are," as James says, "practical beings each with limitations and duties to perform. Each is bound to feel intensely the importance of duties and the significance of the situations that call these forth. But this feeling in each of us is a vital secret for sympathy with which we vainly look to others. The others are too much absorbed in their own vital secrets to take an interest in ours."[1]

It is not possible to suggest in a word the significance which this fact of the isolation and loneliness of the individual—each in his own little world, hugging his own personal secret—assumes

Introduction to *The Shadow of the Plantation* by Charles S. Johnson (Chicago: University of Chicago Press, 1934), pp. xi–xxiv. Reprinted by permission of the publisher.

[1]     William James, *Talks to Teachers on Psychology; and to Students on Some of Life's Ideals.*

in James's interpretation of it. Suffice to say that the fact connects
up directly with a definite philosophy to which James subscribed
and to a theory of knowledge to which—if he did not first formulate it—he lent a powerful support.

## I

My reason for referring to this essay here and to the conception of human relations and of knowledge, which it so persuasively
sets forth, is that it seems to shed light, from an unexpected source,
upon the problem and method of this present study and of social
studies generally, particularly when they are concerned with the
customs and institutions of isolated and provincial peoples; peoples who, though they live close to, and dependent upon us, as
we upon them, are still outside the orbit of our ordinary life and
understanding.

This volume is concerned with the Negro peasants of the southern plantations, but the Negroes of the "black belts" are not the
only peoples in America who live on the outer margins of our
understanding and to whose vital secrets we must confess a certain
blindness. There are other peoples, white peoples, like the Acadi-
ans of southwestern Louisiana; the Mennonites and so-called
Pennsylvania Dutch of Lancaster County, Pennsylvania, and
vicinity. There are also the mountain whites of the Appalachians
and the peoples of mixed racial ancestry like the Mexicans of New
Mexico and the little isolated communities of Indian, Negro, and
white mixtures, scattered about in remote parts of Virginia, North
Carolina, Alabama, and Louisiana. All of these are peoples who
live, to be sure, within the political boundaries of the Unites States
but live nevertheless on the margins of our culture. In this sense,
and for the further reason that they occupy a place somewhere
between the more primitive and tribally organized and the urban
populations of our modern cities, they may be called "marginal
peoples." The distinction between them and the peoples by whom
they are surrounded is that they are not merely people, but folk
people, and their culture, in so far as it differs from that of the
majority of us in the United States, is a folk culture.

What is a folk culture and what is the folk? A very simple way to state the matter is to say that the "folk" is a people whose current history is recorded, if at all, by the ethnologist rather than by the historian or the newspaper. Not that folk peoples do not have history, but it exists for the most part in the form of unrecorded ballads and legends which, with its folk lore, constitutes a tradition that is handed down from generation to generation by word of mouth rather than through the medium of the printed page.

It is characteristic of the folk that it has a habitat and that its culture is local. Gypsies are folk, too, but they are the exception. Though they wander, they manage somehow to preserve a cultural isolation and a tribal solidarity as complete as that of any other preliterate people. In all our various attempts to study human nature we invariably encounter these exceptions. They constitute, in fact, the most valuable data that an investigation ordinarily turns up: first, because they are the starting-points for fresh observation and further reflection; and, second, because in the long run the exceptions always prove the rule.

Redfield in his volume *Tepoztlán*, which is a study of one of the marginal peoples of Mexico, similar in some respects to those in the United States, is at some pains to define what he conceives the folk to be. He says:

Such peoples enjoy a common stock of tradition; they are the carriers of a culture. This culture preserves its continuity from generation to generation without depending upon the printed page. Moreover, such a culture is local; the folk has a habitat. And finally, the folk peoples are country peoples. If folk lore is encountered in the cities it is never in a robust condition, but always diminishing, always a vestige.[2]

And then he adds:

The southern Negro is our one principal folk. He has a local tradition orally transmitted; he makes folk songs. Except for him we have to search for folk peoples in the United States. In the moutains of the

[2]    Robert Redfield, *Tapoztlán, A Mexican Village* (University of Chicago Press, 1930), pp. 1–6.

south and southeast we have a sort of vestigial folk. And here and there, in such occupations as involve long periods of isolation and a relative independence of the printed page—as, for example, among lumbermen or cowboys—a sort of quasi-folk develop, who write anonymous folk songs and sometimes build up, around campfires, folk sagas of the Paul Bunyan variety.

On the other hand, the folk are not to be confused and identified with the peasant who has left the soil to live and work in the city. Such peoples constitute what might be described as the "populus" or, better still, the "proletariat."

So the Negro of the plantation—though the two are closely related and the history of the one goes far to explain the existence of the other—is not to be identified with the mobile and migratory Negro laborers who crowd the slums of southern cities, or, like the hero of Howard Odum's *Rainbow round My Shoulder*, go wandering about the country celebrating their feedom and their loneliness by singing "blues."

These blues, which, by the way, first gained recognition as a form of popular ballad in night clubs of Beale Street, Memphis, are the natural idiom of the Negro proletarian, just as the "spirituals" have been, and to a very considerable extent still are, the natural expression of the mind and the mood of the plantation Negro. The distinction between the folk of the villages and the open country and the proletarians or populus of the city is expressed and symbolized in the difference between the folk song and the popular ballad, the spirituals and the blues.

## II

Marginal peoples, peoples in transit between simpler and primitive and more sophisticated and complex cultures, such as characterize our modern industrial and urban civilization, constitute, as I have suggested, a special problem in method, but one which is after all fundamental to studies of society and human nature everywhere.

There are no special difficulties in describing the external forms and the obvious expressions of a local culture. The difficulty consists in making that culture intelligible; in discovering the meaning and the function of usages, customs, and institutions.

Anthropologists, in their studies of primitive peoples, have distinguished between (1) material and (2) non-material elements of a culture. Material culture is represented by the tools, artifacts, and in general the technical devices employed by a people in their dealings with the external world. Non-material culture, on the other hand, includes all those institutions, ceremonial customs, ritual dances, and what not by which a people maintains its morale and is enabled to act collectively.

Institutions are, generally speaking, devices which come into existence in the effort to act collectively and exist in order to make collective action more effective.

But customs persist and preserve their external forms after they have lost their original meaning and functions. Institutions are borrowed or imposed upon peoples to whose traditions, instincts, and actual needs they are quite foreign, or have not yet been fully assimilated. Fashions change, and with the change institutions, though they still persist, are looked upon with profoundly changed attitudes.

Considerations of this sort have led anthropologists in studying culture to distinguish between form and function, and to emphasize the subjective and less obvious aspects of the cultural complex. The study of a society or of a people turns out under these circumstances to be the study not merely of its institutions but of its mentality.

What is meant by mentality in this sense is stated impressively by Redfield in the concluding chapter of his volume *Tepoztlán*. "If by mentality is understood," he says, "a complex of habits employed in meeting unfamiliar problems," then mentality, too, is an aspect of culture. "If the individual undergoes experiences of a very different sort from those undergone before, he develops a correspondingly new organ, a new mind."

But there is a less obvious aspect of social institutions in which they appear in even more intimate and vital association with the people whose life they serve. It has been observed that as long as their social institutions are functioning normally, primitive peoples ordinarily exhibit an extraordinary zest in the life they lead, even when that life, like that of the Eskimo in the frozen North or the pigmies in the steaming forest of Central Africa, seems to be one of constant privation and hardship.

On the other hand, when some catastrophe occurs which undermines the traditional structure of their society, they sometimes lose their natural lust for life, and that euphoria which enabled them to support the hardships of their primitive existence frequently deserts them. That catastrophe may be, and frequently is, the sudden advent of a more highly civilized people intent upon their improvement and uplift by incorporating them in a more highly organized industrial society.

Under such circumstances, a people may be so completely obsessed by a sense of their own inferiority that they no longer desire to live as a people; and if they live as individuals, they will prefer to identify themselves, as far as they are permitted to do so, with the invading or dominant people.

It is in some such way as this, i.e., by the incorporation of defeated or merely disheartened people into some larger and more complex social unit, that castes are formed.

It is evident, in spite of all that has been written of human nature and of human behavior, that the sources of joy and sorrow are still obscure. It is evident also that, as Stevenson says, in a passage in *Lantern Bearers* quoted by James, "to miss the joy is to miss all." That is to say, if you miss the joy you miss the one aspect of a people's life which more than anything else gives vitality to cultural forms and ensures their persistence, possibly in some new and modified form, under changed conditions. For this reason, the most subjective and least obvious aspect of the life of peoples and cultures is nevertheless one that cannot be neglected, particularly in the case of peoples who, as I have said, are in process of transit and subject to all the vicissitudes of profound cultural change.

This zest for life is just that personal and vital secret which, for each one of us, gives meaning and significance not merely to the life of the individual but of the society, of whatever sort it be, of which he is a member and a part.

## III

Although it describes itself as a study of "social and cultural change," the materials on which this study is based are not those with which anthropologists are familiar or are likely to approve. As a matter of fact, the study starts with a different tradition—the tradition, namely, of the rural sociologist, who conceives his community rather as a statistical aggregate than as a cultural complex. One reason for this is the convenience and the necessity of making use of the available statistics, which have been collected and classified on the basis of existing administrative units rather than of the region or of any other sort of natural area.

Thus the investigation assumed at the outset the character of a survey and study of a population rather than of a people, and the plan, as originally conceived, was, by a process of sampling, to describe and characterize statistically a population area.

The area chosen for this survey was a slice of one of the familiar "black belts," historically the region of cotton culture in the South. Macon County, of which Tuskegee is the county seat, is the seat also of Booker Washington's famous industrial school for Negroes and the county which, during his lifetime, was, so to speak, the rural laboratory in which he carried on his experiments in rural education—experiments which graduates of his school and others, with the assistance of the Rosenwald Fund, have extended to most other parts of the South.

It was assumed, no doubt, that Macon County offered a fair sample of Negro rural population, and that a study of its population would indicate what Negro education—unaccompanied, to be sure, by any special or systematic effort to reorganize on any considerable scale the plantation system—had been able to do to keep the Negro on the soil and, by raising the general level of his intelligence and encouraging him to take the initiative in improving his own condition, to improve the condition of the country as a whole.

There were other reasons why a study of Negro culture should assume the technical form of a survey beside the desirability of starting with the available information in regard to the region. One was the character of the Negro community itself, and of the very tenuous lines of connections which hold the rural population into any sort of solidarity that could be described as communal. Another was the fact that the Negro community is so completely interpenetrated and dependent upon the dominant white community that it is difficult to conceive it as having any independent existence.

Outside of the plantation the only centers of Negro life are the rural churches and rural schools. The social situation is reflected in the human geography of the county.

A bird's-eye view of Macon County discloses a country of softly rolling uplands and interspersed with fragrant, wooded swamps.

Plantation, hamlet, and town, still rather widely dispersed, are connected by a network of rural roads which, except for a few stretches of recently constructed thoroughfare, wind their way leisurely along rolling ridges in order to escape as far as possible the perils of the sometimes heavy spring rains. Closer observation of this same countryside discloses the existence of another, narrower, and less obvious network of footpaths which—unplanned, unplotted, and without official recognition—intersect, connect, and supplement but never compete with the public highways.

These two systems of transportation—the public highways connecting the towns and the plantations and the footpaths connecting the humbler habitations of the Negro tenant farmers—suggest and symbolize the complicated interrelations and divisions between the races in Macon County and in the South generally, suggest also some of the complexities and some of the difficulties of studying one section of a population without taking some account at the same time of the other.

# IV

If the study of culture is to reveal what makes life for individuals or peoples either significant and exciting or merely dull, what are the kinds of facts most likely to disclose this vital secret?

Undoubtedly the most revealing portions of the present study are the candid comments of the peoples studied on thier own lives. As recorded here, in the language and accents in which they were uttered, most of these statements have the character of a human document.

The value of a human document as a datum is that it brings the object that is under investigation closer to the observer. Like a magnifying glass, it brings into view aspects of the object that were before that time not visible or only partially so. It sometimes happens that a casual remark, like a ray of light through a keyhole, will illuminate a whole interior, the character of which could only be guessed at as long as one's observations were confined to the exterior of the structure.

A good many of the remarks recorded in this study are so concrete, so pregnant with human interest, that they might have been written by Julia Peterkin or Du Bose Heyward, whose stories of Negro life exhibit an insight and "acquaintance with" the life they are describing that is unusual even in writers of realistic fiction.

As a rule, the individuals whose conversation and comments are here recorded are not in any sense a selected group of outstanding personalities in the community; rather they are just the ordinary mine-run of the population. A good many of them are old women, grandmothers, who with the freedom traditionally accorded to "old mammies" on the plantation are accustomed to express themselves more vigorously and more volubly than other members of the family. Besides, grandmothers, partly because they are less mobile than other members of the families and therefore more likely to be at home, are in a position to speak with authority in regard to marriages, births, deaths, and all the other facts that the investigators' schedules called for.

The statements recorded, while they do not represent a selected group of individuals, do exhibit an interesting diversity of types such as one would expect the intimate associations of an isolated community would inevitably produce. It is true that every kind of cultural association produces a certain degree of cultural homogeneity, but it invariably produces at the same time characteristic personality types. Among these an occasional individual is sufficiently outstanding to achieve a recognition in this record that is not accorded to the others. This was the case of Zach Ivey, who was clear and convinced that he had had a better time when he was a slave than he had ever had since; and by way of contrast to Zach Ivey there was Riny Biggers, who had early been impressed with the high value of literacy and differed profoundly from the views on slavery which Zach Ivey professed.

It is interesting to know that the relative merits of slavery and freedom are still a matter in regard to which there are differences of opinion among the Negroes on the plantations in the South. It is indicative of the immense weight of the tradition which still supports the plantation system. It makes significant and intelligible a remark made to me years ago by an old Negro farmer in Macon County who, though he could neither read nor write, owned and conducted successfully a plantation of eleven hundred acres. He said, with the peculiar quizzical expression of a man who would like more light on an obscure problem: "You know we'se jus' so ign'rint down heah we don' see much dif'rence 'tween freedom an' slavery, 'cep' den we wuz workin' fer ole marster an' now we'se workin' fer oursel's."

## V

One can hardly escape the impression in viewing the facts of this survey that it is the inheritance of a tradition, embodied in the present plantation system, which more than anything else inhibits the progress, not merely of the black tenant but the white landlord, and that with the persistence of that tradition the small and independent farmer cannot make headway.

Under these conditions the Negro rural school, instead of creating a settled class of Negro peasant proprietors, seems, particularly since the World War, to have conspired with other tendencies to hasten the movement from the rural South to the northern cities. On the whole, the plantation, as at present organized, seems to be a sick and dying institution. It still remains, however, what it was before the Civil War, the focus and center of the Negro life in the rural community; but it is no longer able to maintain either the discipline or the morale of an efficiently functioning institution; and plantation life has apparently lost whatever zest it may ever have had for the generations of white folk and black that it once nourished.

The plight of the cotton plantation is probably due not entirely to its inability to shake off its ancient heritage, which involves among other things the tradition of Negro racial inferiority. The prosperity of the cotton plantation in the southern states is dependent, finally, upon its ability to compete with other cotton-raising areas in the world-market.

Most that is still problematic in the condition of the Negro peasant seems to focus about two quite different institutions: (1) the plantation and (2) the Negro peasant family. What is the future of either or both, since the fate of the one seems to be bound up in that of the other?

The Negro peasant family, as it exists today, is certainly a rather amorphous social organism. In slavery, parents had little or no personal responsibility for the provision and care of their children, since that office was early taken over by the planter or his overseer, who assigned some older and experienced woman to the task. The consequence was that natural maternal affection, rather than any common economic interest, constituted the tie that held the family together. The male member of the family did not count for much in this arrangement. The family was, and still is, matriarchal in character.

It was not until freedom imposed upon the Negro tenant the necessity of making his farm pay that the Negro farmer began to reckon his children as a personal asset. The effect of this was that parents began to discourage the early marriage of their children, the consequence of which would be to deprive them of their children's services.

When a Negro farmer reached the position where he owned property of his own, he had a new incentive and found a new means for maintaining the permanence of the family, since he was eager to transmit this property to his children, who in turn looked forward to inheriting it. The permanence of the property interest became the basis for a continuing family tradition, and for a more consistent life-program for both the family as a whole and its individual members.

As long, however, as the freedman continued to live under the shadow of the plantation, these changes made but slow progress. With the advent of emancipation the status of the Negro on the plantation had been suddenly transformed from that of a field hand to tenant farmer. But the actual change was not as great as might have been expected. The freedman was not able at once to enter into the spirit and tradition of a free competition and industrial society. He had no conception, for example, of the secret terror that haunts the free laborer; the fear, namely, of losing his job and of being out of work. On the contrary, his first conception of freedom was that of a condition in which he would be permanently out of work. So far, therefore, from being possessed by that mania for owning things which is the characteristic, as the communists tell us, of a capitalistic society, his first impulse and aim were to get as deeply in debt as possible. If, therefore, the agents of the "Third International" find that such Negroes are as yet not ripe for communism, it is undoubtedly because they have not had as yet the opportunity to realize the evils of a free and competitive society.

What the findings of this survey suggest, then, is: (1) the necessity of a wider—in fact, a world-wide—and comparative study of the cotton plantation not merely as an economic and industrial but as a cultural unit; and (2) a comparative study of the actual conditions of the world in which the people on the plantation live.

## VI

One thing that complicates any attempt to study Negro peasant institutions and culture is the fact that, though the white man and the Negro have lived and worked together in the United States for three hundred years and more, the two races are still in a certain sense strangers to one another. One way in which this fact finds expression is in the statement that the Negro has not yet been, and perhaps never can be, assimilated. Another and more drastic expression of the same conviction is the familiar statement, repeated in most every part of the world in which Europeans have settled: "This is a white man's country."

It is very curious that anyone in America should still think of the Negro, even the Negro peasant of the "black belts," as in any sense an alien or stranger, since he has lived here longer than most of us, has interbred to a greater extent than the white man with the native Indian, and is more completely a product than anyone of European origin is likely to be of the local conditions under which he was born and bred.

There is, nevertheless, a sense in which the Negro, even though culturally he be a purely native product, is not assimilated, though in just what sense this is true it is difficult to say.

One is reminded of the old lady who, visiting the Indian village at the World's Fair, was moved to speak a friendly word to one of these aborigines. What she said was: "How do you like our country?"

It was her view that, this being a white man's country, an Indian would naturally feel a little strange in it. It did not occur to her that an Indian might not share this common-sense assumption.

It is just these naïve assumptions, which are matters of common sense in one class, caste, sect, or ethnic group but not in others, that seem to constitute the final obstacle to the assimilation of peoples. They reveal social distances between individuals and peoples otherwise unsuspected.

William Graham Sumner has invented a word to describe the state of mind that these innocent and generally unconscious prejudices betray. He calls it "ethnocentrism." In savage people ethnocentrism betrays itself in the disposition to call themselves "men" or "human beings." Others are something else not defined. They are, perhaps, like the flora and fauna, part of the landscape but not human.

This trait is not confined to nature people. We are all disposed to assume that other peoples, with other customs, are not quite human in the sense that we feel this is true of ourselves. This is part of that blindness to which James refers.

The incurable ethnocentrism of peoples makes it difficult to communicate freely and candidly with strangers, particularly when the purpose of the inquirer is to go behind exteriors and discover what is behind their faces, namely, their attitudes.

The great value and the great vogue of psychoanalysis is due to the fact that it has developed a technique for getting behind visible forms and the external expressions of the people to discover the subjective aspect of personal behavior and culture, the thing which at once intrigues and baffles the student of personality and of culture.

If this ethnocentrism makes it difficult, on the one hand, to discover the subjective aspect of a people's culture, it makes it difficult, on the other hand, to describe realistically their customs and usages when one knows that such descriptions are likely to be misinterpreted. One is often tempted under such circumstances to state things in a manner to meet and correct in advance the expected misinterpretation. But that, too, is impracticable and no solution of the difficulty. Realistic descriptions of manners and customs are always likely to be a little shocking. In the final analysis, however, it is undoubtedly true that if anything, at least anything customary and accepted in any human society, seems shocking or merely quaint, it is because that custom or usage is not quite intelligible.

There is an old French adage to the effect that "to comprehend all is to forgive all," and not merely forgive but accept as something not alien but indubitably human, like ourselves.

Only so far as this is anywhere achieved can such studies of human nature as this be said to have wholly achieved their purpose.

**3**

# NEWS AS A FORM OF
# KNOWLEDGE

## I

THERE ARE, as William James and certain others have
observed, two fundamental types of knowledge, namely, (1) "acquaintance with" and (2) "knowledge about." The distinction suggested seems fairly obvious. Nevertheless, in seeking to make it a
little more explicit, I am doubtless doing injustice to the sense of
the original. In that case, in interpreting the distinction, I
am merely making it my own. James's statement is, in part,
as follows:

> *There are two kinds of knowledge* broadly and practically dis-
> tinguishable: we may call them respectively *knowledge of acquaint-
> ance* and *knowledge-about*. . . . In minds able to speak at all there is,
> it is true, *some* knowledge about everything. Things can at least be
> classed, and the times of their appearance told. But in general, the
> less we analyze a thing, and the fewer of its relations we perceive,
> the less we know about it and the more our familiarity with it is of the
> acquaintance-type. The two kinds of knowledge are, therefore, as
> the human mind practically exerts them, relative terms. That is, the
> same thought of a thing may be called knowledge-about it in compari-
> son with a simpler thought, or acquaintance with it in comparison
> with a thought of it that is more articulate and explicit still.[1]

Reprinted from *American Journal of Sociology*, 45 (March, 1940) : 669–86.
There the article is subtitled "A Chapter in the Sociology of Knowledge."

[1]     William James, *The Principles of Psychology* (New York: Henry
Holt & Co., 1896), I, 221–22.

At any rate, "acquaintance with," as I should like to use the expression, is the sort of knowledge one inevitably acquires in the course of one's personal and firsthand encounters with the world about him. It is the knowledge which comes with use and wont rather than through any sort of formal or systematic investigation. Under such circumstances we come finally to know things not merely through the medium of our special senses but through the responses of our whole organism. We know them in the latter case as we know things to which we are accustomed, in a world to which we are adjusted. Such knowledge may, in fact, be conceived as a form of organic adjustment or adaptation, representing an accumulation and, so to speak, a funding of a long series of experiences. It is this sort of personal and individual knowledge which makes each of us at home in the world in which he elects or is condemned to live.

It is notorious that human beings, who are otherwise the most mobile of living creatures, tend nevertheless to become rooted, like plants, in the places and in the associations to which they are accustomed. If this accommodation of the individual to his habitat is to be regarded as knowledge at all, it is probably included in what we call tact or common sense. These are characters which individuals acquire in informal and unconscious ways; but, once acquired, they tend to become private and personal possessions. One might go so far as to describe them as personality traits— something, at any rate, which cannot well be formulated or communicated from one individual to another by formal statements.

Other forms of "acquaintance with" are: (1) clinical knowledge, in so far at least as it is the product of personal experience; (2) skills and technical knowledge; and (3) anything that is learned by the undirected and unconscious experimentation such as the contact with, and handling of, objects involves.

Our knowledge of other persons and of human nature in general seems to be of this sort. We know other minds in much the same way that we know our own, that is, intuitively. Often we know other minds better than we do our own. For the mind is not the mere stream of consciousness into which each of us looks when, introspectively, he turns his attention to the movements of his own thoughts. Mind is rather the divergent tendencies to act of which each of us is more or less completely unconscious, including the ability to control and direct those tendencies in accordance with some more or less conscious goal. Human beings have an extraordinary ability, by whatever mechanism it operates, to sense these tendencies in others as in themselves. It takes a long time, however, to become thoroughly acquainted with any human being, including ourselves, and the kind of knowledge of which this acquaintance consists is obviously not the sort of knowledge we get of human behavior by experiments in a psychological laboratory. It is rather more like the knowledge that a salesman has of his customers, a politician of his clients, or the knowledge which a psychiatrist gains of his patients in his efforts to understand and cure them. It is even more the sort of knowledge which gets embodied in habit, in custom, and, eventually—by some process of natural selection that we do not fully understand—in instinct; a kind of racial memory or habit. Knowledge of this sort, if one may call it knowledge, becomes, finally, a personal secret of the individual man or the special endowment of the race or stock that possesses it.[2]

One may, perhaps, venture this statement since the type of intuitive or instinctive knowledge here described seems to arise out of processes substantially like the accommodations and adaptations which, by some kind of natural selection, have produced the different racial varieties of mankind as well as the plant and animal species. One may object that what one means by knowledge is just what is not inherited and not heritable. On the other hand, it is

---

2     "The biologist ordinarily thinks of development as something very different from such modification of behavior by experience, but from time to time the idea that the basis of heredity and development is fundamentally similar to memory has been advanced. . . . Viewed in this way the whole course of development is a process of physiological learning, beginning with the simple experience of differential exposure to an external factor, and undergoing one modification after another, as new experiences in the life of the organism or of its parts in relation to each other occur" (C. M. Child, *Physiological Foundations of Behavior*, pp. 248–49; quoted by. W. I. Thomas in *Primitive Behavior* [New York: McGraw-Hill Book Co., 1937], p. 25).

certain that some things are learned much more easily than others. What one inherits therefore is, perhaps, not anything that could properly be called knowledge. It is rather the inherited ability to acquire those specific forms of knowledge we call habits. There seems to be a very great difference in individuals, families, and genetic groups as to their ability to learn specific things. Native intelligence is probably not the standardized thing that the intelligence tests might lead one to believe. In so far as this is true studies of intelligence in the future are, I suspect, more likely to be concerned with in the idiosyncrasies of intelligence and the curious individual ways in which individual minds achieve essentially the same results than in measuring and standardizing these achievements.

It is obvious that this "synthetic" (i.e., the knowledge that gets itself embodied in habit and custom, as opposed to analytic and formal knowledge) is not likely to be articulate and communicable. If it gets itself communicated at all, it will be in the form of practical maxims and wise saws rather than in the form of scientific hypotheses. Nevertheless, a wide and intimate acquaintance with men and things is likely to be the bulwark of most sound judgment in practical matters as well as the source of those hunches upon which experts depend in perplexing situations and of those sudden insights which, in the evolution of science, are so frequently the prelude to important discoveries.

In contrast with this is the kind of knowledge that James describes as "knowledge about." Such knowledge is formal, rational, and systematic. It is based on observation and fact but on fact that has been checked, tagged, regimented, and finally ranged in this and that perspective, according to the purpose and point of view of the investigator.

"Knowledge about" is formal knowledge; that is to say, knowledge which has achieved some degree of exactness and precision by the substitution of ideas for concrete reality and of words for things. Not only do ideas constitute the logical framework of all systematic knowledge but they enter into the very nature of the things themselves with which science—natural as distinguished from the historical science—is concerned. As a matter of fact, there seem to be three fundamental types of scientific knowledge: (1) philosophy and logic, which are concerned primarily with ideas; (2) history, which is concerned primarily with events; and (3) the natural or classifying sciences, which are concerned primarily with things.

Concepts and logical artifacts, like the number system, are not involved in the general flux of events and things. For precisely that reason they serve admirably the purpose of tags and counters with which to identify, to describe, and, eventually, to measure things. The ultimate purpose of natural science seems to be to substitute for the flux of events and the changing character of things a logical formula in which the general character of things and the direction of change may be described with logical and mathematical precision.

The advantage of substituting words, concepts, and a logical order for the actual course of events is that the conceptual order makes the actual order intelligible, and, so far as the hypothetic formulations we call laws conform to the actual course of events, it becomes possible to predict from a present a future condition of things. It permits us to speculate with some assurance how, and to what extent, any specific intervention or interference in a present situation may determine the situation that is predestined to succeed it.

On the other hand, there is always a temptation to make a complete divorce between the logical and verbal description of an object or a situation and the empirical reality to which it refers. This seems to have been the cardinal mistake of scholasticism. Scholasticism has invariably tended to substitute logical consistency, which is a relation between ideas, for the relation of cause and effect, which is a relation between things.

An empirical and experimental science avoids a purely logical solution of its problems by checking up its calculation at some point with the actual world. A purely intellectual science is always in danger of becoming so completely out of touch with things that the symbols with which it operates cease to be anything more than mental toys. In that case science becomes a kind of dialectical game. This is a peril which the social sciences, to the extent that they have been disposed to formulate and investigate social problems in the forms in which they have been conventionally defined by some administrative agencies or governmental institution, have not always escaped. Thus investigation has invariably tended to take the form of fact-finding rather than of research. Having found the facts, the agencies were able to supply the interpretations; but they were usually interpretations which were implicit in the policies to which the agencies or institutions were already committed.

These are some of the general characteristics of systematic and scientific knowledge, "knowledge about," as contrasted with the concrete knowledge, common sense and "acquaintance with." What is, however, the unique character of scientific knowledge, as contrasted with other forms of knowledge, is that it is communicable to the extent that common sense or knowledge based on practical and clinical experience is not. It is communicable because its problems and its solutions are stated not merely in logical and in intelligible terms but in such forms that they can be checked by experiment or by reference to the empirical reality to which these terms refer.

In order to make this possible, it is necessary to describe in detail and in every instance the source and manner in which facts and findings were originally obtained. Knowledge about, so far at least as it is scientific, becomes in this way a part of the social heritage, a body of tested and accredited fact and theory in which new increments, added to the original fund, tend to check up, affirm, or qualify, first of all, in each special science and, finally, in all the related sciences, all that has been contributed by earlier investigators.

On the other hand, acquaintance with, as I have sought to characterize it, so far as it is based on the slow accumulation of experience and the gradual accommodation of the individual to his individual and personal world, becomes, as I have said, more and more completely identical with instinct and intuition.

Knowledge about is not merely accumulated experience but the result of systematic investigation of nature. It is based on the answers given to the definite questions which we address to the world about us. It is knowledge pursued methodically with all the formal and logical apparatus which scientific research has created. I might add, parenthetically, that there is, generally speaking, no scientific method which is wholly independent of the intuition and insight which acquaintance with things and events gives us. Rather is it true that, under ordinary circumstances, the most that formal methods can do for research is to assist the investigator in obtaining facts which will make it possible to check up such insights and hunches as the investigator already had at the outset or has gained later in the course of his researches.

One of the functions of this methodical procedure is to protect the investigator from the perils of an interpretation to which a too ardent pursuit of knowledge is likely to lead him. There is, on the other hand, no methodical procedure that is a substitute for insight.

## II

What is here described as "acquaintance with" and "knowledge about" are assumed to be distinct forms of knowledge—forms having different functions in the lives of individuals and of society —rather than knowledge of the same kind but of different degrees of accuracy and validity. They are, nevertheless, not so different in character or function—since they are, after all, relative terms —that they may not be conceived as constituting together a continuum—a continuum within which all kinds and sorts of knowledge find a place. In such a continuum news has a location of its own. It is obvious that news is not systematic knowledge like that of the physical sciences. It is rather, in so far as it is concerned with events, like history. Events, because they are invariably fixed in time and located in space, are unique and cannot, therefore, be classified as is the case with things. Not only do things move about in space and change with time but, in respect to their internal organization, they are always in a condition of more or less stable equilibrium.

News is not history, however, and its facts are not historical facts. News is not history because, for one thing among others, it deals, on the whole, with isolated events and does not seek to relate them to one another either in the form of causal or in the form of teleological sequences. History not only describes events but seeks to put them in their proper place in the historical succession, and, by doing so, to discover the underlying tendencies and forces which find expression in them. In fact, one would not be far wrong in assuming that history is quite as much concerned with the connections of events—the relation between the incidents that precede and those that follow—as it is with the events themselves. On the other hand, a reporter, as distinguished from a historian, seeks merely to record each single event as it occurs and is concerned with the past and future only in so far as these throw light on what is actual and present.

The relation of an event to the past remains the task of the historian, while its significance as a factor determining the future may perhaps be left to the science of politics—what Freeman calls "comparative politics"³—that is to say, to sociology or to some other division of the social sciences, which, by comparative studies, seeks to arrive at statements sufficiently general to support a hypothesis or a prediction.⁴

News, as a form of knowledge, is not primarily concerned either with the past or with the future but rather with the present—what has been described by psychologists as "the specious present." News may be said to exist only in such a present. What is meant here by the "specious present" is suggested by the fact that news, as the publishers of the commercial press know, is a very perishable commodity. News remains news only until it has reached the per-

---

3    Edward A. Freeman, *Comparative Politics* (London, 1873).
4    The sociological point of view makes its appearance in historical investigation as soon as the historian turns from the study of "periods" to the study of institutions. The history of institutions—that is to say, the family, the church, economic institutions, political institutions, etc.—leads inevitably to comparison, classification, the formation of class names or concepts, and eventually to the formulation of law. In the process history becomes natural history, and natural history passes over into natural science. In short, history becomes sociology (R. E. Park and E. W. Burgess, *Introduction to the Science of Sociology* [Chicago: University of Chicago Press, 1921], p. 16).

sons for whom it has "news interest." Once published and its significance recognized, what was news becomes history.

This transient and ephemeral quality is of the very essence of news and is intimately connected with every other character that it exhibits. Different types of news have a different time span. In its most elementary form a news report is a mere "flash," announcing that an event has happened. If the event proves of real importance, interest in it will lead to further inquiry and to a more complete acquaintance with the attendant circumstances. An event ceases to be news, however, as soon as the tension it aroused has ceased and public attention has been directed to some other aspect of the habitat or to some other incident sufficiently novel, exciting, or important to hold its attention.

The reason that news comes to us, under ordinary circumstances, not in the form of a continued story but as a series of independent incidents becomes clear when one takes account of the fact that we are here concerned with the public mind—or with what is called the public mind. In its most elementary form knowledge reaches the public not, as it does the individual, in the form of a perception but in the form of a communication, that is to say, news. Public attention, however, under normal conditions is wavering, unsteady, and easily distracted. When the public mind wanders, the rapport, grapevine telegraph, or whatever else it is that insures the transmission of news within the limits of the public ceases to function, tension is relaxed, communication broken off, and what was live news becomes cold fact.

A news item, as every newspaperman knows, is read in inverse ratio to its length. The ordinary reader will read a column and a half of two- or three-line items about men and things in the home town before he will read a column article, no matter how advertised in the headlines, unless it turns out to be not merely news but a story, i.e., something that has what is called technically "human interest."

News comes in the form of small, independent communications that can be easily and rapidly comprehended. In fact, news performs somewhat the same functions for the public that perception does for the individual man; that is to say, it does not so much inform as orient the public, giving each and all notice as to what is going on. It does this without any effort of the reporter to interpret the events he reports, except in so far as to make them comprehensible and interesting.

The first typical reaction of an individual to the news is likely to be a desire to repeat it to someone. This makes conversation, arouses further comment, and perhaps starts a discussion. But the singular thing about it is that, once discussion has been started, the event under discussion soon ceases to be news, and, as interpretations of an event differ, discussions turn from the news to the issues it raises. The clash of opinions and sentiments which discussion invariably evokes usually terminates in some sort of consensus or collective opinon—what we call public opinion. It is upon the interpretation of present events, i.e., news, that public opinion rests.

The extent to which news circulates, within a political unit or a political society, determines the extent to which the members of such a society may be said to participate, not in its collective life—which is the more inclusive term—but in its political acts. Political action and political power, as one ordinarily understands these terms, are obviously based not merely on such concert and consensus as may exist in a herd or in a crowd. It rests ultimately, it seems, on the ability of a political society, aside from whatever of military or material resources it possesses, to act not only concertedly but consistently in accordance with some considered purpose and in furtherance of some rational end. The world of politics, it seems, is based, as Schopenhauer has said of the world in general, on the organic relation of will and idea. Other and more material sources of political power are obviously merely instrumental.

Freeman, the historian, has said that history is past politics and politics is present history. This puts a great deal of truth into a few words, even if the statement in practice needs some enlargement and some qualification. News, though intimately related to both, is neither history nor politics. It is, nevertheless, the stuff which makes political action, as distinguished from other forms of collective behavior, possible.

Among other kinds of collective behavior are the recognized and conventional forms of ceremonial and religious expression—etiquette and religious ritual—which, in so far as they create unanimity and maintain morale, play directly and indirectly an important role in politics and in political action. But religion has no such intimate connection as politics with the news. News is a purely secular phenomenon.

## III

There is a proverbial saying to the effect that it is the unexpected that happens. Since what happens makes news, it follows, or seems to, that news is always or mainly concerned with the unusual and the unexpected. Even the most trivial happening, it seems, provided it represents a departure from the customary ritual and routine of daily life, is likely to be reported in the press. This conception of news has been confirmed by those editors who, in the competition for circulation and for advertising, have sought to make their papers smart and interesting, where they could not be invariably either informing or thrilling. In their efforts to instil into the minds of reporters and correspondents the importance of looking everywhere and always for something that would excite, amuse, or shock its readers, news editors have put into circulation some interesting examples of what the Germans, borrowing an expression from Homer, have called *geflügelte Wörter*, "winged words." The epigram describing news which has winged its way over more territory and is repeated more often than any other is this: "Dog bites man"—that is not news. But "Man bites dog"—that is. *Nota bene!* It is not the intrinsic importance of an event that makes it newsworthy. It is rather the fact that the event is so unusual that if published it will either startle, amuse, or otherwise excite the reader so that it will be remembered and repeated. For news is always finally, what Charles A. Dana described it to be, "something that will make people talk," even when it does not make them act.

The fact that news ordinarily circulates spontaneously and without any adventitious aids—as well as freely without inhibitions or censorship—seems to be responsible for another character which attaches to it, distinguishing it from related but less authentic types of knowledge—namely, rumor and gossip. In order that a report of events current may have the quality of news, it should not merely circulate—possibly in circuitous underground channels—but should be published, if need be by the town crier or the public press. Such publication tends to give news something of the character of a public document. News is more or less authenticated by the fact that it has been exposed to the critical examination of the public to which it is addressed and with whose interests it is concerned.

The public which thus, by common consent or failure to protest, puts the stamp of its approval on a published report does not give to its interpretation the authority of statement that has been subjected to expert historical criticism. Every public has its local prejudices and its own limitations. A more searching examination of the facts would quite possibly reveal to a more critical and enlightened mind the naïve credulity and bias of an unsophisticated public opinion. In fact, the naïveté and credulity thus revealed may become an important historical or sociological datum. This, however, is merely another and further illustration of the fact that every public has its own universe of discourse and that, humanly speaking, a fact is only a fact in some universe of discourse.[5]

An interesting light is thrown on the nature of news by a consideration of the changes which take place in information that gets into circulation without the sanction which publicity gives to it.

[5]    A universe of discourse is, as the term is ordinarily used, no more than a special vocabulary which is well understood and appropriate to specific situations. It may, however, in the case of some special science include a body of more precisely defined terms or concepts, which in that case will tend to have a more or less systematic character. History, for example, employs no, or almost no, special concepts. On the other hand, sociology, and every science that attempts to be systematic, does. As concepts assume this systematic character, they tend to constitute a "frame of reference."

In such case a report, emanating from some source not disclosed and traveling to a destination that is unknown, invariably accumulates details from the innocent but mainly illicit contributions of those who assist it on its travel. Under these circumstances what was at first mere rumor tends to assume, in time, the character of a legend, that is, something which everyone repeats but no one believes.

When, on the other hand, reports of current events are published with the names, dates, and places which make it possible for anyone concerned to check them, the atmosphere of legend which gathers about and clothes with fantastic detail the news as originally reported is presently dispelled, and what is fact, or what will pass for fact, until corrected by further and later news reports, is reduced to something more prosaic than legend and more authentic than news, i.e., historical fact.

If it is the unexpected that happens, it is the not wholly unexpected that gets into the news. The events that have made news in the past, as in the present, are actually the expected things. They are characteristically simple and commonplace matters, like births and deaths, weddings and funerals, the conditions of the crops and of business, war, politics, and the weather. These are the expected things, but they are at the same time the unpredictable things. They are the incidents and the chances that turn up in the game of life.

The fact is that the thing that makes news is news interest, and that, as every city editor knows, is a variable quantity—one that has to be reckoned with from the time the city editor sits down at his desk in the morning until the night editor locks up the last form at night. The reason for this is that the news value is relative, and an event that comes later may, and often does, diminish the value of an event that turned up earlier. In that case the less important item has to give way to the later and more important.

The anecdotes and "believe it or nots" which turn up in the news are valuable to the editor because they can always be lifted out of the printer's form to make way for something hotter and more urgent. In any case it is, on the whole, the accidents and incidents that the public is prepared for; the victories and defeats

on the ball field or on the battlefield; the things that one fears
and things that one hopes for—that make the news. It is difficult
to understand, nevertheless, considering the number of people who
are killed and maimed annually by automobile accidents (the
number killed in 1938 was 32,600) that these great losses of life
rarely make the front page. The difference seems to be that the
automobile has come to be accepted as one of the permanent features of civilized life and war has not.

News, therefore, at least in the strict sense of the term, is not
a story or an anecdote. It is something that has for the person who
hears or reads it an interest that is pragmatic rather than apprecia-
tive. News is characteristically, if not always, limited to events that
bring about sudden and decisive changes. It may be an incident
like that of the colored family in Philadelphia, Frances and Ben
Mason, who won a fortune in the Irish sweepstakes recently.[6] It
may be a tragic incident like the battle off the coast of Uruguay
which resulted in the destruction of the German battleship, the
"Graf Spee," and the suicide of its captain. These events were not
only news—that is, something that brought a sudden decisive
change in the previously existing situation—but, as they were related in the newspapers and as we reflected upon them, they tended
to assume a new and ideal significance: the one a story of genuine
human interest, the other that of tragedy, something, to use
Aristotle's phrase, to inspire "pity and terror." Events such as these
tend to be remembered. Eventually they may become legends or
be recorded in popular ballads. Legends and ballads need no date
line or the names of persons or places to authenticate them. They
live and survive in our memories and in that of the public because
of their human interest. As events they have ceased to exist. They
survive as a sort of ghostly symbol of something of universal and
perennial interest, an ideal representation of what is true of life
and of human nature everywhere.

Thus it seems that news, as a form of knowledge, contributes
from its record of events not only to history and to sociology but
to folklore and literature; it contributes something not merely to
the social sciences but to the humanities.

6    See *Time*, December 25, 1939, p. 12.

## IV

The sociological horizon has recently taken on new dimensions. Social anthropology, no longer interested in primitive society merely, has begun to study not only the history but the natural history and function of institutions. In doing so it has appropriated more and more the field of sociological interest and research. Psychiatry, likewise, has discovered that neuroses and psychoses are diseases of a personality which is itself a product of a social milieu created by the interaction of personalities. Meanwhile there has grown up in the United States and in Europe a sociology of law which conceives as natural products the norms which the courts are seeking to rationalize, systematize, and apply in specific cases. Finally, there have been some interesting recent attempts to bring the subject of knowledge itself within the limits of a sociological discipline.

Theories of knowledge have existed since the days of Parmenides. They have, however, been less interested in knowledge which is a datum than in truth or valid knowledge which is an idea and an ideal. The question with which the sociology of knowledge is concerned is not what constitutes the validity of knowledge —of a statement of principle or of fact—but what are the conditions under which different kinds of knowledge arise and what are the functions of each.

Most of the forms of knowledge that have achieved the dignity of a science are, in the long history of mankind, of very recent origin. One of the earliest and most elementary forms of knowledge is news. There was a period, and not so long ago, either, when there was neither philosphy, history, nor rational knowledge of any sort. There was only myth, legend, and magic. What we now describe as the exact sciences did not exist until the Renaissance. The social sciences have, roughly speaking, only come into existence in the last fifty years. At least they have only begun within the last half-century to achieve, with the wider use of statistics, anything like scientific precision.

News, so far as it is to be regarded as knowledge at all, is probably as old as mankind, perhaps older. The lower animals were not without a kind of communication which was not unlike news. The "cluck" of the mother hen is understood by the chicks as signifying either danger or food, and the chicks respond accordingly.

This is not to suggest that every kind of communication in a herd or flock will have the character of news. What is ordinarily communicated is merely a kind of contagious excitement—sometimes merely a sense of well-being and security in the gregarious association of the herd, at others a sense of unrest or malaise, manifested and often intensified in the milling of the herd. It seems likely that this pervasive social excitement, which is essential to the existence of the herd as a social unit, serves, also, to facilitate the communication of news, or what corresponds to it in the herd.

There is in naval parlance an expression, "the fleet in being," which means, apparently, that the ships which constitute a fleet are in communication and sufficiently mobilized, perhaps, to be capable of some sort of concerted action. The same expression might be applied to a community, a society, or a herd. A society is "in being" when the individuals that compose it are to such an extent *en rapport* that, whether capable of united and collective action or not, they may be described as participating in a common or collective existence. In such a society a diffuse social excitement tends to envelope, like an atmosphere, all participants in the common life and to give a direction and tendency to their interests and attitudes. It is as if the individuals of such a society were dominated by a common mood or state of mind which determined for them the range and character of their interests and their attitudes or tendencies to act. The most obvious illustration of this obscure social tension or state of mind in a community is the persistent and pervasive influence of fashion.

At certain times and under certain conditions this collective excitement, so essential to communication if not to understanding, rises to a higher level of intensity and, as it does so, tends to limit the range of response but to increase the intensity of impulses not so inhibited. The effect of this is the same as in the case of attention in the individual. Exclusive attention to some things inhibits responses to others. This means in the case of a society a limitation of the range and character of the news to which it will either collectively or individually respond.

The rise of social tension may be observed in the most elementary form in the herd when, for some reason, the herd is restless and begins to mill. Tension mounts as restlessness increases. The effect is as if the milling produced in the herd a state of expectancy which, as it increased in intensity, increased also the certainty that presently some incident, a clap of thunder or the crackling of a twig, would plunge the herd into a stampede.

Something similar takes place in a public. As tension arises, the limits of public interest narrows, and the range of events to which the public will respond is limited. The circulation of news is limited; discussion ceases, and the certainty of action of some sort increases. This narrowing of the focus of public attention tends to increase the influence of the dominant person or persons in the community. But the existence of this dominance depends upon the ability of the community, or its leaders, to maintain tension. It is in this way that dictators arise and maintain themselves in power. It is this that explains likewise the necessity to a dictatorship of some sort of censorship.

News circulates, it seems, only in a society where there is a certain degree of rapport and a certain degree of tension. But the effect of news from outside the circle of public interest is to disperse attention and, by so doing, to encourage individuals to act on their own initiative rather than on that of a dominant party or personality.

Under ordinary circumstances—in a time of peace rather than of war or revolution—news tends to circulate over an ever widening area, as means of communication multiply. Changes in society and its institutions under these circumstances continue to take place, but they take place piecemeal and more or less imperceptibly. Under other conditions—in war or revolution—changes take place violently and visibly but catastrophically.

The permanence of institutions under ordinary conditions is dependent upon their ability, or the ability of the community of which they are a part, to adapt themselves to technological and other less obvious changes. But these changes and their consequences manifest themselves not only directly but rather indirectly in the news. Institutions like the Catholic church or the Japanese state have been able to survive the drastic changes of time because they have been able to respond to changes in the conditions of existence, not merely those physically and obviously imposed upon them but those foreshadowed and reflected in the news.

I have indicated the role which news plays in the world of politics in so far as it provides the basis for the discussions in which public opinion is formed. The news plays quite as important a role in the world of economic relations, since the price of commodities, including money and securities, as registered in the world-market and in every local market dependent upon it, is based on the news.

So sensitive are the exchanges to events in every part of the world that every fluctuation in fashion or the weather is likely to be reflected in the prices on the exchanges. I have said that news is a secular phenomenon. But there come times when changes are so great and so catastrophic that individuals and peoples are no longer interested in worldly affairs. In such case men, frustrated in their ambitions and their hopes, turn away from the world of secular affairs and seek refuge and consolation in a flight from the great world into the security of the little world of the family or of the church. The function of news is to orient man and society in an actual world. In so far as it succeeds it tends to preserve the sanity of the individual and the permanence of society.

Although news is an earlier and more elementary product of communication than science, news has by no means been superseded by it. On the contrary, the importance of news has grown consistently with the expansion of the means of communication and with the growth of science.

Improved means of communication have co-operated with the vast accumulations of knowledge, in libraries, in museums, and in learned societies, to make possible a more rapid, accurate, and thoroughgoing interpretation of events as they occur. The result is that persons and places, once remote and legendary, are now familiar to every reader of the daily press.

In fact, the multiplication of the means of communication has brought it about that anyone, even in the most distant part of the world, may now actually participate in events—at least as listener if not as spectator—as they actually take place in some other part of the world. We have recently listened to Mussolini address his fascist followers from a balcony of Rome; we have heard Hitler speaking over the heads of a devout congregation in the Reichstag, in Berlin, not merely to the President, but to the people, of the United States. We have even had an opportunity to hear the terms of the momentous Munich agreement ten seconds after it had been signed by the representatives of four of the leading powers in Europe and the world. The fact that acts so momentous as these can be so quickly and so publicly consummated has suddenly and completely changed the character of international politics, so that one can no longer even guess what the future has in store for Europe and for the world.

In the modern world the role of news has assumed increased rather than diminished importance as compared with some other forms of knowledge, history, for example. The changes in recent years have been so rapid and drastic that the modern world seems to have lost its historical perspective, and we appear to be living from day to day in what I have described earlier as a "specious present." Under the circumstances history seems to be read or written mainly to enable us, by comparison of the present with the past, to understand what is going on about us rather than, as the historians have told us, to know "what actually happened."

Thus Elmer Davis in a recent article in the *Saturday Review* announces as "required reading" for 1939 two volumes: Hitler's *Mein Kampf* and Thucydides' *History of the Peloponnesian War* (431 B.C.). He recommends the history of the Peloponnesian War because, as he says, "Thucydides was not only a brilliant analyst of human behavior both individual and collective" but was at the same time "a great reporter."[7]

One notes, also, as characteristic of our times, that since news, as reported in American newspapers, has tended to assume the

7    "Required Reading," *Saturday Review of Literature*, October 14, 1939.

character of literature, so fiction—after the newspaper the most popular form of literature—has assumed more and more the character of news.[8]

Emile Zola's novels were essentially reports upon contemporary manners in France just as Steinbeck's *The Grapes of Wrath* has been described as an epoch-making report on the share-cropper in the United States.

Ours, it seems, is an age of news, and one of the most important events in American civilization has been the rise of the reporter.

[8]    See Helen MacGill Hughes, *News and the Human Interest Story* (Chicago: University of Chicago Press, 1940).

# II. Human Ecology

**4**

# THE URBAN COMMUNITY AS A SPATIAL PATTERN AND A MORAL ORDER

SOME THIRTY years ago Professor Eugenius Warming, of Copenhagen, published a little volume entitled *Plant Communities (Plantesamfund)*. Warming's observations called attention to the fact that different species of plants tend to form permanent groups, which he called communities. Plant communities, it turned out, exhibit a good many of the traits of living organisms. They come into existence gradually, pass through certain characteristic changes, and eventually are broken up and succeeded by other communities of a very different sort. These observations later become the point of departure for a series of investigations which have since become familiar under the title "Ecology."

Ecology, in so far as it seeks to describe the actual distribution of plants and animals over the earth's surface, is in some very real sense a geographical science. Human ecology, as the sociologists would like to use the term, is, however, not identical with geography, nor even with human geography. It is not man, but the community; not man's relation to the earth which he inhabits, but his relations to other men, that concerns us most.

Within the limits of every natural area the distribution of population tends to assume definite and typical patterns. Every local group exhibits a more or less definite constellation of the individual units that compose it. The form which this constellation

Reprinted from *The Urban Community*, ed. Ernest W. Burgess (Chicago: University of Chicago Press, 1926), pp. 3–18. Presidential address read before the annual meeting of the American Sociological Society, 1925.

takes, the position, in other words, of every individual in the community with reference to every other, so far as it can be described in general terms, constitutes what Durkheim and his school call the morphological aspect of society.[1]

Human ecology, as sociologists conceive it, seeks to emphasize not so much geography as space. In society we not only live together, but at the same time we live apart, and human relations can always be reckoned, with more or less accuracy, in terms of distance. In so far as social structure can be defined in terms of position, social changes may be described in terms of movement; and society exhibits, in one of its aspects, characters that can be measured and described in mathematical formulas.

Local communities may be compared with reference to the areas which they occupy and with reference to the relative density of population distribution within those areas. Communities are not, however, mere population aggregates. Cities, particularly great cities, where the selection and segregation of the populations has gone farthest, display certain morphological characteristics which are not found in smaller population aggregates.

One of the incidents of size is diversity. Other things being equal, the larger community will have the wider division of labor. An examination a few years ago of the names of eminent persons listed in *Who's Who* indicated that in one large city (Chicago) there were, in addition to the 509 occupations listed by the census, 116 other occupations classed as professions. The number of professions requiring special and scientific training for their practice is an index and a measure of the intellectual life of the community. For the intellectual life of a community is measured not merely by the scholastic attainments of the average citizen, nor even by the communal intelligence-quotient, but by the extent to which rational methods have been applied to the solution of com-

[1]   Geographers are probably not greatly interested in social morphology as such. On the other hand, sociologists are. Geographers, like historians, have been traditionally interested in the actual rather than the typical. Where are things actually located? What did actually happen? These are the questions that geography and history have sought to answer. See *A Geographical Introduction to History*, by M. Lucien Febvre and Lionel Bataillon.

munal problems—health, industry, and social control, for example.

One reason why cities have always been the centers of intellectual life is that they have not only made possible, but have enforced, an individualization and a diversification of tasks. Only as every individual is permitted and compelled to focus his attention upon some small area of the common human experience, only as he learns to concentrate his efforts upon some small segment of the common task, can the vast co-operation which civilization demands be maintained.

In an interesting and suggestive paper read before the American Sociological Society at its meeting in Washington in 1922, Professor Burgess sketched the processes involved in the growth of cities. The growth of cities has usually been described in terms of extensions of territory and increase in numbers. The city itself has been identified with an administrative area, the municipality; but the city, with which we are here concerned, is not a formal and administrative entity. It is rather a product of natural forces, extending its own boundaries more or less independently of the limits imposed upon it for political and administrative purposes. This has become to such an extent a recognized fact that in any thoroughgoing study of the city, either as an economic or a social unit, it has been found necessary to take account of natural, rather than official, city boundaries. Thus, in the city planning studies of New York City, under the direction of the Russell Sage Foundation, New York City includes a territory of 5,500 equare miles, including in that area something like one hundred minor administrative units, cities, and villages, with a total population of 9,000,000.

We have thought of the growth of cities as taking place by a mere aggregation. But an increase in population at any point within the urban area is inevitably reflected and felt in every other part of the city. The extent to which such an increase of population in one part of the city is reflected in every other depends very largely upon the character of the local transportation system. Every extension and multiplication of the means of transportation connecting the periphery of the city with the center tends to bring more people to the central business district, and to bring them there oftener. This increases the congestion at the center; it increases, eventually, the height of office buildings and the values of the land on which these buildings stand. The influence of land values at the business center radiates from that point to every part of the city. If the growth at the center is rapid it increases the diameter of the area held for speculative purposes just outside the center. Property held for speculation is usually allowed to deteriorate. It easily assumes the character of a slum; that is to say, an area of casual and transient population, an area of dirt and disorder, "of missions and of lost souls." These neglected and sometimes abandoned regions become the points of first settlement of immigrants. Here are located our ghettos, and sometimes our bohemias, our Greenwich Villages, where artists and radicals seek refuge from the fundamentalism and the Rotarianism, and, in general, the limitations and restrictions of a Philistine World. Every large city tends to have its Greenwich Village just as it has its Wall Street.

The growth of the city involves not merely the addition of numbers, but all the incidental changes and movements that are inevitably associated with the efforts of every individual to find his place in the vast complexities of urban life. The growth of new regions, the multiplication of professions and occupations, the incidental increase in land values which urban expansion brings—all are involved in the processes of city growth, and can be measured in terms of changes of position of individuals with reference to other individuals, and to the community as a whole. Land values can be reckoned, for example, in terms of mobility of population. The highest land values exist at points where the largest number of people pass in the course of twenty-four hours.

The community, as distinguished from the individuals who compose it, has an indefinite life-span. We know that communities come into existence, expand and flourish for a time, and then decline. This is as true of human societies as it is of plant communities. We do not know with any precision as yet the rhythm of these changes. We do know that the community outlives the individuals who compose it. And this is one reason for the seemingly inevitable and perennial conflict between the interests of the individual and the community. This is one reason why it costs more to police a growing city than one which is stationary or declining.

Every new generation has to learn to accommodate itself to an order which is defined and maintained mainly by the older. Every society imposes some sort of discipline upon its members. Individuals grow up, are incorporated into the life of the community, and eventually drop out and disappear. But the community, with the moral order which it embodies, lives on. The life of the community therefore involves a kind of metabolism. It is constantly assimilating new individuals, and just as steadily, by death or otherwise, eliminating older ones. But assimilation is not a simple process, and, above all else, takes time.

The problem of assimilating the native born is a very real one; it is the problem of the education of children in the homes and of adolescents in the schools. But the assimilation of adult migrants, finding for them places in the communal organization, is a more serious problem: it is the problem of adult education, which we have just in recent years begun to consider with any real sense of its importance.

There is another aspect of the situation which we have hardly considered. Communities whose population increase is due to the excess of births over deaths and communities whose increase is due to immigration exhibit important differences. Where growth is due to immigration, social change is of necessity more rapid and more profound. Land values, for one thing, increase more rapidly; the replacement of buildings and machinery, the movement of population, changes in occupation, increase in wealth, and reversals in social position proceed at a more rapid tempo. In general, society tends to approach conditions which are now recognized as characteristic of the frontier.

In a society in which great and rapid changes are in progress there is a greater need for public education of the sort that we ordinarily gain through the public press, through discussion and conversation. On the other hand, since personal observation and tradition, upon which common sense, as well as the more systematic investigations of science, is finally based, are not able to keep pace with changes in conditions, there occurs what has been described by Ogburn as the phenomenon of "cultural lag." Our political knowledge and our common sense do not keep up with the actual changes that are taking place in our common life. The result is, perhaps, that as the public feels itself drifting, legislative enactments are multiplied, but actual control is decreased. Then, as the public realizes the futility of legislative enactments, there is a demand for more drastic action, which expresses itself in ill-defined mass movements and, often, in mere mob violence. For example, the lynchings in the southern states and the race riots in the North.

So far as these disorders are in any sense related to movements of population—and recent studies of race riots and lynchings indicate that they are—the study of what we have described as social metabolism may furnish an index, if not an explanation, of the phenomenon of race riots.

One of the incidents of the growth of the community is the social selection and segregation of the population, and the creation, on the one hand, of natural social groups, and on the other, of natural social areas. We have become aware of this process of segregation in the case of the immigrants, and particularly in the case of the so-called historical races, peoples who, whether immigrants or not, are distinguished by racial marks. The Chinatowns, the Little Sicilies, and the other so-called "ghettos" with which students of urban life are familiar are special types of a more general species of natural area which the conditions and tendencies of city life inevitably produce.

Such segregations of population as these take place, first, upon the basis of language and of culture, and second, upon the basis of race. Within these immigrant colonies and racial ghettos, however, other processes of selection inevitably take place which bring about segregation based upon vocational interests, upon intelligence, and personal ambition. The result is that the keener, the more energetic, and the more ambitious very soon emerge from their ghettos and immigrant colonies and move into an area of second immigrant settlement, or perhaps into a cosmopolitan area in which the members of several immigrant and racial groups meet and live side by side. More and more, as the ties of race, of language, and of culture are weakened, successful individuals move out and eventually find their places in business and in the professions, among the older population group which has ceased to be identified with any language or racial group. The point is that change of occupation, personal success or failure—changes of economic and social status, in short—tend to be registered in changes of location. The physical or ecological organization of the community, in the long run, responds to and reflects the occupational and the cultural. Social selection and segregation, which create the natural groups, determine at the same time the natural areas of the city.

The modern city differs from the ancient in one important respect. The ancient city grew up around a fortress; the modern city has grown up around a market. The ancient city was the center of a region which was relatively self-sufficing. The goods that were produced were mainly for home consumption, and not for trade beyond the limits of the local community. The modern city, on the other hand, is likely to be the center of a region of very highly specialized production, with a corresponding widely extended trade area. Under these circumstances the main outlines of the modern city will be determined (1) by local geography and (2) by routes of transportation.

Local geography, modified by railways and other major means of transportation, all connecting, as they invariably do, with the larger industries, furnish the broad lines of the city plan. But these broad outlines are likely to be overlaid and modified by another and a different distribution of population and of institutions, of which the central retail shopping area is the center. Within this central downtown area itself certain forms of business, the shops, the hotels, theaters, wholesale houses, office buildings, and banks, all tend to fall into definite and characteristic patterns, as if the position of every form of business and building in the area were somehow fixed and determined by its relation to every other.

Out on the periphery of the city, again, industrial and residential suburbs, dormitory towns, and satellite cities seem to find, in some natural and inevitable manner, their predetermined places. Within the area bounded on the one hand by the central business district and on the other by the suburbs, the city tends to take the form of a series of concentric circles. These different regions, located at different relative distances from the center, are characterized by different degrees of mobility of the population.

The area of greatest mobility, i.e., of movement and change of population, is naturally the business center itself. Here are the hotels, the dwelling-places of the transients. Except for the few permanent dwellers in these hotels, the business center, which is the city *par excellence*, empties itself every night and fills itself every morning. Outside the city, in this narrower sense of the term, are the slums, the dwelling-places of the casuals. On the edge of the slums there are likely to be regions, already in process of being submerged, characterized as the "rooming-house areas," the dwelling-places of bohemians, transient adventurers of all sorts, and the unsettled young folk of both sexes. Beyond these are the apartment-house areas, the region of small families and delicatessen shops. Finally, out beyond all else, are the regions of duplex apartments and of single dwellings, where people still own their homes and raise children, as they do, to be sure, in the slums.

The typical urban community is actually much more complicated than this description indicates, and there are characteristic variations for different types and sizes of cities. The main point, however, is that everywhere the community tends to conform to some pattern, and this pattern invariably turns out to be a constellation of typical urban areas, all of which can be geographically located and specially defined.

Natural areas are the habitats of natural groups. Every typical urban area is likely to contain a characteristic selection of the population of the community as a whole. In great cities the divergence in manners, in standards of living, and in general outlook on life in different urban areas is often astonishing. The difference in sex and age groups, perhaps the most significant indexes of social life, are strikingly divergent for different natural areas. There are regions in the city in which there are almost no children, areas occupied by the residential hotels, for example. There are regions where the number of children is relatively very high: in the slums, in the middle-class residential suburbs, to which the newly married usually graduate from their first honeymoon apartments in the city. There are other areas occupied almost wholly by young unmarried people, boy and girl bachelors. There are regions where people almost never vote, except at national elections;

regions where the divorce rate is higher than it is for any state in the Union, and other regions in the same city where there are almost no divorces. There are areas infested by boy gangs and the athletic and political clubs into which the members of these gangs or the gangs themselves frequently graduate. There are regions in which the suicide rate is excessive; regions in which there is, as recorded by statistics, an excessive amount of juvenile delinquency, and other regions in which there is almost none.

All this emphasizes the importance of location, position, and mobility as indexes for measuring, describing, and eventually explaining, social phenomena. Bergson has defined mobility as "just the idea of motion which we form when we think of it by itself, when, so to speak, from motion we abstract mobility." Mobility measures social change and social disorganization, because social change almost always involves some incidental change of position in space, and all social change, even that which we describe as progress, involves some social disorganization. In the paper already referred to, Professor Burgess points out that various forms of social disorganization seem to be roughly correlated with changes in city life that can be measured in terms of mobility. All this suggests a further speculation. Since so much that students of society are ordinarily interested in seems to be intimately related to position, distribution, and movements in space, it is not impossible that all we ordinarily conceive as social may eventually be construed and described in terms of space and the changes of position of the individuals within the limits of a natural area; that is to say, within the limits of an area of competitive cooperation. Under such interesting conditions as these all social phenomena might eventually become subject to measurement, and sociology would become actually what some persons have sought to make it, a branch of statistics.

Such a scheme of description and explanation of social phenomena, if it could be carried out without too great a simplification of the facts, would certainly be a happy solution of some of the fundamental logical and epistemological problems of sociology. Reduce all social relations to relations of space and it would be possible to apply to human relations the fundamental logic of the physical sciences. Social phenomena would be reduced to the elementary movements of individuals, just as physical phenomena, chemical action, and the qualities of matter, heat, sound, and electricity are reduced to the elementary movements of molecules and atoms.

The difficulty is that in kinetic theories of matter, elements are assumed to remain unchanged. That is, of course, what we mean by element and elementary. Since the only changes that physical science reckons with are changes in space, all qualitative differences are reduced to quantitative differences, and so made subject to description in mathematical terms. In the case of human and social relations, on the other hand, the elementary units—that is to say, the individual men and women who enter into these different combinations—are notoriously subject to change. They are so far from representing homogeneous units that any thoroughgoing mathematical treatment of them seems impossible.

Society, as John Dewey has remarked, exists in and through communication, and communication involves not a translation of energies, such as seems to take place between individual social units, for example, in suggestion or imitation, two of the terms to which sociologists have at various times sought to reduce all social phenomena; but rather communication involves a transformation in the individuals who thus communicate. And this transformation goes on unceasingly with the accumulation of individual experiences in individual minds.

If human behavior could be reduced again, as some psychologists have sought to reduce it, to a few elementary instincts, the application of the kinetic theories of the physical sciences to the explanation of social life would be less difficult. But these instincts, even if they may be said to exist, are in constant process of change through the accumulation of memories and habits. And these changes are so great and continuous that to treat individual men and women as constant and homogeneous social units involves too great an abstraction. That is the reason why we are driven finally, in the explanation of human conduct and society, to psychology. In order to make comprehensible the changes which take place in society it is necessary to reckon with the changes which take place in the individual units of which society seems to be composed. The consequence is that the social element ceases to be the individual and becomes an attitude, the individual's tendency to act. Not individuals, but attitudes, interact to maintain social organizations and to produce social changes.

This conception means that geographical barriers and physical distances are significant for sociology only when and where they define the conditions under which communication and social life are actually maintained. But human geography has been profoundly modified by human invention. The telegraph, telephone, newspaper, and radio, by converting the world into one vast whispering-gallery, have dissolved the distances and broken through the isolation which once separated races and people. New devices of communication are steadily multiplying, and incidentally complicating, social relations. The history of communication is, in a very real sense, the history of civilization. Language, writing, the printing press, the telegraph, telephone, and radio mark epochs in the history of mankind. But these, it needs to be said, would have lost most of their present significance if they had not been accompanied by an increasingly wider division of labor.

I have said that society exists in and through communication. By means of communication individuals share in a common experience and maintain a common life. It is because communication is fundamental to the existence of society that geography and all the other factors that limit or facilitate communication may be said to enter into its structure and organization at all. Under these circumstances the concept of position, of distance, and of mobility have come to have a new significance. Mobility is important as a sociological concept only in so far as it insures new social contact, and physical distance is significant for social relations only when it is possible to interpret it in terms of social distance.

The social organism—and that is one of the most fundamental and disconcerting things about it—is made up of units capable of locomotion. The fact that every individual is capable of movement in space insures him an experience that is private and peculiar to himself, and this experience, which the individual acquires in the course of his adventures in space, affords him, in so far as it is unique, a point of view for independent and individual action. It is the individual's possession and consciousness of a unique experience, and his disposition to think and act in terms of it, that constitutes him finally a person.

The child, whose actions are determined mainly by its reflexes, has at first no such independence and no such individuality, and is, as a matter of fact, not a person.

It is this diversity in the experiences of individual men that makes communication necessary and consensus possible. If we always responded in like manner to like stimulation there would not be, as far as I can see, any necessity for communication, nor any possibility of abstract and reflective thought. The demand for knowledge arises from the very necessity of checking up and funding these divergent individual experiences, and of reducing them to terms which make them intelligible to all of us. A rational mind is simply one that is capable of making its private impulses public and intelligible. It is the business of science to reduce the inarticulate expression of our personal feelings to a common universe of discourse, and to create out of our private experiences an objective and intelligible world.

We not only have, each of us, our private experiences, but we are acutely conscious of them, and much concerned to protect them from invasion and misinterpretation. Our self-consciousness is just our consciousness of these individual differences of experience, together with a sense of their ultimate incommunicability. This is the basis of all our reserves, personal and racial; the basis, also, of our opinions, attitudes, and prejudices. If we were quite certain that everyone was capable of taking us, and all that we regard as personal to us, at our own valuation; if, in other words, we were as naive as children, or if, on the other hand, we were all as suggestible and lacking in reserve as some hysterics, we should probably have neither persons nor society. For a certain isolation and a certain resistance to social influences and social suggestion is just as much a condition of sound personal existence as of a wholesome society. It is just as inconceivable that we should have persons without privacy as it is that we should have society without persons.

It is evident, then, that space is not the only obstacle to communication, and that social distances cannot always be adequately measured in purely physical terms. The final obstacle to communication is self-consciousness.

What is the meaning of this self-consciousness, this reserve, this shyness, which we so frequently feel in the presence of strangers? It is certainly not always fear of physical violence. It is the fear that we will not make a good impression; the fear that we are not looking our best; that we shall not be able to live up to our conception of ourselves, and particularly, that we shall not be able to live up to the conception which we should like other persons to have of us. We experience this shyness in the presence of our own children. It is only before our most intimate friends that we are able to relax wholly, and so be utterly undignified and at ease. It is only under such circumstances, if ever, that communication is complete and that the distances which separate individuals are entirely dissolved.

This world of communication and of "distances," in which we all seek to maintain some sort of privacy, personal dignity, and poise, is a dynamic world, and has an order and a character quite its own. In this social and moral order the conception which each of us has of himself is limited by the conception which every other individual, in the same limited world of communication, has of himself, and of every other individual. The consequence is—and this is true of any society—every individual finds himself in a struggle for status: a struggle to preserve his personal prestige, his point of view, and his self-respect. He is able to maintain them, however, only to the extent that he can gain for himself the recognition of everyone else whose estimate seems important; that is to say, the estimate of everyone else who is in his set or in his society. From this struggle for status no philosophy of life has yet discovered a refuge. The individual who is not concerned about his status in some society is a hermit, even when his seclusion is a city crowd. The individual whose conception of himself is not at all determined by the conceptions that other persons have of him is probably insane.

Ultimately the society in which we live invariably turns out to be a moral order in which the individual's position, as well as his conception of himself—which is the core of his personality—is determined by the attitudes of other individuals and by the standards which the group uphold. In such a society the individual becomes a person. A person is simply an individual who has somewhere, in some society, social status; but status turns out finally to be a matter of distance—social distance.

It is because geography, occupation, and all the other factors which determine the distribution of population determine so irresistibly and fatally the place, the group, and the associates with whom each one of us is bound to live that spacial relations come to have, for the study of society and human nature, the importance which they do.

It is because social relations are so frequently and so inevitably correlated with spatial relations; because physical distances, so frequently are, or seem to be, the indexes of social distances, that statistics have any significance whatever for sociology. And this is true, finally, because it is only as social and psychical facts can be reduced to, or correlated with, spacial facts that they can be measured at all.

# 5

# HUMAN ECOLOGY

## I. *The Web of Life*

NATURALISTS of the last century were greatly intrigued by their observation of the interrelations and co-ordinations, within the realm of animate nature, of the numerous, divergent, and widely scattered species. Their successors, the botanists, and zoölogists of the present day, have turned their attention to more specific inquiries, and the "realm of nature," like the concept of evolution, has come to be for them a notion remote and speculative.

The "web of life," in which all living organisms, plants and animals alike, are bound together in a vast system of interlinked and interdependent lives, is nevertheless, as J. Arthur Thompson puts it, "one of the fundamental biological concepts" and is "as characteristically Darwinian as the struggle for existence."[1]

Darwin's famous instance of the cats and the clover is the classic illustration of this interdependence. He found, he explains, that humblebees were almost indispensable to the fertilization of the heartsease, since other bees do not visit this flower. The same thing is true with some kinds of clover. Humblebees alone visit red clover, as other bees cannot reach the nectar. The inference is that if the humblebees became extinct or very rare in England, the heartsease and red clover would become very rare, or wholly disappear. However, the number of humblebees in any district depends in a great measure on the number of field mice, which

---

Reprinted from *American Journal of Sociology*, 42 (July, 1936): 1–15.

1    *The System of Animate Nature* (Gifford Lectures, 1915–16), II (New York, 1920), 58.

destroy their combs and nests. It is estimated that more than two-thirds of them are thus destroyed all over England. Near villages and small towns the nests of humblebees are more numerous than elsewhere and this is attributed to the number of cats that destroy the mice.[2] Thus next year's crop of purple clover in certain parts of England depends on the number of humblebees in the district; the number of humblebees depends upon the number of field mice, the number of field mice upon the number and the enterprise of the cats, and the number of cats—as someone has added—depends on the number of old maids and others in neighboring villages who keep cats.

These large food chains, as they are called, each link of which eats the other, have as their logical prototype the familiar nursery rhyme, "The House that Jack Built." You recall:

> The cow with the crumpled horn,
> That tossed the dog,
> That worried the cat,
> That killed the rat,
> That ate the malt
> That lay in the house that Jack built.

Darwin and the naturalists of his day were particularly interested in observing and recording these curious illustrations of the mutual adaptation and correlation of plants and animals because they seemed to throw light on the origin of the species. Both the species and their mutual interdependence, within a common habitat, seem to be a product of the same Darwinian struggle for existence.

It is interesting to note that it was the application to organic life of a sociological principle—the principle, namely, of "competitive co-operation"—that gave Darwin the first clue to the formulation of his theory of evolution.

"He projected on organic life," says Thompson, "a sociological idea," and "thus vindicated the relevancy and utility of a sociological idea within the biological realm."[3]

[2]    J. Arthur Thompson, *Darwinism and Human Life* (New York, 1911), pp. 52–53.
[3]    *Ibid.*, p. 72.

The active principle in the ordering and regulating of life within the realm of animate nature is, as Darwin described it, "the struggle for existence." By this means the numbers of living organisms are regulated, their distribution controlled, and the balance of nature maintained. Finally, it is by means of this elementary form of competition that the existing species, the survivors in the struggle, find their niches in the physical environment and in the existing correlation or division of labor between the different species. J. Arthur Thompson makes an impressive statement of the matter in his *System of Animate Nature*. He says:

The hosts of living organisms are not . . . isolated creatures, for every thread of life is intertwined with others in a complex web. . . . Flowers and insects are fitted to one another as hand to glove. Cats have to do with the plague in India as well as with the clover crop at home. . . . *Just as there is a correlation of organs in the body, so there is a correlation of organisms in the world of life.* When we learn something of the intricate give and take, supply and demand, action and reaction between plants and animals, between flowers and insects, between herbivores and carnivores, and between other conflicting yet correlated interests, we begin to get a glimpse of a vast self-regulating organization.

These manifestations of a living, changing, but persistent order among competing organisms—organisms embodying "conflicting yet correlated interests"—seem to be the basis for the conception of a social order transcending the individual species, and of a society based on a biotic rather than a cultural basis, a conception later developed by the plant and animal ecologists.

In recent years the plant geographers have been the first to revive something of the earlier field naturalists' interest in the interrelations of species. Haeckel, in 1878, was the first to give to these studies a name, "ecology," and by so doing gave them the character of a distinct and separate science, a science which Thompson describes as "the new natural history."[4]

The interrelation and interdependence of the species are

---

[4]    "Ecology," says Elton, "corresponds to the older terms Natural History and Bionomics, but its methods are now accurate and precise." See article, "Ecology," *Encyclopædia Britannica* (14th ed.).

naturally more obvious and more intimate within the common habitat than elsewhere. Furthermore, as correlations have multiplied and competition has decreased, in consequence of mutual adaptations of the competing species, the habitat and habitants have tended to assume the character of a more or less completely closed system.

Within the limits of this system the individual units of the population are involved in a process of competitive co-operation, which has given to their interrelations the character of a natural economy. To such a habitat and its inhabitants—whether plant, animals, or human—the ecologists have applied the term "community."

The essential characteristics of a community, so conceived, are those of: (1) a population, territorially organized, (2) more or less completely rooted in the soil it occupies, (3) its individual units living in a relationship of mutual interdependence that is symbiotic rather than societal, in the sense in which that term applies to human beings.

These symbiotic societies are not merely unorganized assemblages of plants and animals which happen to live together in the same habitat. On the contrary, they are interrelated in the most complex manner. Every community has something of the character of an organic unit. It has a more or less definite structure and it has "a life history in which juvenile, adult and senile phases can be observed."[5] If it is an organism, it is one of the organs which are other organisms. It is, to use Spencer's phrase, a superorganism.

What more than anything else gives the symbiotic community the character of an organism is the fact that it possesses a mechanism (competition) for (1) regulating the numbers, and (2) preserving the balance between the competing species of which it is composed. It is by maintaining this biotic balance that the community preserves its identity and integrity as an individual unit through the changes and the vicissitudes to which it is subject in the course of its progress from the earlier to the later phases of its existence.

[5]    Edward J. Salisbury, "Plants," *Encyclopædia Britannica* (14th ed.)

## II. *The Balance of Nature*

The balance of nature, as plant and animal ecologists have conceived it, seems to be largely a question of numbers. When the pressure of population upon the natural resources of the habitat reaches a certain degree of intensity, something invariably happens. In the one case the population may swarm and relieve the pressure of population by migration. In another, where the disequilibrium between population and natural resources is the result of some change, sudden or gradual, in the conditions of life, the pre-existing correlation of the species may be totally destroyed.

Change may be brought about by a famine, an epidemic, or an invasion of the habitat by some alien species. Such an invasion may result in a rapid increase of the invading population and a sudden decline in the numbers if not the destruction of the original population. Change of some sort is continuous, although the rate and pace of change sometimes vary greatly. Charles Elton says:

The impression of anyone who has studied animal numbers in the field is that the "balance of nature" hardly exists, except in the minds of scientists. It seems that animal numbers are always tending to settle down into a smooth and harmonious working mechanism, but something always happens before this happy state is reached.[6]

Under ordinary circumstances, such minor fluctuations in the biotic balance as occur are mediated and absorbed without profoundly disturbing the existing equilibrium and routine of life. When, on the other hand, some sudden and catastrophic change occurs—it may be a war, a famine, or pestilence—it upsets the biotic balance, breaks "the cake of custom," and releases energies up to that time held in check. A series of rapid and even violent changes may ensue which profoundly alter the existing organization of communal life and give a new direction to the future course of events.

The advent of the boll weevil in the southern cotton fields is a minor instance but illustrates the principle. The boll weevil crossed the Rio Grande at Brownsville in the summer of 1892. By

[6]    "Animal Ecology," *ibid.*

1894 the pest had spread to a dozen counties in Texas, bringing destruction to the cotton and great losses to the planters. From that point it advanced, with every recurring season, until by 1928 it had covered practically all the cotton producing area in the United States. Its progress took the form of a territorial succession. The consequences to agriculture were catastrophic but not wholly for the worse, since they served to give an impulse to changes in the organization of the industry long overdue. It also hastened the northward migration of the Negro tenant farmer.

The case of the boll weevil is typical. In this mobile modern world, where space and time have been measurably abolished, not men only but all the minor organisms (including the microbes) seem to be, as never before, in motion. Commerce, in progressively destroying the isolation upon which the ancient order of nature rested, has intensified the struggle for existence over an ever widening area of the habitable world. Out of this struggle a new equilibrium and a new system of animate nature, the new biotic basis of the new world-society, is emerging.

It is, as Elton remarks, the "fluctuation of numbers" and "the failure" from time to time "of the regulatory mechanism of animal increase" which ordinarily interrupts the established routine, and in so doing releases a new cycle of change. In regard to these fluctuations in numbers Elton says:

These failures of the regulating mechanism of animal increase— are they caused by (1) internal changes, after the manner of an alarm clock which suddenly goes off, or the boilers of an engine blowing up, or are they caused by some factors in the outer environment—weather, vegetation, or something like that?[7]

and he adds:

It appears that they are due to both but that the latter (external factor) is the more important of the two, and usually plays the leading rôle.

The conditions which affect and control the movements and numbers of populations are more complex in human societies than

[7]    *Ibid.*

in plant and animal communities, but they exhibit extraordinary similarities.

The boll weevil, moving out of its ancient habitat in the central Mexican plateau and into the virgin territory of the southern cotton plantations, incidentally multiplying its population to the limit of the territories and resources, is not unlike the Boers of Cape Colony, South Africa, trekking out into the high veldt of the central South African plateau and filling it, within a period of one hundred years, with a population of their own descendants.

Competition operates in the human (as it does in the plant and animal) community to bring about and restore the communal equilibrium, when, either by the advent of some intrusive factor from without or in the normal course of its life-history, that equilibrium is disturbed.

Thus every crisis that initiates a period of rapid change, during which competition is intensified, moves over finally into a period of more or less stable equilibrium and a new division of labor. In this manner competition brings about a condition in which competition is superseded by co-operation.

It is when, and to the extent that, competition declines that the kind of order which we call society may be said to exist. In short, society, from the ecological point of view, and in so far as it is a territorial unit, is just the area within which biotic competition has declined and the struggle for existence has assumed higher and more sublimated forms.

## III. *Competition, Dominance and Succession*

There are other and less obvious ways in which competition exercises control over the relations of individuals and species within the communal habitat. The two ecological principles, dominance and succession, which operate to establish and maintain such communal order as here described are functions of, and dependent upon, competition.

In every life-community there is always one or more dominant species. In a plant community this dominance is ordinarily the result of struggle among the different species for light. In a climate which supports a forest the dominant species will invariably be trees. On the prairie and steppes they will be grasses.

Light being the main necessity of plants, the dominant plant of a community is the tallest member, which can spread its green energy-trap above the heads of the others. What marginal exploitation there is to be done is an exploitation of the dimmer light below this canopy. So it comes about in every life-community on land, in the cornfield just as in the forest, that there are layers of vegetation, each adapted to exist in a lesser intensity of light than the one above. Usually there are but two or three such layers; in an oak-wood for example there will be a layer of moss, above this herbs or low bushes, and then nothing more to the leafy roof; in the wheat-field the dominating form is the wheat, with lower weeds among its stalks. But in tropical forests the whole space from floor to roof may be zoned and populated.[8]

But the principle of dominance operates in the human as well as in the plant and animal communities. The so-called natural or functional areas of a metropolitan community—for example, the slum, the rooming-house area, the central shopping section and the banking center—each and all owe their existence directly to the factor of dominance, and indirectly to competition.

The struggle of industries and commercial institutions for a strategic location determines in the long run the main outlines of the urban community. The distribution of population, as well as the location and limits of the residential areas which they occupy, are determined by another similar but subordinate system of forces.

The area of dominance in any community is usually the area of highest land values. Ordinarily there are in every large city two such positions of highest land value—one in the central shopping district, the other in the central banking area. From these points land values decline at first precipitantly and then more gradually toward the periphery of the urban community. It is these land values that determine the location of social institutions and business enterprises. Both the one and the other are bound up in a kind of territorial complex within which they are at once competing and interdependent units.

---

8　H. G. Wells, Julian S. Huxley, and G. P. Wells, *The Science of Life* (New York, 1934), pp. 968–69.

As the metropolitan community expands into the suburbs the pressure of professions, business enterprises, and social institutions of various sorts destined to serve the whole metropolitan region steadily increases the demand for space at the center. Thus not merely the growth of the suburban area, but any change in the method of transportation which makes the central business area of the city more accessible, tends to increase the pressure at the center. From thence this pressure is transmitted and diffused, as the profile of land values discloses, to every other part of the city.

Thus the principle of dominance, operating within the limits imposed by the terrain and other natural features of the location, tends to determine the general ecological pattern of the city and the functional relation of each of the different areas of the city to all others.

Dominance is, furthermore, in so far as it tends to stabilize either the biotic or the cultural community, indirectly responsible for the phenomenon of succession.

The term "succession" is used by ecologists to describe and designate that orderly sequence of changes through which a biotic community passes in the course of its development from a primary and relatively unstable to a relatively permanent or climax stage. The main point is that not merely do the individual plants and animals within the communal habitat grow but the community itself, i.e., the system of relations between the species, is likewise involved in an orderly process of change and development.

The fact that, in the course of this development, the community moves through a series of more or less clearly defined stages is the fact that gives this development the serial character which the term "succession" suggests.

The explanation of the serial character of the changes involved in succession is the fact that at every stage in the process a more or less stable equilibrium is achieved, which in due course, and as a result of progressive changes in life-conditions, possibly due to growth and decay, the equilibrium achieved in the earlier stages is eventually undermined. In such case the energies previously held in balance will be released, competition will be intensified, and change will continue at a relatively rapid rate until a new equilibrium is achieved.

The climax phase of community development corresponds with the adult phase of an individual's life.

In the developing single organism, each phase is its own executioner, and itself brings a new phase into existence, as when the tadpole grows the thyroid gland which is destined to make the tadpole state pass away in favour of the miniature frog. And in the developing community of organisms, the same thing happens—each stage alters its own environment, for it changes and almost invariably enriches the soil in which it lives; and thus it eventually brings itself to an end, by making it possible for new kinds of plants with greater demands in the way of mineral salts or other riches of the soil to flourish there. Accordingly bigger and more exigent plants gradually supplant the early pioneers, until a final balance is reached, the ultimate possibility for that climate.[9]

The cultural community develops in comparable ways to that of the biotic, but the process is more complicated. Inventions, as well as sudden or catastrophic changes, seem to play a more important part in bringing about serial changes in the cultural than in the biotic community. But the principle involved seems to be substantially the same. In any case, all or most of the fundamental processes seem to be functionally related and dependent upon competition.

Competition, which on the biotic level functions to control and regulate the interrelations of organisms, tends to assume on the social level the form of conflict. The intimate relation between competition and conflict is indicated by the fact that wars frequently, if not always, have, or seem to have, their source and origin in economic competition which, in that case, assumes the more sublimated form of a struggle for power and prestige. The social function of war, on the other hand, seems to be to extend the area over which it is possible to maintain peace.

## IV. *Biological Economics*

If population pressure, on the one hand, co-operates with changes in local and environmental conditions to disturb at once

[9]  *Ibid.*, pp. 977–78.

the biotic balance and social equilibrium, it tends at the same time to intensify competition. In so doing it functions, indirectly, to bring about a new, more minute and, at the same time, territorially extensive division of labor.

Under the influence of an intensified competition, and the increased activity which competition involves, every individual and every species, each for itself, tends to discover the particular niche in the physical and living environment where it can survive and flourish with the greatest possible expansiveness consistent with its necessary dependence upon its neighbors.

It is in this way that a territorial organization and a biological division of labor, within the communal habitat, is established and maintained. This explains, in part at least, the fact that the biotic community has been conceived at one time as a kind of superorganism and at another as a kind of economic organization for the exploitation of the natural resources of its habitat.

In their interesting survey, *The Science of Life*, H. G. Wells and his collaborators, Julian Huxley and G. P. Wells, have described ecology as "biological economics," and as such very largely concerned with "the balances and mutual pressures of species living in the same habitat."[10]

"Ecology," as they put it, is "an extension of Economics to the whole of life." On the other hand the science of economics as traditionally conceived, though it is a whole century older, is merely a branch of a more general science of ecology which includes man with all other living creatures. Under the circumstances what has been traditionally described as economics and conceived as restricted to human affairs, might very properly be described as Barrows some years ago described geography, namely as human ecology. It is in this sense that Wells and his collaborators would use the term.

The science of economic—at first it was called Political Economy —is a whole century older than ecology. It was and is the science of social subsistence, of needs and their satisfactions, of work and wealth. It tries to elucidate the relations of producer, dealer, and consumer

[10] *Ibid.*

in the human community and show how the whole system carries on. Ecology broadens out this inquiry into a general study of the give and take, the effort, accumulation and consumption in every province of life. Economics, therefore, is merely Human Ecology, it is the narrow and special study of the ecology of the very extraordinary community in which we live. It might have been a better and brighter science if it had begun biologically.[11]

Since human ecology cannot be at the same time both geography and economics, one may adopt, as a working hypothesis, the notion that it is neither one nor the other but something independent of both. Even so the motives for identifying ecology with geography on the one hand, and economics on the other, are fairly obvious.

From the point of view of geography, the plant, animal, and human population, including their habitations and other evidence of man's occupation of the soil, are merely part of the landscape, of which the geographer is seeking a detailed description and picture.

On the other hand ecology (biologic economics), even when it involves some sort of unconscious co-operation and a natural, spontaneous, and non-rational division of labor, is something different from the economics of commerce; something quite apart from the bargaining of the market place. Commerce, as Simmel somewhere remarks, is one of the latest and most complicated of all the social relationships into which human beings have entered. Man is the only animal that trades and traffics.

Ecology, and human ecology, if it is not identical with economics on the distinctively human and cultural level is, nevertheless, something more than and different from the static order which the human geographer discovers when he surveys the cultural landscape.

The community of the geographer is not, for one thing, like that of the ecologist, a closed system, and the web of communication which man has spread over the earth is something different

11    H. H. Barrows, "Geography as Human Ecology," *Annals Association American Geographers*, 13 (1923) : 1–14. See H. G. Wells, *et al.*, pp. 961–62.

from the "web of life" which binds living creatures all over the world in a vital nexus.

## V. *Symbiosis and Society*

Human ecology, if it is neither economics on one hand nor geography on the other, but just ecology, differs, nevertheless, in important respects from plant and animal ecology. The interrelations of human beings and interactions of man and his habitat are comparable but not identical with interrelations of other forms of life that live together and carry on a kind of "biological economy" within the limits of a common habitat.

For one thing man is not so immediately dependent upon his physical environment as other animals. As a result of the existing world-wide division of labor, man's relation to his physical environment has been mediated through the intervention of other men. The exchange of goods and services have co-operated to emancipate him from dependence upon his local habitat.

Furthermore man has, by means of inventions and technical devices of the most diverse sorts, enormously increased his capacity for reacting upon and remaking, not only his habitat but his world. Finally, man has erected upon the basis of the biotic community an institutional structure rooted in custom and tradition.

Structure, where it exists, tends to resist change, at least change coming from without; while it possibly facilitates the cumulation of change within.[12] In plant and animal communities structure is biologically determined, and so far as any division of labor exists at all it has a physiological and instinctive basis. The social insects afford a conspicuous example of this fact, and one

[12]   Here is, obviously, another evidence of that organic character of the interrelations of organisms in the biosphere to which J. Arthur Thompson and others have referred. It is an indication of the way in which competition mediates the influences from without by the adjustment and readjustment of relations within the community. In this case "within" coincides with the orbit of the competitive process, at least so far as the effects of that process are substantive and obvious. See Simmel's definition of society and the social group in time and space quoted in Park and Burgess, *Introduction to the Science of Sociology* (2d ed.), pp. 348–56.

interest in studying their habits, as Wheeler points out, is that they show the extent to which social organization can be developed on a purely physiological and instinctive basis, as is the case among human beings in the natural as distinguished from the institutional family.[13]

In a society of human beings, however, this communal structure is reinforced by custom and assumes an institutional character. In human as contrasted with animal societies, competition and the freedom of the individual is limited on every level above the biotic by custom and consensus.

The incidence of this more or less arbitrary control which custom and consensus imposes upon the natural social order complicates the social process but does not fundamentally alter it—or, if it does, the effects of biotic competition will still be manifest in the succeeding social order and the subsequent course of events.

The fact seems to be, then, that human society, as distinguished from plant and animal society, is organized on two levels, the biotic and the cultural. There is a symbiotic society based on competition and a cultural society based on communication and consensus. As a matter of fact the two societies are merely different aspects of one society, which, in the vicissitudes and changes to which they are subject remain, nevertheless, in some sort of mutual dependence each upon the other. The cultural superstructure rests on the basis of the symbiotic substructure, and the emergent energies that manifest themselves on the biotic level in movements and actions reveal themselves on the higher social level in more subtle and sublimated forms.

However, the interrelations of human beings are more diverse and complicated than this dichotomy, symbiotic and cultural, indicates. This fact is attested by the divergent systems of human interrelations which have been the subject of the special social sciences. Thus human society, certainly in its mature and more rational expression, exhibits not merely an ecological, but an economic, a political, and a moral order. The social sciences include not merely human geography and ecology, but economics, political science, and cultural anthropology.

13   William Morton Wheeler, *Social Life among the Insects* (Lowell Institute Lectures, March, 1922), pp. 3–18.

It is interesting also that these divergent social orders seem to arrange themselves in a kind of hierarchy. In fact they may be said to form a pyramid of which the ecological order constitutes the base and the moral order the apex. Upon each succeeding one of these levels, the ecological, economic, political, and moral, the individual finds himself more completely incorporated into and subordinated to the social order of which he is a part than upon the preceding.

Society is everywhere a control organization. Its function is to organize, integrate, and direct the energies resident in the individuals of which it is composed. One might, perhaps, say that the function of society was everywhere to restrict competition and by so doing bring about a more effective co-operation of the organic units of which society is composed.

Competition, on the biotic level, as we observe it in the plant and animal communities, seems to be relatively unrestricted. Society, so far as it exists, is anarchic and free. On the cultural level, this freedom of the individual to compete is restricted by conventions, understandings, and law. The individual is more free upon the economic level than upon the political, more free on the political than the moral.

As society matures control is extended and intensified and free commerce of individuals restricted, if not by law then by what Gilbert Murray refers to as "the normal expectation of mankind." The mores are merely what men, in a situation that is defined, have come to expect.

Human ecology, in so far as it is concerned with a social order that is based on competition rather than consensus, is identical, in principle at least, with plant and animal ecology. The problems with which plant and animal ecology have been traditionally concerned are fundamentally population problems. Society, as ecologists have conceived it, is a population settled and limited to its habitat. The ties that unite its individual units are those of a free and natural economy, based on a natural division of labor. Such a society is territorially organized and the ties which hold it together are physical and vital rather than customary and moral.

Human ecology has, however, to reckon with the fact that in human society competition is limited by custom and culture. The cultural superstructure imposes itself as an instrument of direction and control upon the biotic substructure.

Reduced to its elements the human community, so conceived, may be said to consist of a population and a culture, including in the term culture (1) a body of customs and beliefs and (2) a corresponding body of artifacts and technological devices.

To these three elements or factors—(1) population, (2) artifact (technicological culture), (3) custom and beliefs (non-material culture)—into which the social complex resolves itself, one should, perhaps, add a fourth, namely, the natural resources of the habitat.

It is the interaction of these four factors—(1) population, (2) artifacts (technicological culture), (3) custom and beliefs (non-material culture), and (4) the natural resources that maintain at once the biotic balance and the social equilibrium, when and where they exist.

The changes in which ecology is interested are the movements of population and of artifacts (commodities) and changes in location and occupation—any sort of change, in fact, which affects an existing division of labor or the relation of the population to the soil.

Human ecology is, fundamentally, an attempt to investigate the processes by which the biotic balance and the social equilibrium (1) are maintained once they are achieved and (2) the processes by which, when the biotic balance and the social equilibrium are disturbed, the transition is made from one relatively stable order to another.

# 6

# SUCCESSION, AN ECOLOGICAL
# CONCEPT

THE TERM "succession" seems to have first gained currency
and definition as a result of its use in the writings of the plant
ecologists. It has not the same wide application in animal ecology,
and where it has been used elsewhere, as it has by sociological
writers, it seems to be a useful word but without as yet any very
precise connotation. It has been used, for example, in describing
the intra-mural movements and shiftings of population incident to
the growth of the city and of its various "natural areas."

It has been observed, for one thing, that immigrant peoples
ordinarily settle first in or near the centers of cities, in the so-called
areas of transition. From there they are likely to move by stages
(perhaps one might better say, by leaps and bounds) from an area
of first to areas of second and third settlement, generally in the
direction of the periphery of the city and eventually into the suburban area—in any case, from a less to a more stable section of
the metropolitan region. To these movements, seeing in them the
effects of natural tendencies in the life of the urban community,
students have applied the term "succession."

In this same sense the term has been applied to the successive
waves by which the frontier in America advanced from the Atlantic seaboard westward across the plains to the Pacific coast,
each advance marked by a different type of culture and by a different occupational and personality type.

First arrivals were the explorers, trappers, Indian traders, and

Reprinted from *American Sociological Review*, 1 (April, 1936): 171–79.

prospectors, with a sprinkling of outlaws. In the next line of advance were land seekers, squatters and frontier farmers bent on establishing the first frontier settlements. They were followed finally by a swarm of restless enterprising adventurers of all sorts, among them representatives of a frontier *intelligentsia*—the men who eventually became the lawyers, politicians, and newspaper men of the booming settlements.[1]

A similar "territorial succession" may be said to have marked the expansion of European population and European culture during the period of four hundred years in which European commerce has made its conquest of the world.[2]

In a study of Lowell, made by George F. Kenngott and published in 1912, the most striking feature of the study was the succession of immigrant invasions which in the course of the city's history, i.e., from about 1830 to about 1912, the steady demand for labor in the woolen mills had brought to it. This was a study in population succession, though not so designated. It was also a study in progressive cultural change—a progress, however, that was mostly for the worse.[3]

Although the term succession, as originally employed by sociologists, would seem to be more appropriately applied to movements of population and to such incidental social and cultural changes as these movements involve, there seems to be no sound reason why the same term should not be used to describe any orderly and irreversible series of events, provided they are to such an extent correlated with other less obvious and more fundamental social changes that they may be used as indices of these changes.

Thus a series of fundamental inventions like the alphabet, the printing press, the newspaper, and the radio may be said to constitute a succession. At any rate, each may be said to mark an epoch in the history of communication, and in doing this each new invention characterizes the culture of which it is a part and

[1]    Rupert B. Vance, "Frontier: Geographical and Social Aspect," *Encyclopedia of the Social Sciences.*
[2]    E. B. Reuter, *Race and Culture Contacts*, chap. 5.
[3]    George F. Kenngott, *The Record of a City: A Social Survey of Lowell, Massachusetts* (New York, 1920).

defines its place in the historical succession. In the same sense we may speak of the waterwheel as in the same line of succession as the steam engine and the electric motor, each marking a phase in the evolution of the machine age. Manifestly such a series of events represents something more than a mere temporal sequence. It represents rather an irreversible series in which each succeeding event is more or less completely determined by the one that preceded it.

In a recent paper by Edgar T. Thompson on the plantation as an institution of the frontier, the author refers to the fact that a typical plantation society ordinarily passes through a cycle of change, the plantation cycle, and to this he applies the term succession. Thereupon he proceeds to describe in detail the irreversible stages in the natural history of the plantation community.[4]

In a recent study of the "granger movements" in the United States, Thomas C. McCormick pointed out that the different individual movements seemed to be merely the periodic outbreaks of a disease that was endemic in the country, so that the different movements might well be conceived as the recurrent manifestations, the periodic risings and subsidings, of discontents that had their source and origin in a kind of permanent malaise that could be relieved but never quite cured.[5]

Among other things interesting from the point of view of succession which this study showed were: (1) each succeeding rural movement was under way and rising before the one preceding it had wholly subsided: (2) although each wave of utopianism was incontinently followed by a corresponding period of depression and disillusionment, there was, nevertheless, evidence with each recurring wave of a growing realism in the attitudes of the leaders at least. This was manifest in the character of the programs and in the methods for putting them into effect. This is an instance of succession in the psychic or subjective aspect of social change.

A more obvious and impressive example of succession, in the

4     Edgar T. Thompson, "Population Expansion and Plantation System," *American Journal of Sociology*, 41 (November, 1931): 314–26.
5     Thomas C. McCormick, *The Rural Life Movement*, unpublished thesis, The University of Chicago.

very elementary sense in which this term is here used, is the procession of peoples that have invaded and settled South Africa. First came the Bushmen; they were hunters who have left in caves in the mountains, as records of their presence, interesting rock pictures. The Hottentots followed. They were hunters, to be sure, but herdsmen also, and they had a great deal of trouble with the Bushmen who killed their cattle with poisoned arrows. So the Hottentots drove the Bushmen into the Kalahari desert. The Bantu were next. They were hunters and herdsmen but they were more. They cultivated the soil and raised Kaffir corn.

Later still came the Boers, particularly the *voortrekkers*, who settled the Transvaal and the Orange Free State, conquered and enslaved the natives, settled on the land, raised large families, and lived on their wide acres in patriarchal style. Although they were descendants, for the most part, of the earlier Dutch immigrants, with a sprinkling of Huguenots and other Europeans, they had become, as a result of their isolation and their long association with the country, an indigenous folk, having their own language, their own customs and culture.

Then, finally, came the English. They were a sophisticated city folk, and they came in force only after diamonds were discovered in Orange Free State in 1867 and gold was discovered in the Transvaal in 1884. They built Johannesburg, a cosmopolitan city —a world city, in fact, like Calcutta, and Shanghai, and London. In this way they drew South Africa out of its isolation into the current of international trade and the new world civilization.

What makes this instance of succession ecologically interesting is the fact that it illustrates a principle familiar to ethnologists: the principle, namely, that the more primitive the culture of a people the larger the territory needed, in proportion to its numbers, to support its population. A corollary of this is the principle that the land eventually goes to the race or people that can get the most out of it. This, on the other hand, is merely another version of the rule of agricultural economics, which declares that the best lands eventually go to the best farmers.

The thing that makes the settlement of South Africa relevant and significant, as an example of succession, is the fact that it seems to represent not a casual sequence of events but the consequences of an inexorable historical process.

It is evident that in the conception of succession, as here defined and illustrated, there is implicit a more fundamental notion of social change and of society which is nowhere explicitly set forth.

Generally speaking, succession, as the term is used by ecologists, seems to be identical with a notion of social change suggested by Walter Bagehot's phrase, "The cake of custom," in his volume *Physics and Politics*; a conception which has been further elaborated by Frederick Jackson Teggart in his *Theory of History*.[6]

Teggart's is what I have described as the catastrophic theory of history; the theory that each succeeding social order has its origin in the conditions created by the earlier; that society is continually reborn, but that now and then a new and fundamentally different society emerges. In that case, it emerges suddenly and abruptly with the accumulation of minor changes in the course of a long-term trend.

The changes here referred to, have taken place upon the cultural, rather than the biotic level. Nevertheless, they seem to be identical in form, at least, with the kind of change that plant and animal ecologists have called succession, the nature of which is elaborately set forth by F. C. Clements.[7]

On the other hand, the conception of social relations and society on which this account of succession is based is that suggested by J. Arthur Thompson's description of "the web of life" as "a system of inter-related lives." This is a notion that had its origin in a long series of observations and reflections like those from which Darwin arrived at his theory of the origin of the species. It is this concept of a symbiotic society based on physio-

---

6     Walter Bagehot, *Physics and Politics; or Thoughts on the Application of the Principles of "Natural Section" and "Inheritance" to Political Society*, New York, 1873; and Frederick Jackson Teggart, *Theory of History*.

7     F. C. Clements, *Plant Succession* (Washington, D.C.: Carnegie Institution, 1916).

logical correlation rather than culture which has been adopted and elaborated in writings of the plant and animal ecologists.

Perhaps I can make clear the connection of these conceptions of society and social change with the ecological conception of succession if I state briefly certain points of evolutionary and ecological theory. In brief, then, the argument is this:

Man is involved, with all the hosts of other living creatures, in what Darwin calls "the web of life." In certain places and under certain conditions this interdependence of the species, to which Darwin's expression "the web of life" refers, assumes a relatively permanent, structural character. This is true of the so-called plant and animal communities.

The same biotic interdependence of individuals and species, which has been observed and studied in plant and animal communities, seems to exist likewise on the human level, except for the fact that in human society competition and the struggle for existence are limited by custom, convention, and law. In short, human society is, or appears to be, organized on two levels, the biotic and the cultural.

We may distinguish between a society based on symbiosis, and one based on communication and consensus. As a matter of fact, however, the two are but different aspects of one society. The cultural superstructure rests on the basis of a symbiotic substructure, and the emergent energies that manifest themselves on the biotic level in movements and actions which are obvious enough reveal themselves on the higher, social level in more subtle and sublimated forms. The distinction and relation between the two levels of society, the biotic and the cultural, is, or seems to be, analogous to that between the somatic and psychic aspects of the individual organisms of which the society is composed.

Economic competition, as one meets it in human society, is the struggle for existence, as Darwin conceived it, modified and limited by custom and convention. In other respects, however, it is not different from competition as it exists in plant and animal communities.

Society, in the more inclusive sense in which ecologists have defined it, may be said to exist wherever competition has established some sort of order or war has established some sort of peace. It is the area within which an intrinsic and functional social order has succeeded one that was extrinsic and mechanical. This does not imply that the original relations of men were, as Hobbes described them, a war of each against all, a *bellum omnia contra omnes,* but rather that the function and effect of competition has been to bring about everywhere a division of labor which has diminished competition. In the same sense the function of war has been to achieve peace and order, and to create a social organization capable of maintaining it.

There is this difference, however, between a symbiotic and cultural society; namely, that the restraint in the case of symbiotic society (as for example in the plant community) is physical and external. In the case of cultural, i.e., human, society the restraints upon the individual are, so to speak, internal and moral, i.e., based on some sort of consensus.

A social organization on either the biotic or social level, so far as it involves the incorporation of individuals into a more intimate association, imposes limits, control, and direction upon these individual units. One may regard the plant and animal community as an association that is wholly anarchic and free. In that case, however, every form of association on the cultural level will involve a limitation of freedom of the individual.

The individual man, although he has more freedom in some places than in others—more freedom on the economic level than upon the political, more upon the political than the custom or moral level—never has in human society the same absolute freedom to compete with other individuals that plants and animals have.

Competition implies the existence of what J. Arthur Thompson describes as "the self-assertiveness and insurgence of the creature." The adaptations and accommodations which make society possible are for the individual organism or the individual species a partial or temporary solution of its struggles to survive.[8] But they limit freedom.

[8]    "The living creature is by its very nature insurgent and it finds itself encompassed by limitations and difficulties" (Thompson, p. 294).

As the equilibrium we call society becomes relatively fixed in social structure, competition is increasingly diminished. Nevertheless, competition persists in human society and continues to manifest itself, as does the sexual instinct, in manifold indirect and insidious ways.

Every now and then something occurs, however, to disturb the biotic balance and the social equilibrium, thus tending to undermine the existing social order. It may be the advent of a new insect pest, like the boll weevil, or the arrival of a newly invented and perfected artifact, like the automobile. Under these circumstances, forces and tendencies formerly held in check are released, and a period of intense activity and rapid change ensues which then continues until the cycle is completed and a new biotic and social equilibrium is achieved.

Changes, when they are recurrent, so that they fall into a temporal or spatial series—particularly if the series is of such a sort that the effect of each succeeding increment of change reënforces or carries forward the effects of the preceding—constitute what is described in this paper as succession.

In view, however, of the complexity of social change and of the peculiar manner in which change in the social superstructure is involved in change in the biotic or symbiotic substructure, it seems desirable to include within the perspective and purview of the concept, and of the studies of succession, every possible form of orderly change so far as it affects the interrelations of individuals in a community or the structure of the society of which these individual units are a part.

Conceived in this way succession will include studies of the form (morphology) and of the causes (etiology) of social change.

Sometimes the forms of social change are such, as in the case of periodic "psychic epidemics" or recurrent business booms, that their courses can be precisely described in a mathematical equation. In that case it may be possible to predict, with some accuracy, not merely the direction but the duration of change.

Studies of succession, however, seek less to predict the course of change than to make change intelligible, so that it can eventually be controlled by technical devices or political measures. For this reason studies of succession are concerned not only with the form which change takes but even more with the circumstances and events which precede, accompany, and follow change —in short, with its natural history.

The study of succession involves, it seems, not merely the life-cycle of individual types of institution and society, but eventually a study of processes by which new types of society are incubated and, eventually, by which a new social order emerges from the lap of the old.

The problems with which plant and animal ecology have traditionally been concerned are fundamentally population problems. Society, from the ecological point of view is, like the natural as opposed to the institutional family, a symbiotic rather than a social unit. It is a population settled and limited to its habitat. The ties that unite its individual units are those of a free and natural economy, based on a natural division of labor. Such a society is territorially organized, and the ties which hold it together are physical and vital rather than customary and moral. It is, of course, not assumed that this is all of society, but it is one aspect of it.

The changes in which ecology is interested, it follows, are primarily physical and vital. They are the movements of population and of artifacts (commodities), changes in location and in occupation—any sort of change, in fact, which affects an existing division of labor or the relation of the population to the soil.

Human ecology, in approaching the study of society from the aspect presented by its biotic substructure, assumes that the origin of social change, if one could trace it to its source, would be found in the struggle for existence and in the growth, the migration, the mobility, and the territorial and occupational distribution of peoples which this struggle has brought about.

Ecology conceives society as fundamentally a territorial as well as a cultural organization. So far as this conception is valid, it assumes that most if not all cultural changes in society will be correlated with changes in its territorial organization, and every change in the territorial and occupational distribution of the population will effect changes in the existing cultures.

The evolution of society is, therefore, in one of its aspects, the evolution of a territorial organization. Thus, N. B. S. Gras, in his

*Introduction to Economic History*, is able to tell the whole story of economic history by describing the evolution of the metropolitan economy as it has developed through a series of stages which include the village, the town, and the city, and which ends in the metropolitan economy.[9]

In a similar way, the present economic, political and cultural order in Europe has come into existence with the growth in population and the migration and the territorial expansion of Europe. This expansion has been made possible by a series of inventions which have, at different epochs in its history, revolutionized and transformed the prevailing methods of transportation and communication. They are:

(1) The perfecting of ocean-going ships with which, in the age of discovery, Europeans extended their knowledge of the world outside of Europe.

(2) The steamship, by means of which a great commercial highway has been established around the world and has made of the seas, with their seaport cities, the center of the world.

(3) The railways, by which the continental areas have been penetrated and their resources transported to the seaboard, where they have entered into world commerce.

(4) The automobile, which has suddenly further transformed continental areas by spreading out over the land networks of roads which permit rapid and unlimited transportation in every direction.

(5) Finally, there is the airplane, the possibilities of which we are now just beginning to explore.

These changes have literally plowed up the ancient landmarks, undermined the influence of the traditional social order in every part of the world, and released immense social forces which are now seeking everywhere a new equilibrium.

It is from the point of view of these spatial and temporal changes in the interrelation of human beings that ecology seeks to investigate the processes and mechanisms of social and cultural change.

[9]    N. B. S. Gras, *An Introduction to Economic History* (New York, 1922).

# III. Social Process

# 7

# THE NATURAL HISTORY OF
# THE NEWSPAPER

## I. *The Struggle for Existence*

THE NEWSPAPER has a history; but it has, likewise, a natural history. The press, as it exists, is not, as our moralists sometimes seem to assume, the wilful product of any little group of living men. On the contrary, it is the outcome of an historic process in which many individuals participated without foreseeing what the ultimate product of their labors was to be.

The newspaper, like the modern city, is not wholly a rational product. No one sought to make it just what it is. In spite of all the efforts of individual men and generations of men to control it and to make it something after their own heart, it has continued to grow and change in its own incalculable ways.

The type of newspaper that exists is the type that has survived under the conditions of modern life. The men who may be said to have made the modern newspaper—James Gordon Bennett, Charles A. Dana, Joseph Pulitzer, and William Randolph Hearst —are the men who discovered the kind of paper that men and women would read and had the courage to publish it.

The natural history of the press is the history of this surviving species. It is an account of the conditions under which the existing newspaper has grown up and taken form.

A newspaper is not merely printed. It is circulated and read. Otherwise it is not a newspaper. The struggle for existence, in

Reprinted from *American Journal of Sociology*, 29 (November, 1923): 273–89.

the case of the newspaper, has been a struggle for circulation. The newspaper that is not read ceases to be an influence in the community. The power of the press may be roughly measured by the number of people who read it.

The growth of great cities has enormously increased the size of the reading public. Reading which was a luxury in the country has become a necessity in the city. In the urban environment literacy is almost as much a necessity as speech itself. That is one reason there are so many foreign-language newspapers.

Mark Villchur, editor of the Russkoye Slovo, New York City, asked his readers how many of them had read newspapers in the old country. He found that out of 312 correspondents only 16 had regularly read newspapers in Russia; 10 others from time to time read newspapers in the Volast, the village administration center, and 12 were subscribers to weekly magazines. In America all of them were subscribers or readers of Russian newspapers.

This is interesting because the immigrant has had, first and last, a profound influence on the character of our native newspapers. How to bring the immigrant and his descendants into the circle of newspaper readers has been one of the problems of modern journalism.

The immigrant, who has, perhaps, acquired the newspaper habit from reading a foreign-language newspaper is eventually attracted to the native American newspapers. They are for him a window looking out into the larger world outside the narrow circle of the immigrant community in which he has been compelled to live. The newspapers have discovered that even men who can perhaps read no more than the headlines in the daily press will buy a Sunday paper to look at the pictures.

It is said that the most successful of the Hearst papers, the *New York Evening Journal*, gains a new body of subscribers every six years. Apparently it gets its readers mainly from immigrants. They graduate into Mr. Hearst's papers from the foreign-language press, and when the sensationalism of these papers begins to pall, they acquire a taste for some of the soberer journals. At any rate, Mr. Hearst has been a great Americanizer.

In their efforts to make the newspaper readable to the last instructed reader, to find in the daily news material that would thrill the crudest intelligence, publishers have made one important discovery. They have found that the difference between the highbrow and the low-brow, which once seemed so profound, is largely a difference in vocabularies. In short, if the press can make itself intelligible to the common man, it will have even less difficulty in being understood by the intellectual. The character of present-day newspapers has been profoundly influenced by this fact.

## II. *The First Newspapers*

What is a newspaper? Many answers have been given. It is the tribune of the people; it is the fourth estate; the Palladium of our civil liberties, etc.

On the other hand this same newspaper has been characterized as the great sophist. What the popular teachers did for Athens in the period of Socrates and Plato the press has done in modern times for the common man.

The modern newspaper has been accused of being a business enterprise. "Yes," say the newspaper men "and the commodity it sells is news." It is the truth shop. (The editor is the philosopher turned merchant.) By making information about our common life accessible to every individual at less than the price of a telephone call we are to regain, it is urged—even in the complicated life of what Graham Wallas calls the "Great Society"—some sort of working democracy.

The advertising manager's notion is again something different. For him the newspaper is a medium for creating advertising values. The business of the editor is to provide the envelope which encloses the space which the advertising man sells. Eventually the newspaper may be conceived as a sort of common carrier, like the railway or the post office.

The newspaper, according to the author of the *Brass Check*, is a crime. The brass check is a symbol of prostitution. "The brass check is found in your pay envelope every week—you who write and print and distribute our newspapers and magazines. The brass check is the price of your shame—you who take the fair body of truth and sell it in the market place, who betray the virgin hopes of mankind into the loathsome brothel of big business."

This is the conception of a moralist and a socialist—Upton Sinclair.

Evidently the newspaper is an institution that is not yet fully understood. What it is, or seems to be, for anyone of us at any time is determined by our differing points of view. As a matter of fact we do not know much about the newspaper. It has never been studied.

One reason we know so little about the newspaper is that as it exists today it is a very recent manifestation. Beside, in the course of its relatively brief history, it has gone through a remarkable series of transfigurations. The press today is, however, all that it was and something more. To understand it we must see in its historic perspective.

The first newspapers were written or printed letters; newsletters they were called. In the seventeenth century English country gentlemen used to employ correspondents to write them once a week from London the gossip of the court and of the town.

The first newspaper in America, at least the first newspaper that lasted beyond its first issue, was the *Boston News–Letter*. It was published by the postmaster. The village post office has always been a public forum, where all the affairs of the nation and the community were discussed. It was to be expected that there, in close proximity to the sources of intelligence, if anywhere, a newspaper would spring up. For a long time the position of postmaster and the vocation of editor were regarded as inseparable.

The first newspapers were simply devices for organizing gossip and that, to a greater or less extent, they have remained. Horace Greeley's advice to a friend who was about to start a country paper is as good today as it was then.

Begin with a clear conception that the subject of deepest interest to an average human being is himself; next to that, he is most concerned about his neighbors. Asia and the Tongo Islands stand a long way after these in his regard. It does seem to me that most country journals are oblivious as to these vital truths. If you will, so soon as may be, secure a wideawake, judicious correspondent in each village and township of your county, some young lawyer, doctor, clerk in a store, or assistant in a post office who will promptly send you whatever of moment occurs in his vicinity, and will make up at least half your journal of local matter thus collected, nobody in the county can long do without it. Do not let a new church be organized, or new members be added to one already existing, a farm be sold, a new house be raised, a mill be set in motion, a store be opened, nor anything of interest to a dozen families occur, without having the fact duly though briefly chronicled in your columns. If a farmer cuts a big tree, or grows a mammoth beet, or harvests a bounteous yield of wheat or corn, set forth the fact as concisely and unexceptionally as possible.

What Greeley advises friend Fletcher to do with his country paper the city editor of every newspaper, as far as it humanly is possible, is still trying to do. It is not practicable, in a city of 3,000,000 and more to mention everybody's name. For that reason attention is focussed upon a few prominent figures. In a city where everything happens every day, it is not possible to record every petty incident, every variation from the routine of the city life. It is possible, however, to select certain particularly picturesque or romantic incidents and treat them symbolically, for their human interest rather than their individual and personal significance. In this way news ceases to be wholly personal and assumes the form of art. It ceases to be the record of the doings of individual men and women and becomes an impersonal account of manners and life.

The motive, conscious or unconscious, of the writers and of the press in all this is to reproduce, as far as possible, in the city the conditions of life in the village. In the village everyone knew everyone else. Everyone called everyone by his first name. The village was democratic. We are a nation of villagers. Our institutions are fundamentally village institutions. In the village, gossip and public opinion were the main sources of social control.

"I would rather live," said Thomas Jefferson, "in a country with newspapers and without a government than in a country with a government and without newspapers."

If public opinion is to continue to govern in the future as it has in the past, if we propose to maintain a democracy as Jefferson conceived it, the newspaper must continue to tell us about ourselves. We must somehow learn to know our community and its affairs in the same intimate way in which we knew them in the country villages. The newspaper must continue to be the printed diary of the home community. Marriages and divorce, crime and politics, must continue to make up the main body of our news. Local news is the very stuff that a democracy is made of.

But that, according to Walter Lippmann, is just the difficulty. "As social truth is organized today, so he says, "the press is not constituted to furnish from one edition to the next the amount of knowledge which the democratic theory of public opinion demands. . . . When we expect it to supply such a body of truth, we employ a misleading standard of judgment. We misunderstand the limited nature of news, the illimitable complexity of society; we overestimate our own endurance, public spirit, and all-round competence. We suppose an appetite for uninteresting truths which is not discovered by any honest analysis of our own tastes. . . . Unconsciously the theory sets up the single reader as theoretically incompetent, and puts upon the press the burden of accomplishing whatever representative government, industrial organization, and diplomacy have failed to accomplish. Acting upon everybody for thirty minutes in twenty-four hours, the press is asked to create a mystical force called 'public opinion' that will take up the slack in public institutions."[1]

It is evident that a newspaper cannot do for a community of 1,000,000 inhabitants what the village did spontaneously for itself through the medium of gossip and personal contact. Nevertheless the efforts of the newspaper to achieve this impossible result are an interesting chapter in the history of politics as well as of the press.

## III. *The Party Papers*

The first newspapers, the news-letters, were not party papers. Political journals began to supersede the news-letters at the beginning of the eighteenth century. The news with which the reading public was most concerned at that time was the reports of the debates in parliament.

[1]    Walter Lippmann, *Public Opinion*, pp. 361–62.

Even before the rise of the party press certain prying and curious individuals had made a business of visiting the Strangers' Gallery, during the sessions of the House of Commons in order to write up from memory, or from notes taken down surreptitiously, accounts of the speeches and discussions during an important debate. At this time all the deliberations of parliament were secret, and it was not until 100 years later that the right of reporters to attend the sessions of the House of Commons and record its proceedings was officially recognized. In the meantime reporters were compelled to resort to all sorts of subterfuges and indirect methods in order to get information. It is upon this information, gathered in this way that much of our present history of English politics is based.

One of the most distinguished of these parliamentary reporters was Samuel Johnson. One evening in 1770, it is reported, Johnson with a number of other celebrities was taking dinner in London. Conversation turned upon parliamentary oratory. Someone spoke of a famous speech delivered in the House of Commons by the elder Pitt in 1741. Someone else, amid the applause of the company, quoted a passage from this speech as an illustration of an orator who had surpassed in feeling and beauty of language the finest efforts of the orators of antiquity. Then Johnson, who up to that point had taken no part in the discussion, spoke up. "I wrote that speech," he said, "in a garret in Exeter Street."

The guests were struck with amazement. He was asked, "How could it have been written by you, sir?"

"Sir," said Johnson, "I wrote it in Exeter Street. I never was in the gallery of the House of Commons but once. Cave had interest with the doorkeepers; he and the persons employed under him got admittance; they brought away the subjects of discussion, the names of the speakers, the side they took, and the order in which they rose, together with notes of the various arguments adduced in the course of the debate. The whole was afterward communicated to me, and I composed the speeches in the form they now have in the Parliamentary Debates, for the speeches of that period are all printed from Cave's magazine."[2]

---

[2]   Michael MacDonagh, *The Reporters' Gallery*, pp. 139–40.

Someone undertook to praise Johnson's impartiality, saying that in his reports he seems to have dealt out reason and eloquence with an equal hand to both political parties. "That is not quite true," was Johnson's reply. "I saved appearances tolerably well; but I took care that the Whig dogs should not have the best of it."

This speech of William Pitt, composed by Johnson in Exeter Street, has long held a place in school books and collections of oratory. It is the famous speech in which Pitt answered the accusation of the "atrocious crime of being a young man."

Perhaps Pitt thought he delivered that speech. At any rate there is no evidence that he repudiated it. I might add that Pitt, if he was the first, was not the last statesman who is indebted to the reporters for his reputation as an orator.

The significant thing about this incident is that it illustrates the manner in which, under the influence of the parliamentary reporters, something like a constitutional change was effected in the character of parliamentary government. As soon as the parliamentary orators discovered that they were addressing not only their fellow-members but, indirectly, through the medium of the press, the people of England, the whole character of parliamentary proceedings changed. Through the newspapers the whole country was enabled to participate in the discussions by which issues were framed and legislation was enacted.

Meanwhile, the newspapers themselves, under the influence of the very discussions which they themselves instigated, had become party organs. Whereupon the party press ceased to be a mere chronicle of small gossip and came to be what we know as a "journal of opinion." The editor, meanwhile, no longer a mere newsmonger and humble recorder of events, found himself the mouthpiece of a political party, playing a role in politics.

During the long struggle for freedom of thought and speech in the seventeenth century, popular discontent had found literary expression in the pamphlet and broadside. The most notable of these pamphleteers was John Milton, and the most famous of these pamphlets was Milton's *Areopagitica: A Defence of the Liberty of Unlicensed Printing*, published in 1646; "the noblest piece of English prose" it has been called by Henry Morley.

When the newspaper became, in the early part of the eighteenth century, a journal of opinion, it took over the function of the political pamphlet. The opinion that had formerly found expression in a broadside was now expressed in the form of editorial leading articles. The editorial writer, who had inherited the mantle of the pamphleteer, now assumed the role of a tribune of the people.

It was in this role, as the protagonist of the popular cause, that the newspaper captured the imagination of our intelligentsia.

When we read in the political literature of a generation ago references to "the power of the press" it is the editor and the editorial rather than the reporter and the news of which these writers are thinking. Even now, when we speak of the liberty of the press, it is the liberty to express an opinion, rather than the liberty to investigate and publish the facts, which is meant. The activities of the reporter, upon which any opinion that is relevant to existing conditions is likely to be based, are more often regarded as an infringement of our personal rights than an exercise of our political liberties.

The liberty of the press for which Milton wrote the *Areopagitica* was the liberty to express an opinion. "Give me the liberty," he said, "to know, to alter, and to argue freely according to conscience, above all liberties."

Carlyle was thinking of the editorial writer and not of the reporter when he wrote: "Great is journalism! Is not every able editor a ruler of the world, being a persuader of it?"

The United States inherited its parliamentary government, its party system, and its newspapers from England. The role which the political journals played in English politics was re-enacted in America. The American newspapers were a power with which the British government had to reckon in the struggle of the colonies for independence. After the British took possession of New York City, Ambrose Serle, who had undertaken to publish the *New York Gazette* in the interest of the invaders, wrote as follows to Lord Dartmouth in regard to the patriot-party press.

Among other engines which have raised the present commotion, next to the indecent harangues of the preachers, none has had a more extensive or stronger influence than the newspapers of the respective colonies. One is astonished to see with what avidity they are sought after, and how implicitly they are believed by the great bulk of the people.[3]

It was nearly a century later in the person of Horace Greeley, editor of the *New York Tribune* during the anti-slavery struggle, that the journal of opinion reached its highest expression in America. America has had better newspaper men than Horace Greeley, although none, perhaps, whose opinions exercised so wide an influence. "The *New York Tribune*," says Charles Francis Adams, "during those years was the greatest educational factor, economically and morally, this country has ever known."

## IV. *The Independent Press*

The power of the press, as represented by the older type of newspaper, rested in the final analysis upon the ability of its editors to create a party and lead it. The journal of opinion is, by its very nature, predestined to become the organ of a party, or at any rate the mouthpiece of a school.

So long as political activities were organized on the basis of village life, the party system worked. In the village community, where life was and still is relatively fixed and settled, custom and tradition provided for most of the exigencies of daily life. In such a community, where every deviation from the ordinary routine of life was a matter of observation and comment and all the facts were known, the political process was, at any rate, a comparatively simple matter. Under these circumstances the work of the newspaper, as a gatherer and interpreter of the news, was but an extension of the function which was otherwise performed spontaneously by the community itself through the medium of personal contact and gossip.

But as our cities expanded and life grew more complicated, it turned out that political parties, in order to survive, must have

---

[3]   George Henry Payne, *History of Journalism in the United States*, p. 120.

a permanent organization. Eventually party morale became a greater value than the issues for the determination of which the parties are supposed to exist. The effect upon the party press was to reduce it to the position of a sort of house organ of the party organization. It no longer knew from day to day just what its opinions were. The editor was no longer a free agent. It was of this subjugated *Tribune* that Walt Whitman was thinking when he coined the phrase, "the kept editor."

When, finally, the exigencies of party politics, under conditions of life in great cities, developed the political machine, some of the more independent newspapers revolted. This was the origin of the independent press. It was one of the independent papers, the *New York Times* of that day, that first assailed and eventually overthrew, with the aid of a cartoonist, Thomas Nast, the Tweed Ring, the first and most outrageous of the political machines that party politics in this country has so far produced. Presently there was a general breaking away, particularly by the metropolitan as distinguished from the country papers, from the domination of the parties. Party loyalty ceased to be a virtue.

Meanwhile a new political power had arisen and found expression in the press. This power was embodied, not in the editorial and the editorial writer, however, but in the news and the reporter. In spite of the fact that the prestige of the press, up to this time, had rested on its role of champion of popular causes, the older newspapers were not read by the masses of the people.

The ordinary man is more interested in news than he is in political doctrines or abstract ideas. H. L. Mencken has called attention to the fact that the average man does not understand more than two-thirds of what "comes from the lips of the average political orator or clergyman."

The ordinary man, as the *Saturday Evening Post* has discovered, thinks in concrete images, anecdotes, pictures, and parables. He finds it difficult and tiresome to read a long article unless it is dramatized and takes the form of what newspapers call a "story." "News story" and "fiction story" are two forms of modern literature that are now so like one another that it is sometimes difficult to distinguish them.

The *Saturday Evening Post*, for example, writes the news in the form of fiction, while the daily press frequently writes fiction in the form of news. When it is not possible to present ideas in the concrete, dramatic form of a story, the ordinary reader likes them stated in a short paragraph.

It is said that James E. Scripps, of the Scripps, McRae League, which specializes in afternoon papers in secondary cities, built up his whole string of papers upon the basis of the very simple psychological principle that the ordinary man will read newspaper items in the inverse ratio to their length. His method of measuring the efficiency of his newspapers, therefore, was to count the number of items they contained. The paper that had the largest number of items was the best paper. This is just the reverse of Mr. Hearst's methods; his papers have fewer items than other papers.

The old-time journalist was inclined to have a contempt for news. News was for him simply material upon which to base an editorial. If God let things happen that were not in accordance with his conception of the fitness of things, he simply suppressed them. He refused to take the responsibility of letting his readers learn about things that he knew ought not to have happened.

Manton Marble, who was editor of the *New York World* before Joseph Pulitzer took it and made it yellow, used to say there were not 18,000 people in New York City to whom a well-conducted newspaper could offer to address itself. If the circulation of the paper went above that figure he thought there must be something wrong with the paper. Before Mr. Pulitzer took it over the circulation had actually sunk to 10,000. The old *New York World* preserved the type of the old conservative high-brow paper down to the eighties. By that time in the larger cities the political independent newspapers had become the accepted type of journal.

Long before the rise of what was later to be called the independent press, there had appeared in New York two journals that were the forerunners of the present-day newspapers. In 1883 Benjamin Day, with a few associates, started a paper for "mechanics and the masses generally." The price of this paper was 1 cent but the publishers expected to make up by larger circulation and by advertising the loss sustained by the lower price. At that time most of the other New York papers were selling for 6 cents.

It was, however, the enterprise of James Gordon Bennett, the founder of the *New York Herald*, who set the pace in the new form of journalism. In fact, as Will Irwin says in the only adequate account that has ever been written of the American newspaper, "James Gordon Bennett invented news as we know it." Bennett, like some others who have contributed most to modern journalism, was a disillusioned man, and for that very reason, perhaps, a ruthless and cynical one. "I renounce all so-called principles," he said in his announcement of the new enterprise. By principles he meant, perhaps, editorial policies. His salutatory was at the same time a valedictory. In announcing the purposes of the new journalism he bade adieu to the aims and aspirations of the old. Henceforth the editors were to be news gatherers and the newspaper staked its future on its ability to gather, print, and circulate news.

What is news? There have been many answers. I think it was Charles A. Dana, who said, "News is anything that will make people talk." This definition suggests at any rate the aims of the new journalism. Its purpose was to print anything that would make people talk and think, for most people do not think until they begin to talk. Thought is after all a sort of internal conversation.

A later version of the same definition is this: "News is anything that makes the reader say, 'Gee Whiz!' " This is the definition of Arthur McEwen, one of the men who helped make the Hearst papers. It is at the same time the definition of the latest and most successful type of journal, the yellow press. Not all successful journals are, to be sure, yellow. The *New York Times*, for example, is not. But the *New York Times* is not yet a type.

## V. *The Yellow Press*

There seem to be, as Walter Lippmann has observed, two types of newspaper readers. "Those who find their own lives interesting" and "those who find their own lives dull, and wish to live a more thrilling existence." There are, correspondingly, two types of newspapers: papers edited on the principle that readers are mainly interested in reading about themselves, and papers edited upon the principle that their readers, seeking some escape from the dull routine of their own lives, are interested in anything which offers them, what the psychoanalyists call "a flight from reality."

The provincial newspaper with its record of weddings, funerals, lodge meetings, oyster suppers, and all the small patter of the small town represents the first type. The metropolitan press, with its persistent search in the drab episodes of city life for the romantic and the picturesque, its dramatic accounts of vice and crime, and its unflagging interest in the movements of personages of a more or less mythical high society, represents the latter type.

Up to the last quarter of the nineteenth century, that is to say, up to about 1880, most newspapers, even in our large cities, were conducted on the theory that the best news a paper can print is a death notice or marriage announcement.

Up to that time the newspapers had not yet begun to break into the tenements, and most people who supported a newspaper lived in homes rather than in apartments. The telephone had not yet come into popular use; the automobile was unheard of; the city was still a mosaic of little neighborhoods, like our foreign-language communities of the present day, in which the city dweller still maintained something of the provincialism of the small town.

Great changes, however, were impending. The independent press was already driving some of the old-time newspapers to the wall. There were more newspapers than either the public or the advertisers were willing to support. It was at this time and under these circumstances that newspaper men discovered that circulation could be greatly increased by making literature out of the news. Charles A. Dana had already done this in the *Sun*, but there still was a large section of the population for whom the clever writing of Mr. Dana's young men was caviar.

The yellow press grew up in an attempt to capture for the newspaper a public whose only literature was the family story paper or the cheap novel. The problem was to write the news in such a way that it would appeal to the fundamental passions. The formula was: love and romance for the women; sport and politics for the men.

The effect of the application of this formula was to enormously increase the circulation of the newspapers, not only in the great cities, but all over the country. These changes were brought about mainly under the leadership of two men, Joseph Pulitzer and William Randolph Hearst.

Pulitzer had discovered while he was editor of the *St. Louis Post Dispatch* that the way to fight popular causes was not to advocate them on the editorial page but to advertise them—write them up—in the news columns. It was Pulitzer who invented muck-raking. It was this kind of journalism which enabled Pulitzer, within a period of six years, to convert the old *New York World*, which was dying of inanition when he took it, into the most talked about if not the most widely circulated, paper in New York City.

Meanwhile, out in San Francisco Mr. Hearst had succeeded in galvanizing the old moribund *Examiner* into new life, making it the most widely read newspaper on the Pacific Coast.

It was under Mr. Hearst that the "sob sister" came into vogue. This is her story, as Will Irwin told it in *Collier's*, February 18, 1911:

Chamberlain (managing editor of the *Examiner*) conceived the idea that the city hospital was badly managed. He picked a little slip of a girl from among his cub reporters and assigned her to the investigation. She invented her own method; she "fainted" on the street, and was carried to the hospital for treatment. She turned out a story "with a sob for the unfortunate in every line." That was the professional beginning of "Annie Laurie" or Winifred Black, and of a departure in newspaper writing. For she came to have many imitators, but none other could ever so well stir up the primitive emotions of sympathy and pity; she was a "sob squad" all by herself. Indeed, in the discovery of this sympathetic "woman writing," Hearst broke through the crust into the thing he was after.

With the experience that he had gained on the *Examiner* in San Francisco and with a large fortune that he had inherited from his father, Hearst invaded New York in 1896. It was not until he reached New York and started out to make the *New York Journal* the most widely read paper in the United States that yellow journalism reached the limit.

Pulitzer's principal contribution to yellow journalism was muck-raking, Hearst's was mainly "Jazz." The newspaper had been conducted up to this time upon the theory that its business was to instruct. Hearst rejected that conception. His appeal was frankly not to the intellect but to the heart. The newspaper was for him first and last a form of entertainment.

It was about the time the yellow press was engaged in extending the newspaper habit to the masses of people, including women and immigrants—who up to this time did not read newspapers—that the department store was beginning to attract attention.

The department store is, in a sense, a creation of the Sunday newspaper. At any rate, without the advertising that the Sunday newspaper was able to give it, the department store would hardly have gained the vogue it has today. It is important in this connection that women read the Sunday paper before they did the dailies. The women are buyers.

It was in the Sunday newspaper that the methods of yellow journalism were first completely worked out. The men who are chiefly responsible for them are Morrill Goddard and Arthur Brisbane. It was Goddard's ambition to make a paper that a man would buy even if he could not read it. He went in for pictures, first in black and white and then in colors. It was in the *Sunday World* that the first seven-column cut was printed. Then followed the comic section and all the other devices with which we are familiar for compelling a dull-minded and reluctant public to read.

After these methods had been worked out in the Sunday paper, they were introduced into the daily. The final triumph of the yellow journal was Brisbane's "Heart-to-heart editorials"—a column of predigested platitudes and moralizing, with half-page diagrams and illustrations to re-enforce the text. Nowhere has Herbert Spencer's maxim that the art of writing is economy of attention been so completely realized.

Walter Lippmann, in his recent study of public opinion, calls attention to the fact that no sociologist has ever written a book on news gathering. It strikes him as very strange that an institution like the press, from which we expect so much and get so little of what we expect, should not have been the subject of a more disinterested study.

It is true that we have not studied the newspaper as the biologists have studied, for example, the potato bug. But the same may be said of every political institution, and the newspaper is a political institution quite as much as Tammany Hall or the board of aldermen are political institutions. We have grumbled about our political *institutions*, sometimes we have sought by certain magical legislative devices to exercise and expel the evil spirits that possessed them. On the whole we have been inclined to regard them as sacred and to treat any fundamental criticism of them as a sort of blasphemy. If things went wrong, it was not the institutions but the persons we elected to conduct them, and an incorrigible human nature, who were at fault.

What then is the remedy for the existing condition of the newspapers? There is no remedy. Humanly speaking, the present newspapers are about as good as they can be. If the newspapers are to be improved, it will come through the education of the people and the organization of political information and intelligence. As Mr. Lippmann well says, "the number of social phenomena which are now recorded is small, the instruments of analysis are very crude, and the concepts often vague and uncriticized." We must improve our records and that is a serious task. But first of all we must learn to look at political and social life objectively and cease to think of it wholly in moral terms! In that case we shall have less news, but better newspapers.

The real reason that the ordinary newspaper accounts of the incidents of ordinary life are so sensational is because we know so little of human life that we are not able to interpret the events of life when we read them. It is safe to say that when anything shocks us, we do not understand it.

# 8

# RACIAL ASSIMILATION IN
# SECONDARY GROUPS

## I

THE RACE PROBLEM has sometimes been described as a problem in assimilation. It is not always clear, however, what assimilation means. Historically the word has had two distinct significations. According to earlier usage it meant "to compare" or "to make like." According to later usage it signifies "to take up and incorporate."

There is a process that goes on in society by which individuals spontaneously acquire one another's language, characteristic attitudes, habits, and modes of behavior. There is also a process by which individuals and groups of individuals are taken over and incorporated into larger groups. Both processes have been concerned in the formation of modern nationalities. The modern Italian, Frenchman, and German is a composite of the broken fragments of several different racial groups. Interbreeding has broken up the ancient stocks, and interaction and imitation have created new national types which exhibit definite uniformities in language, manners, and formal behavior.

It has sometimes been assumed that the creation of a national type is the specific function of assimilation and that national solidarity is based upon national homogeneity and "like-mindedness." The extent and importance of the kind of homogeneity that individuals of the same nationality exhibit have been greatly

Reprinted from *American Journal of Sociology*, 19 (March, 1914) : 606–23. There the article is subtitled "With Particular Reference to the Negro."

exaggerated. Neither interbreeding nor interaction has created, in what the French term "nationals," a more than superficial likeness or like-mindedness. Racial differences have, to be sure, disappeared or been obscured, but individual differences remain. Individual differences, again, have been intensified by education, personal competition, and the division of labor, until individual members of cosmopolitan groups probably represent greater variations in disposition, temperament, and mental capacity than those which distinguished the more homogeneous races and peoples of an earlier civilization.[1]

What then, precisely, is the nature of the homogeneity which characterizes cosmopolitan groups?

The growth of modern states exhibits the progressive merging of smaller, mutually exclusive, into larger and more inclusive social groups. This result has been achieved in various ways, but it has usually been followed, or accompanied, by a more or less complete adoption, by the members of the smaller groups, of the language, technique, and mores of the larger and more inclusive ones. The immigrant readily takes over the language, manners, the social ritual, and outward forms of his adopted country. In America it has become proverbial that a Pole, Lithuanian, or Norwegian cannot be distinguished, in the second generation, from an American born of native parents.

There is no reason to assume that this assimilation of alien groups to native standards has modified to any great extent fundamental racial characteristics. It has, however, erased the external signs which formerly distinguished the members of one race from those of another.

On the other hand, the breaking-up of the isolation of smaller groups has had the effect of emancipating the individual man, giving him room and freedom for the expansion and development of his individual aptitudes.

What one actually finds in cosmopolitan groups, then, is a superficial uniformity, a homogeneity in manners and fashion, associated with relatively profound differences in individual opin-

[1]    F. Boas, *Journal of American Folk-Lore*, quoted by W. I. Thomas, in *Source Book for Social Origins*, p. 155.

ions, sentiments, and beliefs. This is just the reverse of what one meets among primitive peoples, where diversity in external forms, as between different groups, is accompanied with a monotonous sameness in the mental attitudes of individuals. There is a striking similarity in the sentiments and mental attitudes of peasant peoples in all parts of the world, although the external differences are often great. In the Black Forest, in Baden, Germany, almost every valley shows a different style of costume, a different type of architecture, although in each separate valley every house is like every other and the costume, as well as the religion, is for every member of each separate community absolutely after the same pattern. On the other hand, a German, Russian, or Negro peasant of the southern states, different as each is in some respects, are all very much alike in certain habitual attitudes and sentiments.

What, then, is the role of homogeneity and like-mindedness, such as we find them to be, in cosmopolitan states?

So far as it makes each individual look like every other—no matter how different under the skin—homogeneity mobilizes the individual man. It removes the social taboo, permits the individual to move into strange groups, and thus facilitates new and adventurous contacts. In obliterating the external signs, which in secondary groups seem to be the sole basis of caste and class distinctions, it realizes, for the individual, the principle of *laissez-faire, laissez-aller*. Its ultimate economic effect is to substitute personal for racial competition, and to give free play to forces that tend to relegate every individual, irrespective of race or status, to the position he or she is best fitted to fill.

As a matter of fact, the ease and rapidity with which aliens, under existing conditions in the United States, have been able to assimilate themselves to the customs and manners of American life have enabled this country to swallow and digest every sort of normal human difference, except the purely external ones, like the color of the skin.

It is probably true, also, that like-mindedness of the kind that expresses itself in national types, contributes, indirectly, by facilitating the intermingling of the different elements of the population, to the national solidarity. This is due to the fact that the solidarity of modern states depends less on the homogeneity of population than, as James Bryce has suggested, upon the thorough-going mixture of heterogeneous elements.[2] Like-mindedness, so far as that term signifies a standard grade of intelligence, contributes little or nothing to national solidarity. Likeness is, after all, a purely formal concept which of itself cannot hold anything together.

In the last analysis social solidarity is based on sentiment and habit. It is the sentiment of loyalty and the habit of what Sumner calls "concurrent action," that gives substance and insures unity to the state, as to every other type of social group. This sentiment of loyalty has its basis in a *modus vivendi*, a working relation and mutual understanding, of the members of the group. Social institutions are not founded in similarities any more than they are founded in differences, but in relations, and in the mutual inter-dependence of parts. When these relations have the sanction of custom and are fixed in individual habit, so that the activities of the group are running smoothly, personal attitudes and senti-ments, which are the only forms in which individual minds collide and clash with one another, easily accommodate themselves to the existing situation.

It may, perhaps, be said that loyalty itself is a form of like-mindedness, or that it is dependent in some way upon the like-mindedness of the individuals whom it binds together. This, however, cannot be true, for there is no greater loyalty than that which binds the dog to his master, and this is a sentiment which that faithful animal usually extends to other members of the house-

[2]    "Racial differences and animosities, which have played a large part in threatening the unity of States, are usually dangerous when un-friendly races occupy different parts of the country. If they live intermixed, in tolerably equal numbers, and if in addition they are not of different religions, and speak the same tongue, the antagonism will disappear in a generation or two and especially by intermarriage. . . . But in one set of cases no fusion is possible; and this set of cases forms the despair of statesmen. It presents a problem which no constitution can solve. It is the juxtaposition on the same soil of races of different colors" (James Bryce, *Studies in History and Jurisprudence*, pp. 245–46).

hold to which he belongs. A dog without a master is a dangerous animal, but the dog that has been domesticated is a member of society. He is not, of course, a citizen, although he is not entirely without rights. But he has got into some sort of practical working relations with the group to which he belongs.

It is this practical working arrangement, into which individuals with widely different mental capacities enter as co-ordinate parts, that gives the corporate character to social groups and insures their solidarity.

It is the process of assimilation by which groups of individuals, originally indifferent or perhaps hostile, achieve this corporate character, rather than the process by which they acquire a formal like-mindedness, with which this paper is mainly concerned.

The difficulty with the conception of assimilation which one ordinarily meets in discussions of the race problem, is that it is based on observations confined to individualistic groups where the characteristic relations are indirect and secondary. It takes no account of the kind of assimilation that takes place in primary groups where relations are direct and personal—in the tribe, for example, and in the family.

Thus Charles Francis Adams, referring to the race problem in an address at Richmond, Va., in November, 1908, said:

The American system, as we know, was founded on the assumed basis of a common humanity, that is, absence of absolutely fundamental racial characteristics was accepted as an established truth. Those of all races were welcomed to our shores. They came, aliens; they and their descendants would become citizens first, natives afterward. It was a process first of assimilation and then of absorption. On this all depended. There could be no permanent divisional lines. That theory is now plainly broken down. We are confronted by the obvious fact, as undeniable as it is hard, that the African will only partially assimilate and that he cannot be absorbed. He remains an alien element in the body politic. A foreign substance, he can neither be assimilated nor thrown out.

More recently an editorial in the *Outlook*, discussing the Japanese situation in California, made this statement:

The hundred millions of people now inhabiting the United States must be a united people, not merely a collection of groups of different peoples, different in racial cultures and ideals, agreeing to live together in peace and amity. These hundred millions must have common ideals, common aims, a common custom, a common culture, a common language, and common characteristics if the nation is to endure.[3]

All this is quite true and interesting, but it does not clearly recognize the fact that the chief obstacle to the assimilation of the Negro and the Oriental are not mental but physical traits. It is not because the Negro and the Japanese are so differently constituted that they do not assimilate. If they were given an opportunity the Japanese are quite as capable as the Italians, the Armenians, or the Slavs of acquiring our culture, and sharing our national ideals. The trouble is not with the Japanese mind but with the Japanese skin. The Jap is not the right color.

The fact that the Japanese bears in his features a distinctive racial hallmark, that he wears, so to speak, a racial uniform, classifies him. He cannot become a mere individual, indistinguishable in the cosmopolitan mass of the population, as is true, for example, of the Irish and, to a lesser extent, of some of the other immigrant races. The Japanese, like the Negro, is condemned to remain among us an abstraction, a symbol, and a symbol not merely of his own race, but of the Orient and of that vague, ill-defined menace we sometimes refer to as the "yellow peril." This not only determines, to a very large extent, the attitude of the white world toward the yellow man, but it determines the attitude of the yellow man to the white. It puts between the races the invisible but very real gulf of self-consciousness.

There is another consideration. Peoples we know intimately we respect and esteem. In our casual contact with aliens, however, it is the offensive rather than the pleasing traits that impress us. These impressions accumulate and reinforce natural prejudices. Where races are distinguished by certain external marks these furnish a permanent physical substratum upon which and around

[3]    *Outlook*, August 2, 1913.

which the irritations and animosities, incidental to all human intercourse, tend to accumulate and so gain strength and volume.

## II

Assimilation, as the word is here used, brings with it a certain borrowed significance which it carried over from physiology where it is employed to describe the process of nutrition. By a process of nutrition, somewhat similar to the physiological one, we may conceive alien peoples to be incorporated with, and made part of, the community or state. Ordinarily assimilation goes on silently and unconsciously, and only forces itself into popular conscience when there is some interruption or disturbance of the process.

At the outset it may be said, then, that assimilation rarely becomes a problem except in secondary groups. Admission to the primary group, that is to say, the group in which relationships are direct and personal, as, for example, in the family and in the tribe, makes assimilation comparatively easy, and almost inevitable.

The most striking illustration of this is the fact of domestic slavery. Slavery has been, historically, the usual method by which peoples have been incorporated into alien groups. When a member of an alien race is adopted into the family as a servant, or as a slave, and particularly when that status is made hereditary, as it was in the case of the Negro after his importation to America, assimilation followed rapidly and as a matter of course.

It is difficult to conceive two races farther removed from each other in temperament and tradition than the Anglo-Saxon and the Negro, and yet the Negro in the southern states, particularly where he was adopted into the household as a family servant, learned in a comparatively short time the manners and customs of his master's family. He very soon possessed himself of so much of the language, religion, and the technique of the civilization of his master as, in his station, he was fitted or permitted to acquire. Eventually, also, Negro slaves transferred their allegiance to the state, of which they were only indirectly members, or at least to their masters' families, with whom they felt themselves in most things one in sentiment and interest.

The assimilation of the Negro field hand, where the contact of the slave with his master and his master's family was less intimate, was naturally less complete. On the large plantations, where an overseer stood between the master and the majority of his slaves, and especially on the Sea Island plantations off the coast of South Carolina, where the master and his family were likely to be merely winter visitors, this distance between master and slave was greatly increased. The consequence is that the Negroes in these regions are less touched today by the white man's influence and civilization than elsewhere in the southern states. The size of the plantation, the density of the slave population, and the extent and character of the isolation in which the master and his slave lived are factors to be reckoned with in estimating the influence which the plantation exerted on the Negro. In Virginia the average slave population on the plantation has been estimated at about ten. On the Sea Islands and farther south it was thirty; and in Jamaica it was two hundred.[4]

As might be expected there were class distinctions among the slaves as among the whites, and these class distinctions were more rigidly enforced on the large plantations than on the smaller ones. In Jamaica, for example, it was customary to employ the mulattoes in the lighter and the more desirable occupations about the master's house. The mulattoes in that part of the country, more definitely than was true in the United States, constituted a separate caste midway between the white man and black. Under these conditions the assimilation of the masses of the Negro people took place more slowly and less completely in Jamaica than in the United States.

In Virginia and the border states, and in what was known as the Back Country, where the plantations were smaller and the relation of the races more intimate, slaves gained relatively more of the white man's civilization. The kindly relations of master and slave in Virginia are indicated by the number of free Negroes in that state. In 1860 one Negro in every eight was free and in one county in the Tidewater Region, the county of Nansemond, there

4    *Documentary History of American and Industrial Society*, Vol. I, "Plantation and Frontier": Introduction, pp. 80–81.

were 2,473 Negroes and only 581 slaves. The differences in the Negro population which existed before the Civil War are still clearly marked today. They are so clearly marked, in fact, that an outline of the areas in which the different types of plantation existed before the War would furnish the basis for a map showing distinct cultural levels in the Negro population in the South today.

The first Negroes were imported into the United States in 1619. At the beginning of the nineteenth century there were 900,000 slaves in the United States. By 1860 that number had increased to nearly 4,000,000. At that time, it is safe to say, the great mass of the Negroes were no longer, in any true sense, an alien people. They were, of course, not citizens. They lived in the smaller world of the particular plantation to which they belonged. It might, perhaps, be more correct to say that they were less assimilated than domesticated.

In this respect, however, the situation of the Negro was not different from that of the Russian peasant, at least as late as 1860. The Russian noble and the Russian peasant were likely to be of the same ethnic stock, but mentally they were probably not much more alike than the Negro slave and his master. The noble and the peasant did not intermarry. The peasant lived in the little world of the *mir* or commune. He had his own customs and traditions. His life and thought moved in a smaller orbit and he knew nothing about the larger world which belonged exclusively to the noble. The relations between the serf and the proprietor of the estate to which he was attached were, perhaps, less familiar and less frank than those which existed between the Negro slave and his master. The attitude of the serf in the presence of the noble was more abject. Still, one could hardly say that the Russian peasant had not been assimilated, at least in the sense in which it has been decided to use that term in this paper.

A right understanding of conditions in the South before the War will make clear that the southern plantation was founded in the different temperaments, habits, and sentiments of the white man and the black. The discipline of the plantation put its own impress upon, and largely formed the character of, both races. In the life of the plantation white and black were different but complementary, the one bred to the role of a slave and the other to that of master. This, of course, takes no account of the poor white man who was also formed by slavery, but rather as a by-product.

Where the conditions of slavery brought the two races, as it frequently did, into close and intimate contact, there grew up a mutual sympathy and understanding which frequently withstood not only the shock of the Civil War, but the political agitation and chicane which followed it in the southern states.

Speaking of the difference between the North and the South in its attitude toward the Negro, Booker T. Washington says: "It is the individual touch which holds the races together in the South, and it is this individual touch which is lacking to a large degree in the North."

No doubt kindly relations between individual members of the two races do exist in the South to an extent not known in the North. As a rule, it will be found that these kindly relations had their origin in slavery. The men who have given the tone to political discussion in southern states in recent years are men who did not own slaves. The men from the mountain districts of the South, whose sentiments found expression in a great antislavery document, like Hinton Helper's *Impending Crisis*, hated slavery with an intensity that was only equaled by their hatred for the Negro. It is the raucous note of the Hill Billy and the Red Neck that one hears in the public utterances of men like Senator Vardaman, of Mississippi, and Governor Blease, of South Carolina.

## III

The Civil War weakened but did not fully destroy the *modus vivendi* which slavery had established between the slave and his master. With emancipation the authority which had formerly been exercised by the master was transferred to the state, and Washington, D.C., began to assume in the mind of the freedman the position that formerly had been occupied by the "big house" on the plantation. The masses of the Negro people still maintained their habit of dependence, however, and after the first confusion of the change had passed, life went on, for most of them, much as it had before the War. As one old farmer explained, the only difference he could see was that in slavery he "was working for old Marster and now he was working for himself."

There was one difference between slavery and freedom, nevertheless, which was very real to the freedman. And this was the liberty to move. To move from one plantation to another in case he was discontented was one of the ways in which a freedman was able to realize his freedom and to make sure that he possessed it. This liberty to move meant a good deal more to the plantation Negro than one not acquainted with the situation in the South is likely to understand.

If there had been an abundance of labor in the South; if the situation had been such that the Negro laborer was seeking the opportunity to work, or such that the Negro tenant farmers were competing for the opportunity to get a place on the land, as is so frequently the case in Europe, the situation would have been fundamentally different from what it actually was. But the South was, and is today, what Nieboer called a country of "open," in contradistinction to a country of "closed" resources. In other words there is more land in the South than there is labor to till it. Land owners are driven to competing for laborers and tenants to work their plantations.

Owing to his ignorance of business matters and to a long-established habit of submission the Negro after emancipation was placed at a great disadvantage in his dealings with the white man. His right to move from one plantation to another became, therefore, the Negro tenant's method of enforcing consideration from the planter. He might not dispute the planter's accounts, because he was not capable of doing so, and it was unprofitable to attempt it, but if he felt aggrieved he could move.

This was the significance of the exodus in some of the southern states which took place about 1879, when 40,000 people left the plantations in the Black Belts of Louisiana and Mississippi and went to Kansas. The masses of the colored people were dissatisfied with the treatment they were receiving from the planters and made up their minds to move to "a free country," as they described it. At the same time it was the attempt of the planter to bind the

Negro tenant who was in debt to him, to his place on the plantation, that gave rise to the system of peonage that still exists in a
mitigated form in the South today.

When the Negro moved off the plantation upon which he was
reared he severed the personal relations which bound him to his
master's people. It was just at this point that the two races began
to lose touch with each other. From this time on the relations of
the black man and white, which in slavery had been direct and
personal, became every year, as the old associations were broken,
more and more indirect and secondary. There lingers still the disposition on the part of the white man to treat every Negro famil-
iarly, and the disposition on the part of every Negro to treat every
white man respectfully. But these are habits which are gradually
disappearing. The breaking-down of the instincts and habits of
servitude, and the acquistion, by the masses of the Negro people,
of the instincts and habits of freedom have proceeded slowly but
steadily. The reason the change seems to have gone on more
rapidly in some cases than others is explained by the fact that at
the time of emancipation 10 per cent of the Negroes in the United
States were already free, and others, those who had worked in
trades, many of whom had hired their own time from their masters,
had become more or less adapted to the competitive conditions of
free society.

One of the effects of the mobilization of the Negro has been
to bring him into closer and more intimate contact with his own
people. Common interests have drawn the blacks together, and
caste sentiment has kept the black and white apart. The segregation of the races, which began as a spontaneous movement on the
part of both, has been fostered by the policy of the dominant race.
The agitation of the Reconstruction Period made the division between the races in politics absolute. Segregation and separation in
other matters have gone on steadily ever since. The Negro at the
present time has separate churches, schools, libraries, hospitals,
Y.M.C.A. associations, and even separate towns. There are, perhaps, a half-dozen communities in the United States, every in-
habitant of which is a Negro. Most of these so-called Negro towns
are suburban villages; two of them, at any rate, are the centers of

a considerable Negro farming population. In general it may be said that where the Negro schools, churches, and Y.M.C.A. associations are not separate they do not exist.

It is hard to estimate the ultimate effect of this isolation of the black man. One of the most important effects has been to establish a common interest among all the different colors and classes of the race. This sense of solidarity has grown up gradually with the organization of the Negro people. It is stronger in the South, where segregation is more complete, than it is in the North where, twenty years ago, it would have been safe to say it did not exist. Gradually, imperceptibly, within the larger world of the white man, a smaller world, the world of the black man, is silently taking form and shape.

Every advance in education and intelligence puts the Negro in possession of the technique of communication and organization of the white man, and so contributes to the extension and consolidation of the Negro world within the white.

The motive for this increasing solidarity is furnished by the increasing pressure, or perhaps I should say, by the increasing sensibility of Negroes to the pressure and the prejudice without. The sentiment of racial loyalty, which is a comparatively recent manifestation of the growing self-consciousness of the race, must be regarded as a response and "accommodation" to changing internal and external relations of the race. The sentiment which Negroes are beginning to call "race pride" does not exist to the same extent in the North as in the South, but an increasing disposition to enforce racial distinctions in the North, as in the South, is bringing it into existence.

One or two incidents in this connection are significant. A few years ago a man who is the head of the largest Negro publishing business in this country sent to Germany and had a number of Negro dolls manufactured according to specifications of his own. At the time this company was started Negro children were in the habit of playing with white dolls. There were already Negro dolls on the market, but they were for white children and represented the white man's conception of the Negro and not the Negro's ideal of himself. The new Negro doll was a mulatto with regular features slightly modified in favor of the conventional Negro type. It was a neat, prim, well-dressed, well-behaved, self-respecting doll. Later on, as I understand, there were other dolls, equally tidy and respectable in appearance, but in darker shades with Negro features a little more pronounced. The man who designed these dolls was perfectly·clear in regard to the significance of the substitution that he was making. He said that he thought it was a good thing to let Negro girls become accustomed to dolls of their own color. He thought it important, as long as the races were to be segregated, that the dolls, which like other forms of art, are patterns and represent ideals, should be segregated also.

This substitution of the Negro model for the white is a very interesting and a very significant fact. It means that the Negro has begun to fashion his own ideals and in his own image rather than in that of the white man. It is also interesting to know that the Negro doll company has been a success and that these dolls are now widely sold in every part of the United States. Nothing exhibits more clearly the extent to which the Negro had become assimilated in slavery or the extent to which he has broken with the past in recent years than this episode of the Negro doll.

The incident is typical. It is an indication of the nature of tendencies and of forces that are stirring in the background of the Negro's mind, although they have not succeeded in forcing themselves, except in special instances, into clear consciousness.

In this same category must be reckoned the poetry of Paul Lawrence Dunbar, in whom, as William Dean Howells has said, the Negro "attained civilization." Before Paul Lawrence Dunbar, Negro literature had been either apologetic or self-assertive, but Dunbar "studied the Negro objectively." He represented him as he found him, not only without apology, but with an affectionate understanding and sympathy which one can have only for what is one's own. In Dunbar, Negro literature attained an ethnocentric point of view. Through the medium of his verses the ordinary shapes and forms of the Negro's life have taken on the color of his affections and sentiments and we see the black man, not as he looks, but as he feels and is.

It is a significant fact that a certain number of educated—or rather the so-called educated—Negroes were not at first disposed to accept at their full value either Dunbar's dialect verse or the familiar pictures of Negro life which are the symbols in which his poetry usually found expression. The explanation sometimes offered for the dialect poems was that "they were made to please white folk." The assumption seems to have been that if they had been written for Negroes it would have been impossible in his poetry to distinguish black people from white. This was a sentiment which was never shared by the masses of the people, who, upon the occasions when Dunbar recited to them, were fairly bowled over with amusement and delight because of the authenticity of the portraits he offered them. At the present time Dunbar is so far accepted as to have hundreds of imitators.

Literature and art have played a similar and perhaps more important role in the racial struggles of Europe than of America. One reason seems to be that racial conflicts, as they occur in secondary groups, are primarily sentimental and secondarily economic. Literature and art, when they are employed to give expression to racial sentiment and form to racial ideals, serve, along with other agencies, to mobilize the group and put the masses *en rapport* with their leaders and with each other. In such case art and literature are like silent drummers which summon into action the latent instincts and energies of the race.

These struggles, I might add, in which a submerged people seek to rise and make for themselves a place in a world occupied by superior and privileged races, are not less vital or less important because they are bloodless. They serve to stimulate ambitions and inspire ideals which years, perhaps, of subjection and subordination have suppressed. In fact, it seems as if it were through conflicts of this kind, rather than through war, that the minor peoples were destined to gain the moral concentration and discipline that fit them to share, on anything like equal terms, in the conscious life of the civilized world.

## IV

The progress of race adjustment in the southern states since the emancipation has, on the whole, run parallel with the nationalist movement in Europe. The so-called "nationalities" are, for the most part, Slavic peoples, fragments of the great Slavic race, that have attained national self-consciousness as a result of their struggle for freedom and air against their German conquerors. It is a significant fact that the nationalist movement, as well as the "nationalities" that it has brought into existence, had its rise in that twilight zone, upon the eastern border of Germany and the western border of Russia, and is part of the century-long conflict, partly racial, partly cultural, of which this meeting-place of the East and West has been the scene.

Until the beginning of the last century the European peasant, like the Negro slave, bound as he was to the soil, lived in the little world of direct and personal relations, under what we may call a domestic regime. It was military necessity that first turned the attention of statesmen like Frederick the Great of Prussia to the welfare of the peasant. It was the overthrow of Prussia by Napoleon in 1807 that brought about his final emancipation in that country. In recent years it has been the international struggle for economic efficiency which has contributed most to mobilize the peasant and laboring classes in Europe.

As the peasant slowly emerged from surfdom he found himself a member of a depressed class, without education, political privileges, or capital. It was the struggle of this class for wider opportunity and better conditions of life that made most of the history of the previous century. Among the peoples in the racial borderland the effect of this struggle has been, on the whole, to substitute for a horizontal organization of society—in which the upper strata, that is to say the wealthy or privileged class, was mainly of one race and the poorer and subject class was mainly of another—a vertical organization in which all classes of each racial group were united under the title of their respective nationalities. Thus organized, the nationalities represent, on the one hand, intractable minorities engaged in a ruthless partisan struggle for political privilege or economic advantage and, on the other, they represent cultural groups, each struggling to maintain a sentiment of loyalty to the distinctive traditions, language, and institutions of the race they represent.

This sketch of the racial situation in Europe is, of course, the barest abstraction and should not be accepted realistically. It is intended merely as an indication of similarities, in the broader outlines, of the motives that have produced nationalities in Europe and are making the Negro in America, as Booker Washington says, "a nation within a nation."

It may be said that there is one profound difference between the Negro and the European nationalities, namely, that the Negro has had his separateness and consequent race consciousness thrust upon him, because of his exclusion and forcible isolation from white society. The Slavic nationalities, on the contrary, have segregated themselves in order to escape assimilation and escape racial extinction in the larger cosmopolitan states.

The difference is, however, not so great as it seems. With the exception of the Poles, nationalistic sentiment may be said hardly to have existed fifty years ago. Forty years ago when German was the language of the educated classes, educated Bohemians were a little ashamed to speak their own language in public. Now nationalist sentiment is so strong that, where the Czech nationality has gained control, it has sought to wipe out every vestige of the German language. It has changed the names of streets, buildings, and public places. In the city of Praag, for example, all that formerly held German associations now fairly reeks with the sentiment of Bohemian nationality.

On the other hand, the masses of the Polish people cherished very little nationalist sentiment until after the Franco-Prussian War. The fact is that nationalist sentiment among the Slavs, like racial sentiment among the Negroes, has sprung up as the result of a struggle against privilege and discrimination based upon racial distinctions. The movement is not so far advanced among Negroes; sentiment is not so intense, and for several reasons probably never will be. One reason is that Negroes, in their struggle for equal opportunities, have the democratic sentiment of the country on their side.

From what has been said it seems fair to draw one conclusion, namely: under conditions of secondary contact, that is to say, conditions of individual liberty and individual competition, characteristic of modern civilization, depressed racial groups tend to assume the form of nationalities. A nationality, in this narrower sense, may be defined as the racial group which has attained self-consciousness, no matter whether it has at the same time gained political independence or not.

In societies organized along horizontal lines the disposition of individuals in the lower strata is to seek their models in the strata above them. Loyalty attaches to individuals, particularly to the upper classes, who furnish, in their persons and in their lives, the models for the masses of the people below them. Long after the nobility has lost every other social function connected with its vocation the ideals of the nobility have survived in our conception of the gentleman, genteel manners and bearing—gentility.

The sentiment of the Negro slave was, in a certain sense, not merely loyalty to his master, but to the white race. Negroes of the older generations speak very frequently, with a sense of proprietorship, of "our white folks." This sentiment was not always confined to the ignorant masses. An educated colored man once explained to me "that we colored people always want our white folks to be superior." He was shocked when I showed no particular enthusiasm for that form of sentiment.

The fundamental significance of the nationalist movement must be sought in the effort of subject races, sometimes consciously, sometimes unconsciously, to substitute, for those supplied them by aliens, models based on their own race individuality and embodying sentiments and ideals which spring naturally out of their own lives.

After a race has achieved in this way its moral independence, assimilation, in the sense of copying, will still continue. Nations and races borrow from those whom they fear as well as from those whom they admire. Materials taken over in this way, however, are inevitably stamped with the individuality of the nationalities that appropriate them. These materials will contribute to the dignity, to the prestige, and to the solidarity of the nationality which borrows them, but they will no longer inspire loyalty to the race from which they are borrowed. A race which has attained the character of a nationality may still retain its loyalty to the state of which it is a part, but only in so far as that state incorporates, as an integral part of its organization, the practical interests, the aspirations and ideals of that nationality.

The aim of the contending nationalities in Austria-Hungary at the present time seems to be a federation, like that of Switzerland, based upon the autonomy of the different races composing the empire.[5] In the South, similarly, the races seem to be tending in the direction of a bi-racial organization of society, in which the Negro is gradually gaining a limited autonomy. What the ultimate outcome of this movement may be it is not safe to predict.

5    Aurel C. Popovici, *Die Vereinigten Staaten von Gross-Oestreich, Politische Studien zur Losung der nationalen Fragen u. statsrechtlichen Krisen in Oestreich*, Leipzig, 1906.

# 9

# FOREIGN LANGUAGE PRESS
# AND SOCIAL PROGRESS

THERE are something like forty-three or forty-four languages and dialects spoken by immigrants in the United States. This fact is important because among immigrant people mother-tongue, rather than country of birth, is the basis of association and organization. The world war has emphasized the fact that old political boundaries of Europe did not include homogeneous peoples. It has revealed the fact that within these political boundaries Europe was organized on the basis of languages, and of the memories and traditions which these languages have preserved. It is significant also that when other bonds broke language and tradition held. The nations, which in the break-up of Europe gained their independence, were all language groups, not nationalities.

In America, as in Europe, it is language and tradition rather than political allegiance that united the immigrant populations. People who speak the same language find it convenient to live together. Our great cities, as we discover upon close examination, are mosaics of little language colonies, cultural enclaves, each maintaining its separate existence within the wider circle of the city's cosmopolitan life. Each of these little communities is certain to have some sort of mutual aid society, very likely a church and a school, possibly a theater, but almost invariably a press.

It seems almost certain that there are more foreign language papers in America in proportion to the foreign population than

Reprinted from *Proceedings of the National Conference of Social Work,* Forty-seventh annual session, April 14-21, 1920, pp. 493–500.

there are in Europe in proportion to the native populations. It is certainly true that a very large proportion of the immigrant population read newspapers in America who did not read them in their home country. An article published in the *Russkeye Slove*, based upon information obtained in response to a questionnaire, indicates that even among those who were able to read only about 3 per cent were habitual readers at home.

Peasants and laborers constitute more than 90 per cent of all the Russian immigrants in the United States. A great majority of them felt no need for periodicals or for theatrical performances in their old country. According to the census of 1910, there are 38.4 per cent illiterates among the Russians above fourteen years of age. But even those who are able to read rarely saw newspapers in Russia, and theaters were out of their reach. The Russian village, from which the majority of immigrants came, had no press and no theater.

Out of the three hundred and twelve correspondents only sixteen have regularly read newspapers in Russia; ten others used from time to time to read newspapers in the "volost," the village administrative center; twelve were subscribers to weekly magazines.

In America all of them are subscribers or readers of Russian newspapers. Two hundred of them are theater-goers, and all are visiting the "movies."

Twenty-five per cent of them also read the American newspapers published in the English language. But some mention the fact that they "understand only one word out of five." Others, buying an American daily, just glance over the headlines. "These are easy to understand and you know all the news," writes one of the correspondents.

Most immigrants have been peasants at home. They are likely to be laborers here, participating more or less in all the turbulent cosmopolitan life of our modern industrial cities. In the little, isolated peasant villages from which they came, life was, and is still, relatively fixed and settled. Under such conditions custom and tradition provided for all the exigencies of daily life. Conduct was based on face to face relationships, that is to say, speech and neighborly gossip. In America, where there are vast distances and no traditions, where the population is mobile and everything is in process, the peasant discards his habits and acquires "ideas." In America, above all, the immigrant organizes. These organizations are the embodiment of his new needs and his new ideas. He becomes a socialist or a nationalist, or a member of a fraternal organization, and reads a paper, because practically every immigrant organization publishes some sort of a paper.

There are other explanations for the popularity of the foreign language press. One reason why immigrants are eager to read their own language in this country is that they have not been permitted to do so in their own. Sometimes they have not learned to read before they come here; have not been permitted to do so. Sometimes the journals they might have read were not interesting or not intelligible. Frequently these journals did not exist.

In Lithuania, German Poland, Ukrainia, Slovakia, and Hungary the languages of the native peoples were interdicted. There were in these countries schools and a press, but they were conducted in the language of the dominant race, i.e., German, Russian, Hungarian. The result was that the peasant, who got his education in an alien tongue, never got enough to enable him to read. Besides it is very hard to learn to read in an alien tongue unless you have already learned to read your mother-tongue.

Another reason the immigrant did not read at home was that he could not understand the papers even when they were published in his own language. The papers were, in fact, not addressed to the common man.

A recent writer has called attention, however, to the fact that not only does the average American not speak the English of the books, but he probably does not understand more than two-thirds of what comes from the lips of the average political orator or clergyman.

The reason that the ordinary man does not fully understand the "highbrow" when he is discoursing may be due to the fact that the matter under discussion is itself abstruse. In that case it is even possible that the highbrow does not fully understand it himself. In most instances, however, failure to comprehend is due to the fact that the average man and the academic person do not speak the same language, and no one fully comprehends any form of speech that he does not habitually use. What is interesting and significant in this connection is the fact that, however wide the divergence between the written and the spoken language may be in America, these divergences are considerably less in this country than in any other part of the world.

In no other country is so much effort and ingenuity expended in perfecting the art, not merely of printing, but of publication and publicity. Not only is the language of the press simpler, more direct and incisive, closer to the language of the street, but the distinction between the written and the spoken speech is steadily decreasing in spite of the fact that "the typical literary product of the country is still a refined essay in the *Atlantic Monthly*."

The evidence of this is the enormous circulation of such journals as the *Saturday Evening Post,* and the fact that the number of daily newspapers is decreasing at the same time that circulations are steadily increasing.

In countries where the intellectuals constituted, as they did in Russia, a separate caste, the schools, even where they did exist, did not create a reading habit in the masses of the people, because all the journals were addressed to the highbrow. The American newspaper, with its local news, personal gossip, and its human interest anecdotes, is not the foreigner's conception of journalism.

It is the American's interest in local news that justifies, perhaps, the characterization of America as a "nation of villagers." As a people, it seems we are not interested in ideas but in gossip.

That was undoubtedly the meaning of the cautious observation of a member of the Jewish intelligentsia, whom Hutchins Hapgood met in a Ghetto cafe. In *The Spirit of the Ghetto* (p. 282) he writes:

> In Russia a few men, really cultivated and intellectual, give the tone and everybody follows them. In this country the public gives the tone and the playwright and the literary man simply expresses the public.

In America, however, it becomes necessary for the editors to make some concessions to the intelligence of the immigrant.

The peasant is sentimental; the editors print poetry for him in the vernacular. They fill the paper with cheap fiction and write loud-sounding editorials, double leaded, so that they will be easily read. Sometimes they compromise by writing in the literary language on the editorial pages, discussing the conventional themes, while the rest of the paper is made up of hasty translations from the American newspapers written in jargon, made up of words from the vernacular interspersed with American idioms and American words with foreign endings.

Sometimes the publisher is himself an ignorant man, or at least not an intellectual who looks upon his paper, as the American publisher does, as an advertising medium, which prints news merely to get circulation. It is said that one of the most successful Chinese editors in America cannot read the editorials in his own paper because he does not understand the literary language. Some of the most successful foreign language papers are published by men who do not make any pretensions to education and are regarded by the writers they employ as ignoramuses. These men know their public, however, and insist on printing in the paper what their subscribers are interested in and able to read. When the writers for the press despise both their employers and their public, as they sometimes do, not much can be expected from the newspaper which they succeed in producing.

The effect of this general lowering of the tone of the foreign language papers has been to create a public in this country composed of people who in their home country would have read little or nothing at all. All of the foreign languages have contributed to establish reading habits in the immigrant. It is the socialist press, however, that has taught him to think.

The most interesting of the foreign language papers in America are Yiddish. In the Yiddish press the foreign language newspaper may be said to have achieved form. All the tendencies and all the motives which other divisions of the immigrant press exhibit imperfectly, are here outstanding and manifest. No other press has attained so complete a simplification of the racial language, nor created so large a reading public. No other foreign language press has succeeded in reflecting so much of the intimate life of the people which it represents or reacted so powerfully upon the opinion, thought, and aspiration of the public, for which it exists. This is particularly true of the Yiddish daily newspapers in New York City.

The Jewish socialists were the first among the Jewish immigrants to conceive the idea of a press that would reach and interest the masses of the people. Among the immigrants who sought refuge in America in the early eighties were a number of Jewish students who had participated in the revolutionary agitation that preceded the assassination of Czar Alexander II, in March, 1881. It had been the program of the revolutionists to educate the masses of the people, "to go in among the people" as they termed it, and so prepare them for the international revolution which they, after the manner of millennialists everywhere, believed was impending.

Although there was at this time a popular literature in Yiddish among the Jews in Russia, political discussion was in Russian. There were sermons in Yiddish but no one had ever heard a political speech in the language of the people. The masses of the Jewish immigrants knew nothing of socialism or the labor movement, just as they knew nothing of modern science or modern political thought. All these high matters were the special concern of a few intellectuals who had been permitted to attend a Russian university. William M. Leiserson has said:

On July 27, 1882, occurred the first public meeting of the Russian refugees. For the first time they had an opportunity to enjoy freedom of speech, and on this sweltering day 500 of them jammed to the walls the little Golden Rule Hall on Rivington Street. The speeches were in Russian and German, and many could not understand either of these languages, but they were none the less enthusiastic. Schevitz, editor of the German Volkszeitung, Nelke, a German anarchist, and A. Cahan, on of the Russian students addressed the meeting.

It was Cahan at this meeting who first suggested the idea of using the Yiddish jargon to propagate socialism among the Jews. The suggestion was ridiculed. Who was there that could make speeches in Yiddish? Cahan volunteered to do it; and the following week in the anarchists' hall on Sixth Street the first Yiddish speech was delivered. After that many Jewish meetings were held, but for a long time Cahan continued to be the only Yiddish speaker.

The meetings of the "Propaganda Verein" were marked by the

greatest enthusiasm. The right of free assemblage was a new experience to most of the Jews; but still more new and strange were the speeches in the mother tongue. *The doctrines of socialism which formerly the educated alone could understand were now to be made comprehensible to the ordinary immigrant.* A cry went up among the students: "In the mother tongue must we agitate among the Jews." And for a few months there was great activity in the "Propaganda Verein."

It was not, as it turned out, an easy matter to carry on a political propaganda in the language of a people who had had no political experience. There were no words in Yiddish in which to express the formulas of Marxian socialism. The scholastic discussions of the Russian students did not hold the interest of the common people, eager as they were for the knowledge which the new doctrines promised them.

P. Wiernik, in his *History of the Jews in America* (p. 303, 1912), writes:

In one respect the Hebrew and the Yiddish writers were struggling with the same difficulty—that of making themselves understood by the largest possible number of readers. The method prevailing in Russia, of writing as hard or using as high a language as possible so that the highly intelligent reader—the title to which every reader of a newspaper there at that time laid claim—should take pride in being able to understand the contents, would not attract readers here as it does where scarcity of printed matter makes the public accept with eagerness whatever is offered. But the Hebrew writer came here with a style that may be termed aristocratic, and the Yiddish writer, who had to begin everything anew, had hardly any style. It was all easy as far as the work of the agitator was concerned; denunciations and accusations are always easily understood, and this alone is one of the reasons of their popularity. But when it came to the parts where the writer wanted to describe or to explain, especially in the scientific or semi-scientific articles which a public that had no systematic schooling so eagerly devoured, the language of most of the writers was inadequate and easily misunderstood.

It was not until the appearance of the *Forward*, however, and not until Abraham Cahan returned from his five years' apprenticeship upon an American daily paper that the Jewish socialists succeeded in creating a newspaper that the masses of the Jewish people, and even women, would read. The *Forward*, under Abraham Cahan, may be said to be modelled on the *Yellow Journal* of the period. It was, however, less a copy than an application of methods. The Jewish *Forward* is unquestionably American, but it is unquestionably unique. Its immediate and remarkable popularity was an indication that the Jewish daily press had finally arrived.

*Forward* was born at a Socialist ball fifteen years ago, when Cahan and others passed the hat around to start a Yiddish socialist daily and collected $800. A cooperative publishing company, the Forward Association, was formed almost on the spot. This Association pledged itself to publish the paper and to devote whatever profit accrued to the furthering of socialism and of *Forward*. Today *Forward* and its building bring many thousands of dollars a year profit, not a cent of which goes as dividends to anyone or for any other than these purposes. But as late as ten years ago the *Forward* was not only deep in debt, but also dying.

Its board of managers in despair appealed to Cahan to come and take hold. At that time Cahan was making a name for himself as special writer on the *Sun*, the *Evening Post*, the *Commercial Advertiser*, and other papers. His stories of Jewish life were appearing in the first-class magazines. His novel of East Side life, *Yeki*, had been acclaimed by William Dean Howells and other critics on both sides of the Atlantic as a masterly bit of realism. His *White Terror and Red* and his *Imported Bridegroom and Other Stories* were bringing him a widening English-reading public. But at the call from his comrades he went back to the East Side and threw himself into the task of reviving the dying Yiddish daily.

He found the circulation barely six thousand, the columns full of abstract economic controversy, the tone bitter, and an exaggerated air of the "highbrow" even for the East Side, where Tolstoy, Spencer, Darwin, and similar literature can be bought on pushcarts. Worst of all, it was written in a highly intellectualized, Germanized Yiddish, which only the "intelligentsia" can understand fully.

Cahan at once changed its language to the colloquial, Americanized Yiddish spoken in the street, the shops, the factories, and the homes of the people it desired to reach. "And if you want the public to read this paper and to assimilate Socialism," he told his staff, "you've got to write of things of everyday life, in terms of what they see and feel and find all about them."

So he banished the long abstract essays on economic determinism and the class struggle and presented these things in the form of short actual stories and news from the shop, the street, the market, and the home. The East Side began to read about itself in the news columns of *Forward*. It found its homely everyday problems discussed trenchantly yet sympathetically on the editorial page by Cahan, and read advice to the lovelorn in a department conducted by Rose Pastor, who afterward added Stokes to her name.

Within eight weeks after Cahan had taken hold of *Foward* its circulation trebled. Within two or three years it began to pay a profit; and now (1912) it has a daily circulation of over 130,000 a day.

It is not possible to estimate the changes which the appearance of a genuinely popular press has had upon the life of the Jewish immigrant. Jewish scholars had been sitting for centuries in the synagogues, by the light of sacred candles, poring over the past, brooding over the inner life of the race. Upon this spectacle the common man looked with awe and reverence. The popular press turned the eyes of the Jews outward upon the world. The press was a window on life. The new press was, to be sure, socialistic, but more interesting to the masses of the people than political philosophy was the information it gave them about life, about the physical universe and the world of human nature about them. There had arisen, at this time, a school of writers who devoted themselves to writing popular science in the language of the people. There were a number of these popular writers. Abraham Cahan was one. J. Rombro, who wrote under the name of Philip Kranz, was another. Rombro, like Cahan, was a Russian fugitive. In London he met Morris Winchefsky, the Yiddish poet and writer. Winchefsky, who was at that time editing *The Polish Jew*, the first socialist Yiddish paper to be published in England, asked him to write a description of the riots against the Jews in Russia. "It was a hard job for me," he wrote to Leo Wiener, "and it took me a long time to do it. I never thought of writing in the Jewish jargon, but fate ordered otherwise, and, contrary to all my aspirations, I am now nothing more than a poor jargon journalist." To which the author of the *History of Yiddish Literature* adds this comment:

The author's evil plight has, however, been the people's gain, for to his untiring activity is due no small amount of the enlightenment that they have received in the last ten years.

The most picturesque figure among the popular writers in Yiddish is Shaikevitch, the man who popularized the "heften." The "heften" were unsigned novels, popular stories, that had an immense vogue until the daily papers began publishing them serially. The competition of daily papers, which sometimes published as many as five or six stories at a time, destroyed the vogue of the "heften."

Shaikevitch, in an interview with Hutchins Hapgood, said this of his own work:

My works are partly pictures of the life of the Jews in the Russian villages of fifty years ago, and partly novels about the old history of the Jews. Fifty years ago the Jews were more fanatical than they are now. They did nothing but study the Talmud, pray and fast, wear long beards and wigs and look like monkeys. I satirized all this in my novels. I tried to teach the ignorant Jews that they were ridiculous, that they ought to take hold of modern, practical life and give up all that was merely formal and absurd in the old customs. I taught them that a pious man might be a hypocrite, and that it is better to do good than to pray. My works had a great effect in modernizing and educating the ignorant Jews. In my stories I pictured how the Jewish boy might go out from his little village into the wide, gentile world, and make something of himself. In the last twenty-five years, the Jews, owing to my books, have lost a great deal of their fanaticism. At that time they had nothing but my books to read, and so my satire had a great effect.[1]

[1]    Hutchins Hapgood, *The Spirit of the Ghetto*, chap. 10, "Odd Characters," pp. 274–75.

Through the medium of the popular press the learning which had been the privilege of the few became the common possession of the many. The intellectual ferment, which this new contact with modern science produced, was scattered broadcast and under the influence of the new ideas and the unrest which it created, the whole structure of Jewish life crumbled. The younger generation, particularly the more ardent and intellectual among them, went over to socialism *en masse.* Socialism gave the common man a point of view from which he could, at any rate, think about actual life. It made the sweatshop an intellectual problem.

Under the same influences socialism itself changed. It ceased to be a mere political doctrine and became a criticism of life. The socialist press ceased to be the mere organ of the doctrinaries, and became an instrument of general culture. All the intimate, human, and practical problems of life found a place in its columns. It founded a new literature and a new culture, based on the life of the common man.

A fact in regard to the immigrant, which is not generally understood, is that there exists in certain parts of Europe, as a result of the suppression of the folk languages and because of some rather drastic efforts at naturalization, what has been characterized as an "artificial illiteracy." With the growth of socialism and of nationalism, the two political movements which immigrant peoples are able to understand, there has been an intellectual awakening of the masses of the people. There is in all the back areas of Europe, as a matter of fact, a genuine renaissance, a widespread desire to know and to participate in the conscious life of the world from which they have hitherto been shut out. This new and vivid interest in life—modern life, science, and even literature—has been intensified by the new, strange, confusing but stimulating encounters with the American environment, the organization of the great industries, and the vast and cosmopolitan life of modern cities. It is to this interest that the foreign language press, and particularly the socialistic, communistic, and I.W.W. press, appeals. But after all the worst that can be said in regard to the great majority of the so-called radical immigrant papers, is, that while they aim at being edifying, they succeed in being dull. This is not true of the whole radical press, it is not true of the Yiddish papers. It is far from true of the *Forward*, the most successful and important of them all. But the *Forward* has long since ceased to be a purely radical paper and has become, more completely than any other paper in this country, a form of literature and a transcript of life.

# 10

# THE SOCIAL FUNCTION OF WAR

BY MAKING warfare more efficient and more terrible, modern technology has made war itself our No. 1 social problem. There is a vast literature on war and peace; but, aside from what has been written about the science and art of warfare, there is little or nothing in the literature that throws light on the nature of war or its role and function in the life and natural history of society. Furthermore, what we have learned about the effects of war, while it has made peace more desirable, has not made war any less inevitable.

Most of what has been written in recent years in regard to the problem of war and of peace may be fairly summed up in the vigorous language of General Sherman's apology for his "march to the sea." "War," said he, "is hell"—that is to say, it is cruel, barbarous, economically disastrous and politically atavistic, and generally unconscionable. This recognizes the problem but contributes nothing to its solution. I might add that problems which can be fairly described only in epithets are notoriously hard to deal with. In so far as this is true in the case of war, it seems to be because we have no adequate working conception of what war is.

The immediate consequences of war are obvious enough, but we do not know the long-run effect of wars and the preparations for wars upon society and human nature. It is inevitable that struggles which involve the very existence of peoples have had and will continue to have, as long and as often as they are repeated, a profound effect upon the nature of men, their attitudes and institutions. "Peace," it has been said, "has been the dream of wise men but war has been the history of nations." When, however, we seek

Reprinted from *American Journal of Sociology*, 46 (January, 1941): 551–70.

to make war the subject of systematic and scientific investigation, we do not seem to have language in which to describe these influences in general terms. We need to ask ourselves: What is war?

We do not know whether to regard war as a natural phenomenon, like an earthquake or a pestilence, or to classify it as a social phenomenon, like a political contest or an elementary form of judicial procedure, like the ancient trial by battle—an institution which may be said to survive at present in Germany and elsewhere in Continental Europe in the form of the duello. In short, we do not know whether war is to be conceived as a social institution or as a biological and social process.

Trial by combat seems to have been a peculiar custom of certain German tribes and was imported by them into western Europe in the course of the Germanic invasions. It was, according to Gibbon, first made a legal institution in Burgundy by an edict of King Gundobald in A.D. 501 and was later "propagated and established in all the monarchies of Europe from Sicily to the Baltic." The church and the clergy were, for various reasons, opposed to the institution, and it is recorded that the King, in defending his edict against the objections and complaints of one of his bishops, disposed of the matter finally with this appeal to common sense and the consensus of mankind. "Is it not true," he said, "that the event of national wars and private combats is directed by the judgment of God; and that his providence awards the victory to the juster cause?"[1]

The conception of war as a procedure in which issues that cannot otherwise be adjudicated are decided, if not by force of arms, at least by physical combat, has persisted to the present day in several interesting forms—the strike, for example.[2] Taking account of the changes in the modes of thought which have taken place since Gundobald made his defense of trial by battle, it is interesting and, in a sense, reassuring to note that the conception of war upon which warfare is conducted today is not substantially

[1]     Edward Gibbon, *The Decline and Fall of the Roman Empire*, vol. 3, chap. 38, p. 331.
[2]     E. T. Hiller, *The Strike: A Study in Collective Action* (Chicago: University of Chicago Press, 1928).

different from what it was fourteen hundred years ago. Treitschke in his lectures on politics, in which he set forth fully the Prussian conception of war, defined its function in much the same language as King Gundobald. He says: "Between civilized nations also war is the form of litigation by which states make their claims valid. The arguments brought forward in these terrible law suits of the nations compel as no arguments in civil suits ever can do."

In illustrating and enforcing his conception of war as an instrument of political policy and a method by which states may, if they can, "make their claims valid," Treitschke reminds his students, to whom these lectures are addressed, that "often as we have tried by theory to convince the small states that Prussia alone can be the leader in Germany, we had to produce the final proof upon the battlefields of Bohemia and the Main."

Treitschke's notion that war may be conceived as a form of litigation between states, whether wholly valid or not, helps to make war intelligible in so far as he seems to identify the role of modern war with that of the ancient custom of trial by battle. "It is important," Treitschke adds, "not to look upon war always as a judgment from God. Its consequences are evanescent but the life of a nation is reckoned in centuries, and the final verdict can be pronounced only after a survey of the whole epoch," a sentence which reminds one of Schiller's famous dictum, *"Die Weltgeschichte ist das Weltgericht."*

When and how far war may be conceived as a judicial procedure remains a question. While the institution of trial by battle seems to have been based, like war, on a purely nonrational procedure, these contests did, nevertheless, have the character of a judicial procedure in so far as they were duly regulated by custom and sanctioned by tradition.

The same may be said, with some qualifications, to be sure, of war. Even in the little wars of primitive people intertribal etiquette usually prescribed some formalities for the declaration of war and the conclusion of peace. In the great wars of more civilized peoples there have always been some accepted rules of warfare, though not always rigidly enforced. The so-called "laws of war" were mainly designed to lessen the cruelties and hardships of warfare, particularly for the innocent bystanders, namely, the neutrals and civilian populations.[3]

One of the more important actions taken for the regulation of warfare between European peoples was the Declaration of Paris, adopted in 1856 at the close of the Crimean War. This was followed by the Red Cross Convention of 1864, providing for certain immunities for doctors, nurses, and other persons engaged in caring for the sick and wounded.

Not only civilians, however, but military experts and professional soldiers acknowledging that there are "technical limits at which war ought to yield to the requirements of humanity," have from time to time sought to regulate by international understanding the consequences of unrestricted warfare. In 1868 the Russian czar called an international conference, composed entirely of military officers and experts, to secure an agreement to limit the use of a type of bullet which inflicted needless suffering. The recommendations of this conference were embodied in the Declaration of St. Petersburg, binding the parties to renounce, among other things, the use of "projectiles weighing less than 400 grammes (about 14 ounces) which are explosive or charged with fulminating or inflammable substance." The Hague conferences of 1899 and 1907 followed, and, as a result of these and other conferences, an elaborate code for the conduct of war was drawn up and adopted. However, in view of the uncertainties of the interpretation and enforcement of these "laws" under actual conditions of warfare the code was happily supplemented by a proviso in the preamble which provided that, until a more complete system of regulation should be agreed upon, "inhabitants and belligerents should remain under the protection and the rule of the principles of the law of nations, as they result from the usages established among civilized peoples, from the laws of humanity and the dictates of the public conscience."[4]

Since that time warfare, with the rapid advance in the technology of war, has assumed ever vaster proportions and achieved an

3    *Encyclopaedia of the Social Sciences* (New York, 1935), XV, 359.
4    *Ibid.*, p. 361.

ever more terrible efficiency. International politics, meantime, has become more realistic and more cynical. "Total warfare," so called, is limited neither to the heavens above nor to the waters under the earth, and, with the advent of the new "strategy of treachery and terror," war has invaded the realm of the spirit—the last stronghold of free souls. Under these circumstances a "peace offensive" may be as effective a means of conquest as physical warfare.

Since propaganda has come to be recognized as one of the weapons of warfare, it has, by means of the radio and other forms of communication, not only broken down the last effective barrier dividing nations but abolished the distinction that once existed between peace and war. William James said thirty years ago in an article that sounds as if it had been written yesterday:

> "Peace" in military mouths today is a synonym for "war expected." The word has become a pure provocative, and no government wishing peace sincerely should allow it ever to be printed in a newspaper. Every up-to-date dictionary should say that "peace" and "war" mean the same thing, now *in posse*, now *in actu*. It may even reasonably be said that the intensely sharp competitive *preparation* for war by the nations *is the real war*, permanent, unceasing; and that the battles are only a sort of public verification of the mastery gained during the "peace"-internal.[5]

Under these conditions it is difficult to conceive of war as a form of judicial procedure even as elementary as the ancient trial by battle. It is even doubtful whether it can any longer be regarded, as it once was, as an "institution recognized by international law."[6] This is true in spite of the German War Book and other treatises in which the rules of the game have been rigorously defined.[7]

War has, in a summary way, settled international disputes but

5    *The Moral Equivalent of War*, a leaflet published in 1910 and circulated by the Association for International Conciliation and republished in part in the *Saturday Review of Literature*, October 12, 1940.
6    Herman Lutz, "War Guilt," *Encyclopaedia Britannica*, XXIII, 356.
7    See "Kriegsbrauch im Landkriege," translated by J. H. Morgan in *Encyclopaedia of the Social Sciences*, XV, 361.

not always in accordance with any recognized principle of justice or necessity inherent in the international situation. Otherwise, each new war as it occurred would have provided a precedent not merely for defining progressively the rules of warfare but for determining the issues involved in these "terrible lawsuits." As a matter of fact the precedents do exist. They make up a large part of the subject matter of our histories. But no principle seems to have emerged from them that is likely to enable us to deal with the issues of new wars as they arise. More often, so far from adjudicating international disputes in accordance with some general understanding or tradition, not to say principle, of international law, war has been an innovating and revolutionary force tending to overturn the existing international order and to challenge the tradition and principles upon which that order at any time has rested.

Thus World War II, which began with the assumption that its purpose was to revise the treaties with which World War I was concluded, is now proclaiming itself a world-revolution. It is no longer, as was once announced, a war to enforce the claims of the Have-Nots against the Haves. It is rather an ideological war—a war to establish a new order based upon a new political philosophy and a new philosophy of life.

This, then, is the interesting but anomalous status which war seems to occupy in the international social order. It is an institution—a political institution—in process; an institution whose function has not been defined, whose structure is not yet fixed in custom and in tradition. Such usages governing the conduct of wars as have grown up and been accepted in the past have, indeed, tended to legitimatize wars and give them an institutional character. But legitimacy is a characteristic that attaches to something regarding which we know what to expect. We do not know what to expect of war any more.

Considering the manner in which wars are now waged and the definition of "total war" by General Ludendorff,[8] the modern

8    "Every individual in the nation is expected to give his entire strength either at the front or at home, and this he can only do when he realizes that it is an immutable and inviolable truth that war is being waged solely for the existence of the nation. A totalitarian policy must put

world, whatever it may do in practice, has accepted, as an intellectual proposition, Professor George Mead's dictum that war "as a policy for adjudicating national differences is utterly discredited." It is discredited because, as Professor Mead concludes, "if logically pursued it leaves nothing to be adjudicated, not even the enemy nations themselves."[9]

The obvious, if not insuperable, difficulties of bringing war within the limitations of an institutional order where its function would be defined and its excesses controlled has led some students of political society to conceive war in biological rather than in sociological terms and to define its function accordingly as biological rather than social. Thus, Spencer Wilkinson, professor of military science at Oxford University, in an article on war in the *Encyclopaedia Britannica,* introduces the subject with a reference to an observation upon which Malthus based his theory of population and Darwin his theory of the origin of the species—namely, the observation that living organisms multiply more rapidly than the food supply, and for that reason there is "a perpetual competition among all living creatures, including human beings, for the means of subsistence." Among the higher organisms, certainly in the case of man, competition often assumes the form of conflict. As a matter of fact, animals "are usually equipped with organs of attack and of protection or evasion. On the one hand teeth, tusks, paws, claws, electricity; on the other hand shells, hides, scales and devices of camouflage."

Because he is not only a gregarious animal like sheep but a social and rational creature as well, man carries on the "struggle for existence," as Darwin described it, not merely by individual

---

at the disposal of such a war the strength of the nation and preserve it and only a conformity to the fundamental racial and spiritual laws will succeed in welding nation, conduct of war, and politics into that powerful unity which is the basis of national preservation" (General Erich Ludendorff, *The Nation at War* [London, 1936], p. 54).

9     George H. Mead, "National-Mindedness and International-Mindedness," *International Journal of Ethics,* 39 (July, 1929) : 400–404.

competition but by the conflict of organized groups or societies. Such a conflict between organized groups is war, and the instruments by which wars are carried on are armies.

The author pushes the biological interpretation still further. He conceives the army as itself an organism, "a society within a society." The weapons with which an army fights are—like the claws, paws, and tusks with which the lower animals are equipped —the instruments with which nations and peoples carry on the struggle for existence. So conceived, war becomes a form of natural selection, its function being to determine the survival not so much of individuals as of peoples and of the institutions by means of which nations and peoples carry on their collective life. The conception of war in terms of Darwin's theory of evolution, since it seems to accept war as fatally rooted in the very nature of human relations and of society, has not been accepted by the advocates of international peace. Militarists, on the other hand, even when they make no apologies for it, are likely to regard war as an inevitable incident of international relations, just as conflict has invariably been an incident and an instrument of political action wherever a political society has existed.

Von Moltke, who led the Prussian army in the three wars which brought about the establishment of the Second German Reich, wrote in a letter that has become famous: "Perpetual peace is a dream and not even a happy dream." From other statements one gathers that Moltke conceived of war, as others have before and since, as one of the instruments of God's mysterious providence designed not to settle international disputes but (1) to purge society of a political regime and a social order which were decadent and doomed to destruction and (2) to supersede these with forms more vigorous and fit to live.[10]

The attempt to put war into a biological category goes astray,

[10]    See Dr. G. F. Nicolai, *The Biology of War* (New York, 1918), pp. 521–22. Written during World War I and translated from the German by Constance A. Grande and Julian Grande, this volume by a professor of physiology is perhaps the most thoroughgoing criticism of the biological conception of war in the literature of the subject.

it seems to me, not so much from a failure to distinguish between the social and biological aspects of wars as from a failure to distinguish between competition and conflict as different aspects of the "struggle for existence." As a matter of fact, the existing species have not survived merely because they were "superior" to those that perished but rather because they were the "fitter," i.e., they fitted the "niches" in the natural economy in which they occur. Thus the first effect of competition has not been to destroy but to distribute the different organisms and species as they have successively appeared in the evolutionary series. It is as if each individual and each species had been condemned to be forever seeking the particular spot in the biosphere where it could live, and to survive by reproducing its kind. In turn, this distribution has been one of the instruments for the evolution of new species. The dispersion of the species, their diversification and preservation in all their diversity, as described by the older naturalists and their successors, the plant and animal ecologists, is one of the most fascinating chapters in the story of biological evolution.[11]

Dispersion was facilitated by the fact that competition between organisms of the same species, since they make similar demands on the habitat, is more intense than the competition between organisms of different species. Dispersion is an incident of the food quest. A further consequence of this dispersion has been the formation of associations, like that of the vine and the fig tree, of mutually interdependent species. This interdependence, like that of the predacious animal and its prey, does not necessarily result in the extirpation of either species but rather in the preservation of both.

It is by competition in the first instance that the dispersion and diversity of organisms is made possible; but it is by competition, also, that what is called the "balance of life" is maintained and the diversity of the species is preserved. This mutual interdependence of organisms has been described as "the web of life."

Within the limits of a geographical habitat the interdepend-

11    See Richard Hesse, *Ecological Animal Geography*, trans. and ed. W. C. Allee and Karl P. Schmidt (New York, 1937).

ence of the species inhabiting it tends to become more intimate and more vital. Such a region in which plants and animals maintain a kind of biological economy is described by ecologists as a "community." This is, however, a community, *nota bene*, without institutions. Such a community is, in fact, a kind of society, since it is composed of individual organisms living together; but it is different from the so-called animal societies, like those of the social insects, in this important respect—it is composed of species which, because they do not interbreed, have no "family ties." They have no instincts, as is the case of the social insects, which hold the individual units of the family or of other genetic groups together during the periods of reproduction and of the infancy of the progeny. Animal societies are, after all, merely great families. Communities, as the term is used by ecologists, are associations organized territorially in which the nexus which holds individual organisms of the divergent species together is purely economic. Societies, as the term applies to animals, are associations of individuals genetically related and organized on a familial pattern.

The two fundamental types of association which I have sought to distinguish as they exist among the inferior species—namely, (1) the territorial and ecological or economic and (2) the familial or social—are reproduced, with substantially the same differences, in the interrelations of races and peoples. This is true even though the different races, being of the same species, interbreed freely where the opportunity offers, as organisms of different species do not.

Generally speaking, the type of association that I have called "communal"—using the word in the sense in which that term is employed in ecology—is identical with that widespread system of relationships which commerce has spun among the peoples of the world, a form of association which is likely to be more intimate and personal among neighbors but more impersonal and less intimate among those who are either wholly unaware of their biotic and economic interdependence or know it only at second hand. This net of economic relationships in which, individually and collectively, races and peoples are ineluctably bound together corresponds in a general way to the "web of life" in which all living creatures are involved.[12]

On the other hand, within this wide-ranging economy, which at the present time extends to the limits of the habitable world, kinship ties and economic relationships are, in human society, further complicated by the existence of institutions—familial, economic, political, and religious—which do not exist in animal societies.

It is quite possible, as some anthropologists have contended, that primitive man—the genuinely primitive man—being a gregarious creature, may have lived for long periods of time wandering about in the forests in flocks or herds, without formal organization or institutions of any sort. There are, at any rate, in remote corners of the world peoples like the Semangs in the tropical forest of the Malay Peninsula, the Veddas of Ceylon, or the blameless Punan of Borneo whose mode of life is said to approach in its simplicity that of the lower animals. In this age of innocence, where there were no formal social order and no institutions, there

---

[12] We have studied the forms of life, and we have considered the adaptation of these forms to the exigencies of this or that habitat. In every habitat we find that there is a sort of community or society of organisms not only preying upon but depending upon each other and that certain balance, though often a violently swaying balance, is maintained between the various species so that the community *keeps on*. The particular name given to this subject of vital balances and interchanges is "Ecology.' "Economics" is used only for human affairs; ecology is really an extension of economics to the whole world of life. Man is always beginning his investigations too close to himself and finding later that he must extend his basis of inquiry. The science of economics—at first it was called political economy—is a whole century older than ecology. It tries to elucidate the relations of producer, dealer, and consumer in the human community and show how the whole system carries on. Ecology broadens out this inquiry into a general study of the give and take—the effort, accumulation, and consumption in every province of life. Economics, therefore, is merely human ecology; it is the narrow and special study of the ecology of the very extraordinary community in which we live. It might have been a better and brighter science if it had begun biologically (H. G. Wells, Julian S. Huxley, G. P. Wells, *The Science of Life* [New York, 1931], III, 961).

were, we are told, no wars.[13] As soon, however, as men came together to carry on any common enterprise, under circumstances where it was necessary to preserve discipline and maintain tension over any considerable length of time, some more efficient sort of organization was needed. It was under these circumstances that institutions seem to have come into existence.

Institutions, generally speaking, have had their origins in some collective action—some common enterprise or social movement that required concert and continuity of action over a considerable period of time. The most elementary form which these movements take is undoubtedly that of mass migration. The connection and correlations between mass migration and war in the historical process have been discussed in a recent volume by Frederick Teggart.[14] Other social movements are those that seek to bring about some sort of reform in the manners or in the economic and political organization of existing society, like the feminist or the prohibition movement. But there are also other movements that aim at more drastic changes, for example the revolutionary and religious movements initiated by political sects—fascism, communism, and socialism.

All these movements entail a more or less consistent collective action over a considerable period of time; but, compared with the changes which are ordinarily described as evolutionary, they are relatively sudden and catastrophic. They are, however, different, not merely in degree but in kind, from those more gradual and evo-

[13]    The Punan of Boreo are among the most primitive people, culturally speaking, in the world. For untold ages they have lived in the forests of Borneo, well out of the way of the great movements that have swept through the archipelago, carrying culture from India to the East. There is no reason to believe that they had been influenced strongly by any food-producing people until the Kayan and kindred tribes came up into the central watershed on their way toward Sarawak.

In the Punan we have a food-gathering people of good physique and bright intelligence who have remained comparatively undisturbed and therefore present to us typical conditions among really primitive peoples in general (see G. Elliot Smith, *Human History* [New York, 1929], p. 199).

[14]    *Rome and China: A Study of Correlations in Historical Events* (University of California Press, 1939).

lutionary, sometimes insensible, changes which take place with the slow accumulations of time—changes which are the results of the minor innovations, accommodations, and adaptations of a multitude of individuals who, like these little marine animals (Anthozoa) which build the coral islands, co-operate unconsciously to bring into existence a structure of whose character and dimensions they are hardly conscious.

Such changes as social movements bring about might be characterized as "mutations"—mutations that are planned and promoted. Social changes that are planned, particularly when they are planned on a grand scale, almost always have consequences that can never quite be foreseen. These consequences, therefore, are very largely just what happens rather than what was planned. Society is so far from being a closed system that one cannot deal with it either as an artifact or as a system of mechanical forces.[15]

Of all the common enterprises and of all the collective actions that men have undertaken, war is undoubtedly the most imposing in the amount and quality of the effort men put forth; the most devastating and revolutionary in its consequences. Into war—a great war, a total war—man puts all that he has: his wealth, his science, his indomitable will, and eventually his very existence. It is certain, therefore, that as far as man has sought to control his destiny by his collective planning and collective action, these titanic contests—the death struggles of superorganisms—have had the most tremendous effects, not only upon society and its institutions, but upon man himself, his spirit, his personality, and his terrestrial career. The amount of effort that man puts forth in war, however, as well as the passions and sentiments that these efforts arouse, are due not merely to the fact that man is here com-

[15] Where will you find in history a case of a great purpose rationally adopted by a great society and carried through to the intended result and then followed by the expected consequences in the way of social advantage? You can find no such thing. Men act from immediate and interested motives like these for which they have waged war and the consequences may be advantageous or disadvantageous to men. The story of these acts and consequences makes up human history (*Essays of William Graham Sumner*, edited, with prefaces, by Albert Galloway Keller and Maurice R. Davie [New Haven: Yale University Press, 1934], p. 148).

peting with other men but that he is conscious of those with whom
he is in competition, not only of their acts, but of their purposes
and intentions. Under these circumstances competition becomes
conflict; a competitor an enemy.

Cooley, who seems to have been the first to undertake to give
an account of competition in sociological terms, says its function
is "to assign each individual his place in the social system." He
adds that "competition is not necessarily a hostile contention nor
even something of which the competing individual is always conscious," since "from our infancy onward throughout life judgments are daily forming regarding us of which we are unaware,
but go to determine our careers."

Cooley does not, however, distinguish the very different consequences that ensue (1) when competition is not conscious and
(2) when it is, i.e., when it is conflict. Competition does indeed
determine our place in the economic system since it assigns us to
the job and function we can perform rather than to the one we
should choose to perform. But status, whether it is occupational or
social—in any of the various senses of that term—gets its peculiar
character because it is a result of conscious competition, i.e.,
emulation, personal conflict, war; because, in short, it is the outcome of a struggle, not merely for a spot in the sun or for a job but
for recognition and a place in an existing social order.

Gaetano Mosca in his *Elementi di scienza politica*, recently
translated under the title of *The Ruling Class*, referring to the
attempts to introduce Darwin's doctrine of evolution of the species
into the social sciences, declared that its application to social relations is based upon a fundamental confusion, since it identifies
"the struggle for existence" which is characteristic of the lower
animals with "the struggle for pre-eminence" which is characteristically human and "a constant phenomenon that arises in all
human societies, from the most highly civilized down to such as
have barely issued from savagery." Incidentally, Mosca points out
that conflict, like competition, is not merely a means of biological
selection. On the contrary, like competition, it is the principle of
organization. Its function is not to destroy but ultimately to assimilate the vanquished. This involves the imposition upon them of the

status of a subject people and, incidentally, the assignment to them of a function in the territorial economy within which the victors are dominant. Mosca's statement is:

In a struggle between two human societies, the victorious society as a rule fails to annihilate the vanquished society, but subjects it, assimilates it, imposes its own type of civilization upon it. In our day in Europe and America war has no other result than political hegemony for the nation that proves superior in a military sense, or perhaps the seizure of some bit of territory.[16]

Although the struggle for status or, as Mosca calls it, the struggle for "pre-eminence" is an obvious characteristic of human society, it has by no means diminished or taken the place of the unceasing, if silent, struggle of races and peoples for survival. Comparative studies of vital statistics of different peoples and population groups show that.[17] Rather has the struggle for pre-eminence, as Corrado Gini's demographic investigations indicate, had a profound effect upon biotic competition, "the competition of life," as Sumner calls it. This is a consequence of the fact that every population group tends to die at the top. Pre-eminence as it is achieved by any group or class is accompanied by a declining birth rate in the pre-eminent class. "As a rule," says Gini, "the upper classes are less fertile than the middle, and these, as a rule, are less so than the lower classes."[18] The effect of this is "to provoke a current from the middle classes to the upper, and from the lower to the middle" in order to fill the gaps that have been created by the decline of fertility in the upper classes or the decline in birth rate from whatever causes.

These and other considerations to which recent population studies have called attention indicate that the struggle for exist-

16 Translated by Hannah D. Kahn and edited and revised with Introduction by Arthur Livingston ([New York and London, 1939], p. 29).
17 See S. J. Holmes, *The Negro's Struggle for Survival* (University of California Press, 1937); also Romanzo Adams, *Interracial Marriage in Hawaii: A Study of the Mutually Conditioned Processes of Acculturation and Amalgamation* (New York, 1937).
18 Corrado Gini, Shiroshi Nasu, Oliver E. Baker, and Robert Kuczynski, *Population* ("Lectures on the Harris Foundation" [Chicago, 1929]).

ence, i.e., the competition of life and for space—*Lebensraum*, to use the German expression—whether it takes the form of biotic competition or the more obvious form of struggle for pre-eminence, is a more complicated matter than has been assumed by those who have sought to explain war as an incident of natural selection and the struggle for existence.

From this point of view competition, as distinguished from conflict, appears as an individuating, not to say analytic, process. It tends to dissolve the traditional social order into its individual elements in order that it may bring about a greater specialization and wider division of labor in an ever wider circle of those economically interdependent individuals and groups which constitute the economic community. The communal order, where it exists, is thus an effect of competition. Conflict, on the other hand, tends to bring about an integration and a superordination and subordination of the conflict groups, whether they be familial and tribal in character, as among the simpler peoples, or national, racial, and religious, as among more sophisticated peoples.

These two terms—community and society—employed in this restricted sense, designate two aspects—biological and cultural— of a single entity which presents itself in one aspect as a biotic community, i.e., a population occupying a territory, settled in a habitat, and in the other as an institutional and cultural unit, a society organized to act collectively and eventually politically.

However one may finally conceive the role which war has played in the long process of history, it is obvious that its function has not been merely that of an adjudicator of intertribal or international disputes. Rather, these disputes and the wars that grew out of them have provided the occasion and the necessity for an organization of society which, as it evolved, has become immeasurably superior, for the purposes of collective action at least, to the gregariousness of the primitive horde or the animal herd.

The effect of hostility upon the organization and solidarity of the groups in conflict has been frequently noted, but no one has stated it in more memorable terms than William Graham Sumner in his *Folkways*, where, discussing the mechanisms of "we-group" and the "others-group" relationships, he says:

The relation of comradeship and peace in the we-group and that of hostility and war towards others-groups are correlative to each other. The exigencies of war with outsiders are what make peace inside, lest internal discord should weaken the we-group for war. These exigencies also make government and law in the in-group, in order to prevent quarrels and enforce discipline. Thus war and peace have reacted on each other and developed each other, one within the group, the other in the intergroup relation. The closer the neighbors, and the stronger they are, the intenser is the warfare, and then the intenser is the internal organization and discipline of each.[19]

In insuring peace within as its consequence, war has created (1) in the family and in societies organized on a familial pattern a moral solidarity based on personal loyalties and piety and (2) in the state a political institution which has made collective action possible on a scale of which there is no promise in primitive society.[20] The fact that in the division of labor between the sexes man was not only the hunter but the fighter, who now and then brought home a strange woman, is responsible for putting him at the head of the family. It is probably one reason why, in primitive society, the matriarchate has, in most cases, been succeeded by the patriarchate—a change which Sumner believes may have been the greatest and most revolutionary in history.[21]

It was, however, not merely war but the life-long intimacy and dependency of every member of the family on every other, the sense of security in the family circle and the terror of all that was outside of it, which created the moral solidarity so characteristic

[19]    (New York, 1906), p. 12; see also Sumner's essay "War" in the *Essays of William Graham Sumner*, II, 136–73.

[20]    When for the first time in the history of the world the group of people who happened to be living in Egypt abandoned the nomadic life and began to till the soil they were accomplishing a vastly greater revolution in the affairs of mankind than the mere invention of the crafts of the farmer and the irrigation engineer. They were committing themselves to the much more formidable task of erecting the complicated edifice of civilization and formulating the fantastic doctrine of the state system which has dominated the world ever since (Smith, *Human History*, pp. 252–53).

[21]    See Sumner, *Folkways*, pp. 355–56; see also Maurice R. Davie, "War and Women," in his *The Evolution of War: A Study of Its Role in Early Societies* (Yale University Press, 1929), pp. 96–102.

of familial society including the clan and the tribe. As soon as man achieved a more or less settled existence and began to accumulate property, wars were undertaken for less romantic purposes and for less interesting and more manageable booty. In fact, war became with pastoral peoples not merely an adventure but a vocation. Robbery among many of the Bedouin tribes was considered as legitimate a method of gaining a livelihood as agriculture. Lippert refers to it as "Bedouin livelihood."

It happens occasionally today in North Africa that desert tribes come to terms with a settled population, whom they have long regarded as their legitimate prey, by accepting tribute in lieu of the booty they were accustomed to carry off. In such case it is part of the agreement that the erstwhile marauders become the protectors of their erstwhile victims, holding off other tribesmen who would otherwise plunder them. Sometimes, however, mobile and warlike desert tribes have not been content merely to exact tribute from, but have chosen to make a conquest of, their sedentary neighbors. This, in fact, seems to have been the way in which the state has normally come into existence, i.e., by the conquest of an agricultural by a pastoral and nomadic people. Friedrich Ratzel says:

The war-like character of the nomads is a great factor in the creation of states. It finds expression in the immense nations of Asia controlled by nomad dynasties and nomad armies, such as Persia, ruled by the Turks; China, conquered and governed by the Mongols and Manchus; and in the Mongol and Radjaputa states of India, as well as in the states on the border of the Soudan.[22]

In any case, sociologists and historians who have investigated the subject seem to agree that the state not only had its origin in war but that its chief business is still, as Dealey says, "to be ready for war and to wage it whenever national safety or national interest demand it."[23]

As states have come into existence by war, it has seemed to certain writers that they are forever condemned to continue their

[22]   Quoted by Franz Oppenheimer, *The State: Its History and Development Viewed Sociologically* (Indianapolis, 1914), p. 54.
[23]   See Davie, *The Evolution of War*, where (p. 166) James Q. Dealey, *State and Government*, is quoted.

conquests in order to maintain their existence. Nothing is more demoralizing to an army or to a military state than peace, and nations to survive must act. There must always be some great collective enterprise on the national agenda in which all classes can actively participate. "It is not yesterday, tradition, the past, which is the decisive, the determining force in the nation. . . . Nations are made and go on living by having a program for the future."[24]

War has been and still is the greatest, the most strenuous, if no longer the most glorious, enterprise in which nations can engage; and there seems to be, as George Mead has insisted in his reply to William James, no substitute for war. "The age of discussion" has not yet, as Walter Bagehot believed it should and would, superseded the age of war.[25]

What is probably taking place is that the issues in international controversies are being steadily narrowed by the increase of political knowledge, i.e., a more searching analysis of international situations and a more realistic conception of the processes involved in the functioning of political societies. Even discussions are more fruitful when they are based on facts. But facts assume the existence of some common assumptions, either implicitly or explicitly accepted by the parties to the discussion. In political controversies they involve the existence of a common body of tradition and of constitutional, that is to say fundamental, understandings, by reference to which what was a datum becomes a fact. In most wars what I have called "constitutional understandings" are involved, as they were, for example, in our war between the states, as they are in the present World War. In such cases neither discussion nor "appeasement" is likely to bring a solution. Where no common interest appears that makes compromise possible, wars seem inevitable. But men like Mead believe there is, or should be, no such instance; no situation that would not eventually yield to an intelligent analysis of the facts.[26]

---

[24]    José Ortega y Gasset, *Invertebrate Spain*, trans. Mildred Adams (New York, 1937), p. 26.

[25]    Walter Bagehot, "The Age of Discussion," *Physics and Politics* (New York, 1904), chap. 5, pp. 156–204.

[26]    Mead, "National-Minedness and International-Mindedness," pp. 355–407.

As states brought into existence a society that was organized on the basis of territory rather than on common race and culture, it was more or less inevitable that they should seek to expand their territories. In carrying on their wars for that purpose, however, they were always seeking a frontier which they could defend; always seeking to find a boundary behind which the state could stabilize society and live in peace. But always the frontiers receded as the armies approached them. A land-hungry population was always moving beyond the established frontiers, and new means of travel and transportation were constantly extending the area over which it was possible and necessary to exercise sovereignty in order to maintain peace.

With the organization of the city-state there began, in contrast with the dispersion of peoples characteristic of primitive life, a movement for the coming-together and integration of races and peoples—a tendency which is characteristic of cities and civilized life. The city, as we must remember, has been not merely the market place and focal center of a constantly expanding trade area or market. It has been at the same time the seat and center of an expanding dominion—a dominion and an authority which was invariably dispersed or relaxed in times of peace but constantly tightened and intensified when the beacons on the hilltops announced the approach of war. For war and peace are, as Sumner suggests, so intimately related that one may say that peace creates the problem that war is required to solve.

While the struggle for possession of the land has provided the occasion for most international wars, there have been other wars, like the Crusades to gain possession by Christians of the Holy Sepulcher or the Islamic wars to win the world for Allah and Mahomet. These so-called holy wars were actually ideological wars, seeking primarily to propagandize a cult. But all wars, imperialistic wars, that seek to expand the territory of the state always turn out, as in the case of the present World War, to have an ideological core. They are wars "to end war" or they are wars to defend the democratic way of life from the invasions of a collectivistic and totalitarian imperialism.

On the other hand, ideological wars turn out, likewise, to be struggles for land and living space. This is because, in order to maintain the different ways of life represented by the parties to these conflicts, political control and sovereignty of a territory in which they can survive is indispensable.

What can one say, finally, in regard to the nature of war and its function? Generally speaking, one may say that war is politics. It is, generally speaking, politics in its original, noninstitutional, and nonrational form—a form in which the belligerent states or parties seek by force of arms (1) to extend the territorial limits of their sovereignty and (2) to establish and impose upon the nations and peoples with whom they are in conflict a political and economic order which is in the interest of the dominant party, race, or nation. This gives a new significance to Freeman's statement that "history is past politics" and "politics is present history."

Historically, the function of war has been (1) to extend the area over which it is possible to maintain peace, (2) to create and organize within that area a political power capable of enforcing it, and, finally, at least in most cases, (3) to establish an ideology which rationalizes, and a cult which idealizes and so gains understanding and acceptance for, the new political and social order which the victor has imported or imposed upon the vanquished. This is the way that war settles issues. It is in this sense that one may say with Schiller: "The world's history is the world's judgment" on the acts of men and of nations.

# IV. Person in Social Process

## 11

# THE BASES OF RACE PREJUDICE

PREJUDICE even race prejudice, no matter how reprehensible in itself, is a profoundly human phenomenon. As such, it deserves, perhaps, to be defended against those who inveigh against it, as if it were not a common human weakness in which we all, more or less, share. It is not, however, in precisely this sense that President John Grier Hibben, of Princeton, wrote some years ago his "Defense of Prejudice." He sought to show that prejudice was, as he says, "a natural factor in any thinking, and not to be regarded in any sense as an abnormal and disturbing element."

### Defense of Prejudice

When the matter is stated in this fundamental way, it serves merely to call attention to the fact that primarily men are practical creatures; that thought is, after all, merely an incident of action, and that reflection arises, and gets its justification, in our efforts to achieve ends. We are biased by our own purposes, and in the final analysis, knowledge is relative to them. The fact is, we come into the world with certain predispositions, and we acquire others. Tradition into which we are born, and which we imbibe with our mothers' milk, is infused with prejudices. "There is," as President Hibben puts it, "no thought, however original, that does not rest upon a credit basis." A man without prejudices is a man without conviction, and ultimately without character.

Reprinted from *Annals of the American Academy of Political and Social Science*, CXL (November, 1928), pp. 11–20.

Common sense, "that diffuse sagacity which eludes all attempt at definition," is a tissue of hunches and prejudices that have not been, and in most cases cannot be justified on general and rational grounds. Our friendships, our hobbies, our amiable but irrational predilections for certain places and certain persons all are manifestations of what, under certain circumstances, we are likely to condemn as prejudices. It is notorious, for example, that friendships corrupt politics. The situation has been defined in the phrase, "What is the constitution among friends?" What, indeed, is the constitution or any other formal principle of action in the presence of the elementary claims of friendship, and the personal prejudices which such friendships imply?

As it seems impossible to conceive of a world without friendships, so it seems improbable, in such a world, that life should go on without enmities, for these two things are, in some sense and in some degree, correlative, so that the bias with which we view the qualities of our friends makes it difficult if not impossible to do justice to the virtues of our enemies and theirs. There is always and everywhere the inevitable dichotomy between those who call each other "we," and the outsiders whom one refers to as "they." As William Graham Sumner puts it,

> The relation of comradeship and peace in the "we-group" and that of hostility and war toward the "other-groups" are correlative to each other. . . . Sentiments are produced to correspond. Loyalty to the group, sacrifice for it, hatred and contempt for outsiders, brotherhood within, warlikeness without—all grow together, common products of the same situation.

All our sentiments, love, loyalty, patriotism, homesickness, contempt, arrogance, hate, are based upon and supported by prejudices. Furthermore, mankind is incurably sentimental, and sentiments and prejudices are part of the stuff from which our human life is made.

The thing reduces itself to this, that prejudice, defined in this broad and inclusive way, has its source and origin in the very nature of men and their relation to one another. It gets itself fixed and sublimated in the habits of individuals, and enters into the very structure of society. In short, prejudice is an attitude, a social attitude.

## Race Prejudice

There is no reason to believe that attitudes based upon race are fundamentally different from any other attitudes. Race prejudice is like class and caste prejudices—merely one variety of a species. So far as it can be described in these terms, race prejudice may be regarded as a phenomenon of status. Most of us are familiar with the fact that thought, particularly scientific thought, proceeds by the method of classification. According to the rules of Aristotelian logic—which is the logic of common sense—we may be said to know a thing when we are able to classify it. We have not always recognized that the thinking of the ordinary man proceeds, if less consciously, still substantially, in the same manner.

We are all dependent, to a degree that we do not recognize, upon our categories, and this is true in a very special sense with respect to our knowledge of human beings. Every individual we meet inevitably finds a place in our minds in some category already defined. He is either a friend, a neighbor, a mere acquaintance, or, as we often say, a complete stranger. The category into which he falls determines, more or less automatically, and with very little conscious reflection on our part, the attitude we assume toward each individual figure in the changing scene of our daily experiences. Furthermore, our attitudes, our fundamental attitudes at any rate, are substantially alike. Each of us has, of course, his own preferences and his own opinions, and we are all likely to be a little proud of our independence of thought. On the other hand, any very marked divergence from the generally accepted opinion is invariably shocking, and frequently quite unintelligible. Most of our "opinions" are merely justifications and apologies for what are, after all, rather slight deviations from views that are orthodox in the society in which we happen to live. Opinions are individual, but the attitudes upon which they are based are collective.

On the whole and in the large, in every society, things have very much the same meaning. That is merely to say that every society has its own universe of discourse, and that is what Walter Lippman means when he says that the public thinks only in stereotypes. There is, in fact, no other way in which the public can think. Where there is substantial agreement as to the categories, as there is bound to be in every stable society, there the status of every individual is defined by the class in which, by tradition or general consensus, he happens to find himself. The individual who is in no class at all is a pariah and an outlaw. The man who seeks to rise, or who rises suddenly, from a lower to a higher class is an upstart and a parvenu. The man who loses his status and sinks to a lower class is what the French describe as *déclassé*.

The point is that every change in status, whether of an individual or of a group, involves a change in social organization. Prejudice—that is caste, class and race prejudice—in its more naïve and innocent manifestations, is merely the resistance of the social order to change. Every effort of the Negro—to take the most striking example—to move, to rise and improve his status, rather than his condition, has invariably met with opposition, aroused prejudice and stimulated racial animosities. Race prejudice, so conceived is merely an elementary expression of conservatism.

As a matter of fact, changes in status are constantly taking place in every society. Certain individuals and certain classes rise and invade the higher levels of society. As a consequence the prestige of other individuals and other classes is diminished, with the result that they are forced to decline and to accept a lower position. In America, where changes in underlying conditions proceed more rapidly than they do elsewhere, changes in status are correspondingly rapid. There seems, under ordinary conditions, to be no barrier in America to advancement—except failure to succeed. Lindbergh, a small town boy from the Middle West, flies across the Atlantic and becomes a national hero. Gene Tunney, yesterday a prize fighter, today moves in the most exclusive circles. Prohibition has created a new generation of plutocrats, composed of retired "bootleggers." The spectacle of American life is amazing and inspiring. No man, it seems, is so far down that he cannot hope to rise. Every boy born in America may aspire to be president, even if he be a Catholic.

It may strike the disinterested observer as a little strange that in America, where, humanly speaking, there are no class distinctions, there is still so much race prejudice, particularly when we consider that as far as race relations are concerned, racial minorities are merely social classes. What is the answer?

First of all we ordinarily confuse racial prejudice with racial antagonism. There is probably less racial prejudice in America than elsewhere, but there is more racial conflict and more racial antagonism. There is more conflict because there is more change, more progress. The Negro is rising in America and the measure of the antagonism he encounters is, in some very real sense, the measure of his progress. The fact seems to be that racial prejudices do not always and everywhere express themselves in racial animosities. Animosities arise in conflict, and racial animosities are an incident of the struggles in which racial classes are formed. When, however, conflict ceases; when some sort of accommodation of the contending is achieved, animosities subside. In that case the sentiments change. They are no longer hostile, or are only potentially so. On the other hand, the racial prejudices, which are the basis of this hostility, may and often do persist.

## Race Relations

Where there are social classes there will invariably be corresponding attitudes and sentiments. Racial distinctions, when they exist, will always be supported by racial prejudices. But where distinctions based on class, caste, and race, are part of the established social order, as they invariably are in a static society, each caste and class lives within the limitations of its own world and accepts the definition imposed upon it as if it were a part of the order of nature. Under such circumstances each class and caste, having its own internal organization, maintains its own norms of conduct, and each expects and demands that every individual will live up to the standards of his own class. So far as this normal expectancy is maintained, good-will will exist, and each class will respect the other.

Something approaching this condition existed in the southern states before the Civil War, particularly in the far South, where slavery was firmly established and race relations, especially the relation of master and slave, assumed that fixed and irrevocable character which simulated the permanence of physical nature.

It was, however, during this period, and under the influences of the associations thus established, that those intimate and friendly relations between master and slave were established which are still so unintelligible to those who have looked upon slavery as if it were, always and everywhere, something inhuman and monstrous.

It was, nevertheless, during this same period that there grew up, out of the daily experience of master and slave, that conception of the Negro, according to which he was predestined by God and Nature, to be forever a hewer of wood and a drawer of water, "a servant of servants unto his brethren."

There is evidence to show that, on the whole, the black man accepted the position to which the white man assigned him. Negro servants spoke habitually in a proprietary sense of their masters' families as "our white folks." And, on the other hand, the masters' families thought of the slaves on their plantations as "our Negroes." In short, the plantation population, in spite of differences of race and status, constituted what I have described as a we-group. This was conspicuously the case of the members of the families and the house servants, between whom a lifelong intimacy existed.

Every large plantation in the South tended to assume the character of a little feudal state, each relatively independent of the others. In the intimacy of that isolated life, racial antipathy, such as existed elsewhere, and especially in the North, disappeared. Nathaniel S. Shaler, who knew this life intimately, says:

It is an interesting fact, if my observations on the matter are correct, that the instinctive dislike to the Negro disappears more quickly than prejudices against others less remote in quality of body from ourselves. I have never known an instance in which it persisted, provided contacts were intimate.[1]

---

[1]    N. S. Shaler, *The Neighbor: The Natural History of Human Contacts* (Boston, 1904), p. 166.

On the other hand, race and class distinctions within this feudal society were rigidly enforced. Writing of the plantation overseer, John Spencer Bassett says:

It was not even his fortune to be esteemed for what he did. He was patronized by the benign planters and condemned by the heedless. He might belong to the same church with the planter, but he usually preferred some plain form of worship, as in the churches of Methodists or Baptists. If the two found themselves worshipping in the same place they sat apart quite distinctly. Their children did not visit one another nor intermarry. Each was a class in society, and between them in social matters was a frozen ocean.

When there was illness in the overseer's family there was much kindness for him in the mansion. The mistress on a Southern plantation knew no caste in time of distress. . . . But she knew, and the overseer knew, that her visits of mercy were not visits of social equality. And he suffered nothing in his mind because of his lower place on the ladder. He was born to it. His wife was born to it. His children would never have aught else so far as the existing environment was concerned. Being a sensible man, he was not discontented. He took the best he could get of what life offered to overseers, finding his wife and marrying off his children in the ranks of such people as himself. If he did not like this prospect, and sometimes he was in revolt against it, he might turn to the frontier, which always had a welcome for a man with courage and industry.[2]

One may suspect that the distances which separated the families of the planter and the overseer, if they were not so great as those between master and slave, were more rigidly maintained. However, the very definiteness with which the position of the overseer was defined within the plantation hierarchy, is an indication of the solid character of the institution. The structure within which master and slave had lived for two hundred and fifty years was not at once dissolved by the publication of the emancipation proclamation. The old order, which was fixed in the habits and customs of both races, persisted long after the institution of slavery had been deprived of its legal sanctions. In many of its characteristic features it exists today; but it is crumbling.

[2]     John Spencer Bassett, *The Southern Plantation Overseer* (Northampton, Mass., 1925), pp. 2–3.

## Effects of Social Dissolution

The effect of the gradual dissolution of the traditional social order was to release interests and passions which, on the plantation if not in the cities, had achieved something like a stable equilibrium. The resulting struggles and conflicts, with the incidental disorganization, released all the latent animosities in the old social order, and created antipathies and prejudices between the races which previously did not exist.

Prejudices against the Negro in the South were, and are still, prejudices in favor of an order that is changing or no longer exists. "The Negro," Southern people were wont to say, "is all right in his place." On the whole, and so far as one may make any general statement of the matter, race prejudice in the southern states is caste prejudice. If the Negro were content to remain in a subordinate position to which the white man's prejudices—prejudices which have grown up through long and intimate association—assigned him, racial animosities would probably not exist.

As far as the South is concerned, it is where racial prejudices, and the social order which they perpetuated, are breaking down, that racial animosities are most intense. It is when the Negro invades a new region that race riots occur; it is when he seeks a place in a new occupation or a new profession that he meets the most vigorous opposition; it is when he seeks to assume a new dignity that he ceases to be quaint and becomes ridiculous.

The Negro achieved in slavery a definite position in the social organization and the cultural life of the South. In the South the black man is a native and has his roots in the soil; he has a place in tradition and is a figure in literature. The folk-songs of the South are Negro songs. Tradition assigns him a place in the social order, and race prejudice has made it difficult for him to get out of it.

Not so in the North. There, until very recently, the Negro has been, in the main, a sojourner and a stranger. He has had more freedom, but his status is precarious and undefined. It is true that, in the more liberal atmosphere of the Northern cities, the Negro has contributed something of his tradition to literature, and something of his temperament to the stage. On the other hand, as a serious figure either in literature or on the stage, he is still a good deal of a novelty and his contributions to our culture have the interest of something exotic.

Antagonism to the Negro in the North is different from that which he meets in the South. In the North it is less prejudice than antipathy, which is something more elementary and more insidious.

Racial antipathies, in a somewhat more positive sense than is true of racial prejudices, have their sources in fundamental human nature. This does not mean, however, that any particular prejudice nor the antipathies with which it is so often associated are instinctive; that is to say, biologically fixed and inalterable, so that the individual who grows up without the customary and expected race consciousness and the corresponding race prejudice, is to be regarded as in some sense abnormal—an aberrant individual.

Race consciousness, like the racial reserves, antipathies, and tabus in which it finds expression, is invariably, as far as observation goes, an acquired trait, quite as much as the taste for olives or the mania for collecting stamps. Children do not have it. They take the world of human beings in which they find themselves as part of the order of nature and respond to a black or yellow face as readily as they do to a white, depending upon the character and intimacy of the association. In the South it is a mark of distinction to have had a "black mammy," and the lasting affections which have so frequently grown out of that early intimacy are unquestionably the normal and natural consequences of human associations of this description everywhere.

## Race Instinctiveness

The fact seems to be that what we ordinarily regard as instinctive, and biologically determined in our behavior and attitudes toward peoples and races other than our own, is merely, in the first instance at least, the spontaneous response of most sentient creatures—including men and dogs—to what is strange and unfamiliar. We are always keenly conscious of whatever in our experience is novel and undefined, and we are invariably interested in other creatures like ourselves, especially if they are at the same time different. Man is notoriously the most unstable and unpredictable element in the environment. Nature, physical nature, is changing and moody; but behind those brooding human faces that men wear, and particularly behind those faces that we do not know, who can tell what things are going on?

On the whole, we may define the situation in which races meet, as one of vague apprehension tinged with and qualified by curiosity. The first effect is to provoke in us a state of tension—a more vivid awareness and readiness to act—and with that a certain amount of reserve and self-consciousness which is incident to every effort at self-control. In all this there is so far neither prejudice nor antipathy, but merely expectancy. The strange new creature may prove to be attractive, even fascinating. The reports of the first meetings of primitive peoples with Europeans are instructive on this point. The first Europeans to reach Mexico were received ceremonially and regarded as superior beings.

On the other hand, if we seek to get at the very core of this so-called instinctive element in race prejudice, it seems to have its locus just here. If the strange creature approach too suddenly, or if on further acquaintance he seems to behave in outlandish and incalculable ways, we may retain our interest, but we maintain our distance. In that case, anything approaching intimacy may leave us with a vague sense of insecurity and malaise which effectually limits intercourse and understanding.

It is in such situations, I suspect, that those antipathies arise which seem to constitute the most irrational, and at the same time the most invincible, elements in racial prejudice. The sense of insecurity which the presence of the stranger inspires, when not dispelled by more intimate acquaintance, crystallizes into an attitude. Sentiments grow about it which give it substance and support. The racial mark becomes a symbol of these sentiments, the core of which is a sense of insecurity. We do not know what, under certain circumstances, a creature so unlike ourselves will do. Even after a prolonged and rather intimate acquaintance with an individual of another race, there usually remains a residue of uncertainty and vague apprehension, particularly if the stranger maintains a reserve that we cannot fully penetrate. Under such circumstances it is inevitable that rumors and legends will arise and gain general currency which purport to describe and explain racial differences, but in fact serve merely to give support to apprehensions and vague terrors for which there is no real ground in fact. Anything that tends to make a mystery of divergent and alien races, even biological theories which suggest remote and ill-defined dangers of contact and intimacy, tends to intensify antipathies and lend support to racial prejudices. For racial differences in which we are ultimately interested are not the obviously physical and biological marks by which one race is distinguished from another, but the less obvious mental and moral traits of which these physical characters are assumed to be an index and a symbol. The more obvious the differences in physical traits, the greater the presumption of fundamentally divergent moral characteristics.

## Antipathies

Racial antipathies are intensified by anything which arouses disgust. For this reason we tend to contract many of our racial antipathies, so to speak, through the nose. Some writers have gone so far as to suppose that the sense of smell is, in some subtle way, a guide to moral differences in individuals.[3] At any rate, it seems to be a fact that races and individuals have each a distinctive smell, and this odor becomes, in certain cases, the sensuous basis for racial antipathies. The Hindi, for example, who are so meticulous about their contacts with aliens, as well as with members of the different castes of their own people, profess a special abhorrence to the smell of the Anglo-Saxon. A few years ago a Hindu acquaintance of mine, in explaining the opposition of his family to his marriage to an American woman, confessed that his father

[3]    W. H. Hudson, *A Hind in Richmond Park* (New York, 1923), pp. 77 ff.

had written him saying he hoped, if no other considerations were sufficient, that the smell of an Anglo-Saxon would be sufficient to prohibit such a misalliance. W. H. Hudson, in his volume "A Hind in Richmond Park," discussing the sense of smell in animals, devotes a chapter to the explanation of the fact that those who have a nose for these things are sensitive to the smell of other races, but quite oblivious to the odor of their own. He relates an incident, by way of illustration, which I quote in his own words:

Many and curious are the tricks our olfactories play us. . . . A young army doctor in India and at Bombay zealously set himself to win a good private practice. He made himself well known in the society of the place, and his servant had strict instructions to come always into the church where he attended Sunday morning service to call him out to a supposed urgent case.

The natives just then were in a state of political excitement, and he was desirous of finding out all he could about their aspirations, intentions, and so on. One day he told his servant that he wished to attend a big meeting about to be held in a quarter of the town he was not well acquainted with, to listen to the speeches of the orators, and he asked his man to take him there and get him admitted. Accordingly they went on an oppressively hot evening, and he sat in a huge densely-packed hall for about half an hour, then came out. After taking a few deep breaths he exclaimed: "What a relief to get out! In another ten minutes I should have collapsed. The smell!"

To which his servant promptly replied: "Ah, Sahib, *now* you will understand what I suffer every Sunday when I have to go right to the middle of the church to call you out! . . ."

The extraordinary readiness, the candour, the spontaneity, and even the glee, with which he brought out his words made it impossible for his master to doubt his perfect sincerity. He had taken it for granted that his master *would* understand, and after his own unhappy experience at the native meeting would be ready to sympathise with his servant's sufferings in the performance of that painful Sunday duty. . . . And what did it mean? Why, that we white-skinned Westerns, lords of creation, have our smell just as the blacks and bi-colored races and the lower animals have theirs; that we are unconscious of this fact with regard to ourselves—our own race—but are quite conscious of it with regard to the others.[4]

[4]     *Ibid.*, pp. 76–77.

It is because smell is so definitely associated with the organic reactions that it is the least intellectual of the senses. For the same reason, no doubt, it is so intimately related to the antipathies and the sentiments generally. At any rate, racial antipathies are frequently concerned with touch and smell. If these antipathies have, as many persons contend, a biological significance, it is because they seem to inhibit intimate and ultimately sexual contacts. They are a bar to miscegenation. There seems to be just as good reason for adopting, as some writers do, the opposite view. It is the strange woman who is sexually the more stimulating; and it is the man from abroad to whom the most romantic interest attaches. This is one explanation of exogamy.

The facts seem to indicate that racial antipathies and tabus have a conventional rather than a natural and instinctive origin. The man who arrives with a strange new, pungent odor may arouse digust, but he may, under other circumstances, evoke a sentiment of awe and respect. We are most of us familiar with the odor of sanctity that attaches to saints and sacred edifices. It seems, therefore, that antipathy and prestige may, and perhaps often do, rest on the same sensuous basis. To a Hindu, the mere thought of eating meat is disgusting. The Japanese are shocked to see men and women embrace in public. Whether a stranger entering an unfamiliar society will be treated with consideration or contempt, is apparently uncertain, except in so far as the situation is controlled by ceremonial and etiquette. It is notorious that representatives of every race and color have been received at one time and another in the most select and intimate circles. Marco Polo was received with distinction at the court of Kubla Kahn, and Booker T. Washington dined with President Roosevelt at the White House. It seems as if there are no instinctive racial antipathies that cannot be overcome by scrupulous adherence to etiquette.

## Ceremonial and Social Ritual

While etiquette and ceremonial are at once a convenience and a necessity in facilitating human intercourse, they serve even more effectively to maintain social distances and to preserve the rank and order of individuals and classes, which seems to be essential to social organization and effective collective action. This is the significance of the ceremonial and social ritual so rigidly enforced in the South, by which racial distinctions are preserved amid all the inevitable changes and promiscuity of an expanding industrial and democratic society. Thus white folk and colored, in the small town at any rate, eat at the same restaurant, if it is conducted by a Negro, but not at the same tables.

A colored nurse may ride, without objection, in a Pullman coach if she has a white baby in her arms. On the other hand, if a white nurse should appear in the same car with a colored baby, no one knows what would happen. There is no provision in the social ritual for the unprecedented.

Southern people have difficulty in addressing a colored man as "Mr.," even though he may have achieved an eminent position in the world. In that case it is possible to avoid the difficulty, as one man is reported to have done in the case of Booker Washington, by calling him "Professor." A distinguished clergyman in the Southern Episcopal Church, after some mental conflict, announced a few years ago that he had resolved that thenceforth when a colored woman was decently married, to address her as "Mrs.," "out of respect," as he explained, "for the holy estate of matrimony."

On the other hand, in a little Negro town in Oklahoma, Boley, where at the time no separate provision was made for white visitors, a traveling salesman appealed to the Negro hotel keeper to give him a table apart, because, as he said, with a certain amount of pathos in his voice, "I am from Mississippi, and I just can't eat with you niggers."

These are illustrations of what Ogburn calls "cultural lag." The situation changes, but the cultural form persists.

There exists in the South, and in the North too, for that matter, a great body of materials which no student of race problems has, so far as I know, seen fit or found time to collect and interpret. These are the legends, anecdotes, and racial myths current in the South in which each race, in perfect good faith, and often with very real insight, has characterized the follies and foibles, and occasionally the more excellent qualities, of the other. These materials, because they do not get into print, are a kind of folklore, a form of verbal literature which passes sometimes for history, and sometimes for scientific fact. In this as in every other form of literature, the wishes—and particularly the conflicting wishes— of the two races are unconsciously reflected. As might be expected, the stories which circulate among white people concerning Negroes tend to support the traditional social order, which assigns every Negro to a position inferior to that of every white man. On the other hand, the stories which circulate among Negroes are those which show that the old order is cracking or exhibit the traditional racial distinctions in some paradoxical or logically untenable and ridiculous form.

For example, a white farmer in Alabama, one of the so-called "poor whites," became greatly interested in the farm demonstration work which a colored agent was carrying on among the Negroes. The white man invited the colored agent to come over and look at his place and advise him about his crops. Eventually he invited him to stay to dinner. He arranged the matter simply. The colored man sat at one table, and the white man at another, close enough to continue their discussions. The white man's wife waited upon them both. This was merely reversing the situation in which a white man visits a Negro planter and perhaps remains all night. In that case the white man eats in the dining room, and the colored man more than likely eats in the kitchen. In both cases the social amenities are served, and what amounts, in these cases, to caste distinctions are preserved. They are part of the etiquette which makes intercourse and cooperation among the races in the South possible.

## Change in Race Relations

Originally race relations in the South could be rather accurately represented by a horizontal line, with all the white folk above, and all the Negro folk below. But at present these relations are assuming new forms, and in consequence changing in character and meaning. With the development of industrial and professional classes within the Negro race, the distinction between the races tends to assume the form of a vertical line. On one side of this line the Negro is represented in most of the occupational and professional classes; on the other side of the line the white man is similarly represented. The situation *was* this:

All white

---

All colored

It is *now* this:

| *White* | *Colored* |
|---|---|
| Professional occupation | Professional occupation |
| Business occupation | Business occupation |
| Labor | Labor |

The result is to develop in every occupational class professional and industrial bi-racial organizations. Bi-racial organizations preserve race distinction, but change their content. The distances which separate the races are maintained, but the attitudes involved are different. The races no longer look up and down: they look across. These bi-racial organizations, so far as I know, are a unique product of the racial struggle in this country; they do not exist outside the United States.

# HUMAN NATURE AND
# COLLECTIVE BEHAVIOR

RECENT ATTEMPTS to apply to the study of human conduct the methods of investigation first employed in the study of animal behavior have profoundly influenced the point of view not merely of psychology, but of social psychology and of sociology. Psychology, in becoming objective—that is to say, behavioristic—has emphasized what it calls overt response. Incidentally, consciousness either has been dismissed from any consideration whatever or has been relegated to the position of an incident in a cycle of events which begins with the physiological reflexes and terminates in an act; what Thurstone calls "the psychological act."[1]

What the students of animal behavior actually have done in their laboratories is to put animals under test conditions and then incite them to appropriate action. The mouse, in a maze, tries to find its way out. The lowly earthworm, which, as reported in a local newspaper, a Harvard professor sought to educate, was incited by hunger and the proximity of food to find the easiest and the least painful way of getting it. Under these circumstances the animal responded in every case, not to a single stimulus, but to a situation; and the response was not that of a single reflex or instinct, but that of the organism as a whole. In other words, the response which the situation called forth was not a reaction, if

---

Reprinted from *American Journal of Sociology*, 32 (March, 1927) : 733–41. The article had previously appeared in *Zeitschrift für Völkersychologie*, September, 1926.

[1]    L. L. Thurstone, *The Nature of Intelligence* (New York, 1924).

we may be permitted to make a distinction, but an act. A reaction presupposes the existence of a reflex, habit, conditioned reflex, or pattern, in which the response to a stimulus is predetermined. But an act implies, relatively speaking, new adjustment, co-ordination, and integration of the existing physiological mechanism.

The thing which distinguishes an organism from a mere aggregation of individuals, or of parts, is the capacity for concerted action—the disposition of the parts, under certain conditions, to act as a unit. The structure of an organism, inherited or acquired, serves to facilitate this concerted action. This is as true of a social as of a biological organism. The fundamental differences between organisms, the character which permits us to arrange them in a progressive series, are the different degrees to which the different parts of which they are composed have been integrated and organized for the purpose of corporate action. What constitutes the organism, then, as distinguished from the mere assemblage of its parts, is, according to Child, an action-pattern, which controls and co-ordinates the reaction of the parts so as to give to the behavior of the organism the character which I have described as an act.

We speak of organisms as individuals, meaning that each organism represents a more or less definite and discrete order and unity; in other words, a pattern, which not only determines its structure and the relations of its parts to each other, but enables it to act as a whole with respect to the world about it. . . . Organismic behavior is, then, the behavior of the organism as a whole as distinguished from the behavior of single parts. . . . On the other hand the integration of behavior is not limited by the individual organism. Organisms may be integrated into social groups of various sorts and orders of magnitude, and in such groups the behavior of the constituent individuals is more or less integrated into the social behavior of the group.[2]

On the whole, the social group behaves like an organism, and the differences between groups may be described in terms of the action-pattern which determines the behavior of each. The fundamental difference between a city and a village, from the point of view of sociology, is not the mere size of the aggregates or the num-

[2]    Charles M. Child, *Physiological Foundations of Behavior* (New York, 1924).

ber of individuals of which they are composed, but the degree to which these different aggregates have been integrated and organized for concerted action. This suggests that in a study of the social group, as of the biological organism, the point of departure is, properly, not structure, but activity. The thing that gives a community the character of a society is not its structure, but its capacity for concerted action.

The capacity for corporate action is, to be sure, facilitated by structure, but is not dependent upon it. The crowd becomes a society, not by the mere fact that a group of persons are gathered together at a given moment and in a particular spot, but by the fact that this aggregation of individuals is capable of action. Action may take place in the crowd with a minimum of organization or with no organization at all, except what has been called by Le Bon "psychological organization."

Action is first; but the effect of action is to create an action pattern. This action pattern, as may be observed in the crowd, is frequently extremely fragile and ephemeral, and may exist without any clearly defined organization. Permanence of the action pattern, however, is dependent upon the existence of structure, upon a division of labor, and upon some degree of specialization in the individuals who compose the group. When the role of the individuals in the action of the group has become fixed in habit, and particularly when the role of different individuals and their special functions have become recognized in custom and tradition, the social organization gains a new stability and permanence which permits it to be transmitted to succeeding generations. In this way the life of the community and of society may be prolonged beyond the lives of the individuals who compose it.

Institutions and social structures of every sort may be regarded as products of collective action. War, famine, revolution, the struggle against an external enemy and against internal disorganization —any of the ordinary exigencies of communal and collective life which call for collective action—may set a social pattern which repetition fixes in habits, and which eventually become institutionalized in customs and traditions.

Looked at from the point of the individual organism or the individual member of a community, this functioning of the social group and this evolution of society and of institutions presents itself as a response, an accommodation, and eventually a biological adaptation of the individual to habitat; a physical environment and a social milieu. In this habitat the individual becomes, in the course of time, a person, and perhaps a citizen.

The same forces which co-operate to create the characteristic social organization and the accepted moral order of a given society or social group determine at the same time, to a greater or lesser extent, the character of the individuals who compose that society. The individual inherits from his forbears and from a long series of his animal ancestors the potentialities which are realized in specific characters in the course of his association—particularly during childhood and adolescence—with his fellows. The extent to which these potentialities are actually realized and the specific forms which they eventually take is determined, not merely by the general conditions which every society and every social milieu imposes upon its members, but rather more by the extent to which, in any given society, a division of labor has been achieved. It is the division of labor, quite as much as anything else, which determines the degree to which the individual is depedent upon, and incorporated in, the social organization of which he is a member.

Adam Smith long ago recognized that the most striking differences between individuals are due to the division of labor. It is not that these differences were not implicit in the individuals themselves, existing there as potentialities, but it is the division of labor and the discipline imposed by society upon its members that has developed them.

The difference of natural talents in different men is, in reality, much less than we are aware of; and the very different genius which appears to distinguish men of different professions, when grown up to maturity, is not upon many occasions so much the cause, as the effect, of the division of labor. The difference between the most dissimlar characters, between a philosopher and a common street porter, for example, seems to arise not so much from nature, as from habit, custom, and education. When they came into the world, and for the first six or eight years of their existence, they were perhaps very much alike, and neither their parents nor playfellows could perceive any remarkable difference. About that age, or soon after, they come to be employed in different occupations. The difference of talents comes then to be taken notice of, and widens by degrees, till at last the vanity of the philosopher is willing to acknowledge scarce any resemblance. But without the disposition to truck, barter, and exchange, every man must have procured to himself every necessary and conveniency of life which he wanted. All must have had the same duties to perform, and the same work to do, and there could have been no such difference of employment as could alone give occasion to any great difference of talent. . . .

As it is the power of exchanging that gives occasion to the division of labor, so the extent of this division must always be limited by the extent of that power, or, in other words, by the extent of the market. . . . There are some sorts of industry, even of the lowest kind, which can be carried on nowhere but in a great town.[3]

It is not, however, a division of labor, but the fact of social control that characterizes human society. It is not, in other words, the unconscious competition and co-operation of individual men and women within the limits of a human habitat that has impressed upon human nature and human society their most distinctive traits. It is rather the conscious participation in a common purpose and a common life, rendered possible by the fact of speech and by the existence of a fund of common symbols and meanings. The lower animals have neither words nor symbols; nothing, for them, has what we may describe as meaning. The lower animals have, in the words of Durkheim, no "collective representations." They do not organize processions and carrry banners; they sing, and sometimes, we are told, even dance, but they do not celebrate; they acquire habits which are sometimes transmitted as a kind of social tradition, but they have no customs, and for them nothing is either sacred or lawful. Above all, the animals are natural and naïve, and not concerned, as human beings are, about their reputations and their conduct. They are not tortured by moral scruples. "They do not," as Walt Whitman has put it, "sweat and whine about their condi-

[3]    Adam Smith, *An Iquiry into the Nature and Causes of the Wealth of Nations*, B.I, chap. 2.

tion. They do not lie awake in the dark and weep for their sins."
And "over the whole earth there is not one that is respectable or
unhappy."

But it is just this sort of behavior—which makes Walt Whitman, as he says, "sick," so that he thinks he could turn and live
with the animals, "they are so placid and self-contained"—that is
most characteristic of human nature and human behavior. For
man is a creature such that when he lives at all, he lives in his
imagination, and, through his imagination, in the minds of other
men, who share with him not merely their possessions, but their
hopes and their dreams. By suggestion, by imitation, by expressions of sympathy and antipathy, men invade one another's lives
and participate one with another in their efforts to direct, control,
and give expression to their own conflicting impulses.

In human society every act of every individual tends to become
a gesture, since what one does is always an indication of what one
intends to do. The consequence is that the individual in society
lives a more or less public existence, in which all his acts are antici-
pated, checked, inhibited, or modified by the gestures and the intentions of his fellows. It is in this social conflict, in which every
individual lives more or less in the mind of every other individual,
that human nature and the individual may acquire their most
characteristic and human traits.

It is probably no mere historical accident, as I have said elsewhere, that the word "person," in its first meaning, is a mask. It is
rather a recognition of the fact that everyone is always and everywhere, more or less consciously, playing a role. We are parents
and children, masters and servants, teachers and students,
clients and professional men, Gentiles and Jews. It is in these
roles that we know each other; it is in these roles that we know
ourselves.[4]

One thing that distinguishes man from the lower animals is the
fact that he has a conception of himself, and once he has defined
his role he strives to live up to it. He not only acts, but he dresses
the part, assumes quite spontaneously all the manners and attitudes that he conceives as proper to it. Often enough it happens

[4]   Robert E. Park, "Behind Our Masks," *Survey Graphic*, May, 1926,
pp. 135–39.

that he is not fitted to the role which he chooses to play. In any case, it is an effort for any of us to maintain the attitudes which we assume; all the more difficult when the world refuses to take us at our own estimates of ourselves. Being actors, we are consciously or unconsciously seeking recognition, and failure to win it is, at the very least, a depressing, often a heartbreaking, experience. This is one of the reasons why we all eventually conform to the accepted models and conceive ourselves in some one or other of the conventional patterns.

The consequence of this, however, is that we inevitably lead a dual existence. We have a private and a public life. In seeking to live up to the role which we have assumed, and which society has imposed upon us, we find ourselves in constant conflict with ourselves. Instead of acting simply and naturally, as a child, responding to each natural impulse as it arises, we seek to conform to accepted models, and conceive ourselves in some one of the conventional and socially accepted patterns. In our efforts to conform, we restrain our immediate and spontaneous impulses, and act, not as we are impelled to act, but rather as seems appropriate and proper to the occasion.

Under these circumstances our manners, our polite speeches and gestures, our conventional and proper behavior, assume the character of a mask. Our very faces are living masks, which reflect, to be sure, the changing emotions of our inner lives, but which more and more tend to conform to the type we are seeking to impersonate. Not only every race, but every nationality has its characteristic "face," its conventional mask. As Emerson points out in his *English Traits,* "every religious sect has its physiognomy. The Methodists have acquired a face, the Quakers a face, the nuns a face. An Englishman will point out a dissenter by his manner. Trades and professions carve their own lines on faces and forms."

In a sense, and in so far as this mask represents the conception which we have formed of ourselves, the role which we are striving to live up to, this mask is our "truer self," the self we should like to be. So, at any rate, our mask becomes at last an integral part of our personality; becomes second nature. We come into the world as individuals, achieve character, and become persons.

Human behavior, so far as it can be distinguished from that of the lower animals, is conscious and conventional; socially controlled, in short. Behavior that is controlled in this way we may call conduct; that is to say, behavior morally sanctioned and subjectively conditioned. This subjectivity, so characteristic of human nature, is at once a condition and a product of collective life. So far as it is subjective it cannot be adequately described as the stricter sect of behaviorists insist it should be, in physiological terms; but so far as it is social it cannot be described in terms of individual behavior, and for this reason psychology, so far as it deals with persons and personality, inevitably becomes social psychology. The motives which compel men to commit suicide, to write poetry, and to go to war are frequently the outcome of long and painful conflict. The acts in which they terminate have, therefore, an antecedent history, and it is necessary to know this history to understand the acts. This is true of most overt acts, as it is of individual opinion, religious creeds, and political doctrines. Opinions, creeds, and doctrines become intelligible to us only when we know their history; when we know, in other words, the experiences out of which they have sprung. The reason why history and biography exist is not merely to record overt acts, but to make them intelligible.

No only is it true that we all participate directly or indirectly in making up the minds and determining the overt acts of our fellows, but the craving for this participation in a common life—the desire for sympathy, recognition, understanding, for example—is one of the most fundamental traits of human nature. Just as history is, to a very large extent, the record of the struggles of nations and peoples for prestige and status in an international society, so the humbler, more garrulous, and provincial chronicle of the local newspaper is largely a record of the conflicts of individual men and women in seeking to find a place and a position in some tribe, clan, neighborhood, or household.

It is because human actions must be interpreted in order to make them intelligible that documents—human documents—are more important for the study of human nature than statistics or formal facts. The documents are valuable, therefore, not merely because they describe events, but because they throw light upon motives; that is to say, upon the subjective aspects of events and acts in which human nature manifests itself. Not merely events, but institutions as well become intelligible when we know their histories, and particularly when we know the individual experiences of men and women in which they had their origin and on which they finally rest.

The most significant document, of course, is the one that is most expressive and revealing, and this, on the whole, has been the life-history, using that term in the sense in which Thomas and Znaniecki have defined it in their monumental study, *The Polish Peasant in Europe and America.*[5]

If it is not practical or desirable to confine our investigations of human nature to the overt response, as the behaviorists define that term, the attempt to study human nature objectively has, at any rate, done sociology and social psychology a good turn in so far as it has directed attention to the psychological act rather than to the physiological reaction as a unit of investigation and analysis. For society, as well as mental life, has come into existence not merely in the efforts of individuals to act, but in their efforts to act collectively.

From this point of view the moral struggles of individual men and women and the political conflicts of nations turn out to be merely incidents in the processes by which society and social groups integrate and organize the individual units of which they are composed and mobilized them for collective action. Furthermore, just as the individual person may in some sense be conceived as the product of individual acts, so social institutions may be regarded as the product of collective actions. Just as custom in the group may be regarded as the objective aspect of habit in the individual, so morality in the individual may be construed as the subjective aspect of organization and morale in the group.

[5] W. I. Thomas and Florian Znaniecki, *The Polish Peasant in Europe and America: Monograph of an Immigrant Group,* 5 vols. (Boston, 1918).

# HUMAN MIGRATION AND THE
# MARGINAL MAN

STUDENTS of the great society, looking at mankind in the long perspective of history, have frequently been disposed to seek an explanation of existing cultural differences among races and peoples in some single dominating cause or condition. One school of thought, represented most conspicuously by Montesquieu, has found that explanation in climate and in the physical environment. Another school, identified with the name of Arthur de Gobineau, author of *The Inequality of Human Races,* has sought an explanation of divergent cultures in the innate qualities of races biologically inherited. These two theories have this in common, namely, that they both conceive civilization and society to be the result of evolutionary processes—processes by which man has acquired new inheritable traits—rather than processes by which new relations have been established between men.

In contrast to both of these, Frederick Teggart has recently restated and amplified what may be called the catastrophic theory of civilization, a theory that goes back to Hume in England, and to Turgot in France. From this point of view, climate and innate racial traits, important as they may have been in the evolution of races, have been of only minor influence in creating existing cultural differences. In fact, races and cultures, so far from being in any sense identical—or even the product of similar conditions and forces—are perhaps to be set over against one another as contrast

Reprinted from *American Journal of Sociology,* 33 (May, 1928): pp. 881–93.

effects, the results of antagonistic tendencies, so that civilization may be said to flourish at the expense of racial differences rather than to be conserved by them. At any rate, if it is true that races are the products of isolation and inbreeding, it is just as certain that civilization, on the other hand, is a consequence of contact and communication. The forces which have been decisive in the history of mankind are those which have brought men together in fruitful competition, conflict, and co-operation.

Among the most important of these influences have been— according to what I have called the catastrophic theory of progress —migration and the incidental collisions, conflicts, and fusions of people and cultures which they have occasioned.

"Every advance in culture," says Bücher, in his *Industrial Evolution,* "commences, so to speak, with a new period of wandering," and in support of this thesis he points out that the earlier forms of trade were migratory, that the first industries to free themselves from the household husbandry and become independent occupations were carried on itinerantly. "The great founders of religion, the earliest poets and philosophers, the musicians and actors of past epochs, are all great wanderers. Even today, do not the inventor, the preacher of a new doctrine, and the virtuoso travel from place to place in search of adherents and admirers—notwithstanding the immense recent development in means of communicating information?"[1]

The influences of migrations have not been limited, of course, by the changes which they have effected in existing cultures. In the long run, they have determined the racial characteristics of historical peoples. "The whole teaching of ethnology," as Griffith Taylor remarks, "shows that peoples of mixed race are the rule and not the exception."[2] Every nation, upon examination, turns out to have been a more or less successful melting-pot. To this constant sifting of races and peoples, human geographers have given the title "the historical movement," because, as Miss Semple says

[1]    Carl Bücher, *Industrial Evolution*, p. 347.
[2]    Griffith Taylor, *Environment and Race: A Study of the Evolution, Migration, Settlement, and Status of the Races of Men*, p. 336.

in her volume *Influences of Geographic Environment,* "it underlies most written history and constitutes the major part of unwritten history, especially that of savage and nomadic tribes."[3]

Changes in race, it is true, do inevitably follow, at some distance, changes in culture. The movements and mingling of peoples which bring rapid, sudden, and often catastrophic, changes in customs and habits are followed, in the course of time, as a result of interbreeding, by corresponding modifications in temperament and physique. There has probably never been an instance where races have lived together in the intimate contacts which a common economy enforces in which racial contiguity has not produced racial hybrids. However, changes in racial characteristics and in cultural traits proceed at very different rates, and it is notorious that cultural changes are not consolidated and transmitted biologically, or at least to only a very slight extent, if at all. Acquired characteristics are not biologically inherited.

Writers who emphasize the importance of migration as an agency of progress are invariably led to ascribe a similar role to war. Thus Waitz, commenting upon the role of migration as an agency of civilization, points out that migrations are "rarely of a peaceful nature at first." Of war he says: "The first consequence of war is that fixed relations are established between peoples, which render friendly intercourse possible, an intercourse which becomes more important from the interchange of knowledge and experience than from the mere interchange of commodities."[4] And then he adds:

Whenever we see a people, of whatever degree of civilization, not living in contact and reciprocal action with others, we shall generally find a certain stagnation, a mental inertness, and a want of activity, which render any change of social and political condition next to impossible. These are, in times of peace, transmitted like an everlasting disease, and war appears then, in spite of what the apostles

---

[3]   Ellen Churchill Semple, *Influences of Geographic Evironment,* p. 75.
[4]   Theodore Waitz, *Introduction to Anthropology,* p. 347.

of peace may say, as a saving angel, who rouses the national spirit, and renders all forces more elastic.[5]

Among the writers who conceive the historical process in terms of intrusions, either peaceful or hostile, of one people into the domain of another, must be reckoned such sociologists as Gumplowicz and Oppenheim. The former, in an effort to define the social process abstractly, has described it as the interaction of heterogeneous ethnic groups, the resulting subordination and superordination of races constituting the social order—society, in fact.

In much the same way, Oppenheim, in his study of the sociological origin of the state, believes he has shown that in every instance the state has had its historical beginnings in the imposition, by conquest and force, of the authority of a nomadic upon a sedentary and agricultural people. The facts which Oppenheim has gathered to sustain his thesis show, at any rate, that social institutions have actually, in many instances at least, come into existence abruptly by a mutation, rather than by a process of evolutionary selection and the gradual accumulation of relatively slight variations.[6]

It is not at once apparent why a theory which insists upon the importance of catastrophic change in the evolution of civilization should not at the same time take some account of revolution as a factor in progress. If peace and stagnation, as Waitz suggests, tend to assume the form of social disease; if, as Sumner says, "society needs to have some ferment in it" to break up this stagnation and emancipate the energies of individuals imprisoned within an existing social order; it seems that some "adventurous folly" like the crusades of the middle ages, or some romantic enthusiasm like that which found expression in the French Revolution, or in the more recent Bolshevist adventure in Russia, might serve quite as effectively as either migration or war to interrupt the routine of existing habit and break the cake of custom. Revolutionary doc-

5     *Ibid.*, p. 348.
6     Franz Oppenheim, *The State: Its History and Development Viewed Sociologically* (1914).

trines are naturally based upon a conception of catastrophic rather than of evolutionary change. Revolutionary strategy, as it has been worked out and rationalized in Sorel's *Reflections on Violence,* makes the great catastrophe, the general strike, an article of faith. As such it becomes a means of maintaining morale and enforcing discipline in the revolutionary masses.[7]

The first and most obvious difference between revolution and migration is that in migration the breakdown of social order is initiated by the impact of an invading population, and completed by the contact and fusion of native with alien peoples. In the case of the former, revolutionary ferment and the forces which have disrupted society have ordinarily had, or seem to have had, their sources and origins mainly if not wholly within, rather than without, the society affected. It is doubtful whether it can be successfully maintained that every revolution, every *Aufklärung,* every intellectual awakening and renaissance has been and will be provoked by some invading population movement or by the intrusion of some alien cultural agency. At least it seems as if some modification of this view is necessary, since with the growth of commerce and communication there is progressively and relatively more movement and less migration. Commerce, in bringing the ends of the earth together, has made travel relatively secure. Moreover, with the development of machine industry and the growth of cities, it is the commodities rather than men which circulate. The peddler, who carries his stock on his back, gives way to the traveling salesman, and the catalog of the mail order house now reaches remote regions which even the Yankee peddler rarely if ever penetrated. With the development of a world-economy and the interpenetration of peoples, migrations, as Bücher has pointed out, have changed their character:

The migrations occurring at the opening of the history of European peoples are migrations of whole tribes, a pushing and pressing of collective units from east to west which lasted for centuries. The migrations of the Middle Ages ever affect individual classes alone; the knights in the crusades, the merchants, the wage craftsmen, the jour-

[7]     Georges Sorel, *Reflections on Violence* (New York, 1914).

neymen hand-workers, the jugglers and minstrels, the villeins seeking protection within the walls of a town. Modern migrations, on the contrary, are generally a matter of private concern, the individuals being led by the most varied motives. They are almost invariably without organization. The process repeating itself daily a thousand times is united only through the one characteristic, that it is everywhere a question of change of locality by persons seeking more favourable conditions of life.[8]

Migration, which was formerly an invasion, followed by the forcible displacement or subjugation of one people by another, has assumed the character of a peaceful penetration. Migration of peoples has, in other words, been transmuted into mobility of individuals, and the wars which these movements so frequently occasioned have assumed the character of internecine struggles, of which strikes and revolutions are to be regarded as types.

Furthermore, if one were to attempt to reckon with all the forms in which catastrophic changes take place, it would be necessary to include the changes that are effected by the sudden rise of some new religious movement like Mohammedanism or Christianity, both of which began as schismatic and sectarian movements, and which by extension and internal evolution have become independent religions. Looked at from this point of view, migration assumes a character less unique and exceptional than has hitherto been conceived by the writers whom the problem has most intrigued. It appears as one, merely, of a series of forms in which historic changes may take place. Nevertheless, regarded abstractly as a type of collective action, human migration exhibits everywhere characteristics that are sufficiently typical to make it a subject of independent investigation and study, both in respect to its form and in respect to the effects which it produces.

Migration is not, however, to be identified with mere movement. It involves, at the very least, change of residence and the breaking of home ties. The movements of gypsies and other pariah peoples, because they bring about no important changes in cultural life, are to be regarded rather as a geographical fact than a

[8]   Carl Bücher, *Industrial Evolution*, p. 349.

social phenomenon. Nomadic life is stabilized on the basis of movement, and even though gypsies now travel by automobile, they still maintain, comparatively unchanged, their ancient tribal organization and customs. The result is that their relation to the communities in which they may at any time be found is to be described as symbiotic rather than social. This tends to be true of any section or class of the population—the hobos, for example, and the hotel dwellers—which is unsettled and mobile.

Migration as a social phenomenon must be studied not merely in its grosser effects, as manifested in changes in custom and in the mores, but it may be envisaged in its subjective aspects as manifested in the changed type of personality which it produces. When the traditional organization of society breaks down, as a result of contact and collision with a new invading culture, the effect is, so to speak, to emancipate the individual man. Energies that were formerly controlled by custom and tradition are released. The individual is free for new adventures, but he is more or less without direction and control. Teggart's statement of the matter is as follows:

As a result of the breakdown of customary modes of action and of thought, the individual experiences a "release" from the restraints and constraints to which he has been subject, and gives evidence of this "release" in aggressive self-assertion. The overexpression of individuality is one of the marked features of all epochs of change. On the other hand, the study of the psychological effects of collision and contact between different groups reveals the fact that the most important aspect of "release" lies not in freeing the soldier, warrior, or berserker from the restraint of conventional modes of action, but in freeing the individual judgment from the inhibitions of conventional modes of thought. It will thus be seen (he adds) that the study of the *modus operandi* of change in time gives a common focus to the efforts of political historians, of the historians of literature and of ideas, of psychologists, and of students of ethics and the theory of education.[9]

Social changes, according to Teggart, have their inception in events which "release" the individuals out of which society is composed. Inevitably, however, this release is followed in the course

[9]　Frederick J. Teggert, *Theory of History*, p. 196.

of time by the reintegration of the individuals so released into a new social order. In the meantime, however, certain changes take place—at any rate they are likely to take place—in the character of the individuals themselves. They become, in the process, not merely emancipated, but enlightened.

The emancipated individual invariably becomes in a certain sense and to a certain degree a cosmopolitan. He learns to look upon the world in which he was born and bred with something of the detachment of a stranger. He acquires, in short, an intellectual bias. Simmel has described the position of the stranger in the community, and his personality, in terms of movement and migration.

"If wandering," he says, "considered as the liberation from every given point in space, is the conceptual opposite of fixation at any point, then surely the sociological form of the stranger presents the union of both of these specifications." The stranger stays, but he is not settled. He is a potential wanderer. That means that he is not bound as others are by the local proprieties and conventions. "He is the freer man, practically and theoretically. He views his relation to others with less prejudice; he submits them to more general, more objective standards, and he is not confined in his action by custom, piety or precedents."

The effect of mobility and migration is to secularize relations which were formerly sacred. One may describe the process, in its dual aspect, perhaps, as the secularization of society and the individuation of the person. For a brief, vivid, and authentic picture of the way in which migration of the earlier sort, the migration of a people, has, in fact, brought about the destruction of an earlier civilization and liberated the peoples involved for the creation of a later, more secular, and freer society, I suggest Gilbert Murray's introduction to *The Rise of the Greek Epic*, in which he seeks to reproduce the events of the Nordic invasion of the Aegean area.

What ensued, he says, was a period of chaos:

A chaos in which an old civilization is shattered into fragments, its laws set at naught, and that intricate web of normal expectation which forms the very essence of human society torn so often and so utterly by continued disappointment that at last there ceases to be any normal expectation at all. For the fugitive settlers on the shores that were afterwards Ionia, and for parts too of Doris and Aeolis, there were no tribal gods or tribal obligations left, because there were no tribes. There were no old laws, because there was no one to administer or even to remember them; only such compulsions as the strongest power of the moment chose to enforce. Household and family life had disappeared, and all its innumerable ties with it. A man was now not living with a wife of his own race, but with a dangerous strange woman, of alien language and alien gods, a woman whose husband or father he had perhaps murdered—or, at best, whom he had bought as a slave from the murderer. The old Aryan husbandman, as we shall see hereafter, had lived with his herds in a sort of familiar connexion. He slew "his brother the ox" only under special stress or for definite religious reasons, and he expected his women to weep when the slaying was performed. But now he had left his own herds far away. They had been devoured by enemies. And he lived on the beasts of strangers whom he robbed or held in servitude. He had left the graves of his fathers, the kindly ghosts of his own blood, who took food from his hand and loved him. He was surrounded by the graves of alien dead, strange ghosts whose names he knew not, and who were beyond his power to control, whom he tried his best to placate with fear and aversion. One only concrete thing existed for him to make henceforth the centre of his allegiance, to supply the place of his old family hearth, his gods, his tribal customs and sanctities. It was a circuit wall of stones, a *Polis*; the wall which he and his fellows, men of diverse tongues and worships united by a tremendous need, had built up to be the one barrier between themselves and a world of enemies.[10]

It was within the walls of the *polis* and in this mixed company that Greek civilization was born. The whole secret of ancient Greek life, its relative freedom from the grosser superstitions and from fear of the gods, is bound up, we are told, with this period of transition and chaos, in which the older primitive world perished and from which the freer, more enlightened social order sprang into existence. Thought is emancipated, philosophy is born, public opinion sets itself up as an authority as over against tradition and custom. As Guyot puts it, "The Greek with his festivals, his songs, his poetry, seems to celebrate, in a perpetual hymn, the liberation of man from the mighty fetters of nature."[11]

[10]    Gilbert Murray, *The Rise of the Greek Epic*, pp. 78–79.
[11]    A. H. Guyot, *Earth and Man* (Boston, 1857), cited by Franklin Thomas, *The Environmental Basis of Society* (New York, 1911), p. 205.

What took place in Greece first has since taken place in the rest of Europe and is now going on in America. The movement and migration of peoples, the expansion of trade and commerce, and partciularly the growth, in modern times, of these vast melting-pots of races and cultures, the metropolitan cities, has loosened local bonds, destroyed the cultures of tribe and folk, and substituted for the local loyalties the freedom of the cities; for the sacred order of tribal custom, the rational organization which we call civilization.

In these great cities, where all the passions, all the energies of mankind are released, we are in position to investigate the processes of civilization, as it were, under a microscope.

It is in the cities that the old clan and kinship groups are broken up and replaced by social organization based on rational interests and temperamental predilections. It is in the cities, more particularly, that the grand division of labor is effected which permits and more or less compels the individual man to concentrate his energies and his talents on the particular task he is best fitted to perform, and in this way emancipates him and his fellows from the control of nature and circumstance which so thoroughly dominates primitive man.

It happens, however, that the process of acculturation and assimilation and the accompanying amalgamation of racial stocks does not proceed with the same ease and the same speed in all cases. Particularly where peoples who come together are of divergent cultures and widely different racial stocks, assimilation and amalgamation do not take place so rapidly as they do in other cases. All our so-called racial problems grow out of situations in which assimilation and amalgamation do not take place at all, or take place very slowly. As I have said elsewhere, the chief obstacle to the cultural assimilation of races is not their different mental, but rather their divergent physical traits. It is not because of the mentality of the Japanese that they do not so easily assimilate as do the Europeans. It is because

the Japanese bears in his features a distinctive racial hallmark, that he wears, so to speak, a racial uniform which classifies him. He cannot become a mere individual, indistinguishable in the cosmopolitan mass of the population, as is true, for example, of the Irish, and, to a lesser extent, of some of the other immigrant races. The Japanese, like the Negro, is condemned to remain among us an abstraction, a symbol— and a symbol not merely of his own race but of the Orient and of that vague, ill-defined menace we sometimes refer to as the "yellow peril."[12]

Under such circumstances peoples of different racial stocks may live side by side in a relation of symbiosis, each playing a role in a common economy, but not interbreeding to any great extent; each maintaining, like the gypsy or the pariah peoples of India, a more or less complete tribal organization or society of their own. Such was the situation of the Jew in Europe up to modern times, and a somewhat similar relation exists today between the native white and the Hindu populations in Southeast Africa and in the West Indies.

In the long run, however, peoples and races who live together, sharing in the same economy, inevitably interbreed, and in this way if in no other, the relations which were merely co-operative and economic become social and cultural. When migration leads to conquest, either economic or political, assimilation is inevitable. The conquering peoples impose their culture and their standards upon the conquered, and there follows a period of cultural endosmosis.

Sometimes relations between the conquering and the conquered peoples take the form of slavery; sometimes they assume the form, as in India, of a system of caste. But in either case the dominant and the subject peoples become, in time, integral parts of one society. Slavery and caste are merely forms of accommodation, in which the race problem finds a temporary solution. The case of the Jews was different. Jews never were a subject people, at least not in Europe. They were never reduced to the position of an inferior caste. In their ghettos in which they first elected, and then were forced, to live, they preserved their own tribal traditions and their cultural, if not their political, independence. The Jew who left the ghetto did not escape; he deserted and became that execrable object, an apostate. The relation of the ghetto Jew to the

[12]   "Racial Assimilation in Secondary Groups," *Publications of the American Sociological Society*, vol. 8 (1914).

larger community in which he lived was, and to some extent still is, symbiotic rather than social.

When, however, the walls of the medieval ghetto were torn down and the Jew was permitted to participate in the cultural life of the peoples among whom he lived, there appeared a new type of personality, namely, a cultural hybrid, a man living and sharing intimately in the cultural life and traditions of two distinct peoples; never quite willing to break, even if he were permitted to do so, with his past and his traditions, and not quite accepted, because of racial prejudice, in the new society in which he now sought to find a place. He was a man on the margin of two cultures and two societies, which never completely interpenetrated and fused. The emancipated Jew was, and is, historically and typically the marginal man, the first cosmopolite and citizen of the world. He is, par excellence, the "stranger," whom Simmel, himself a Jew, has described with such profound insight and understanding in his *Sociologie*. Most if not all the characteristics of the Jew, certainly his pre-eminence as a trader and his keen intellectual interest, his sophistication, his idealism and lack of historic sense, are the characteristics of the city man, the man who ranges widely, lives preferably in a hotel—in short, the cosmopolite. The autobiographies of Jewish immigrants, of which a great number have been published in America in recent years, are all different versions of the same story—the story of the marginal man; the man who, emerging from the ghetto in which he lived in Europe, is seeking to find a place in the freer, more complex and cosmopolitan life of an American city. One may learn from these autobiographies how the process of assimilation actually takes place in the individual immigrant. In the more sensitive minds its effects are as profound and as disturbing as some of the religious conversions of which William James has given us so classical an account in his *Varieties of Religious Experience*. In these immigrant autobiographies the conflict of cultures, as it takes place in the mind of the immigrant, is just the conflict of "the divided self," the old self and the new. And frequently there is no satisfying issue of this conflict, which often terminates in a profound disillusionment, as described, for example, in Lewisohn's autobiography *Up Stream*.

But Lewisohn's restless wavering between the warm security of the ghetto, which he has abandoned, and the cold freedom of the outer world, in which he is not yet quite at home, is typical. A century earlier, Heinrich Heine, torn with the same conflicting loyalties, struggling to be at the same time a German and a Jew, enacted a similar role. It was, according to his latest biographer, the secret and the tragedy of Heine's life that circumstance condemned him to live in two worlds, in neither of which he ever quite belonged. It was this that embittered his intellectual life and gave to his writings that character of spiritual conflict and instability which, as Browne says, is evidence of "spiritual distress." His mind lacked the integrity which is based on conviction: "His arms were weak" —to continue the quotation—"because his mind was divided; his hands were nerveless because his soul was in turmoil."

Something of the same sense of moral dichotomy and conflict is probably characteristic of every immigrant during the period of transition, when old habits are being discarded and new ones are not yet formed. It is inevitably a period of inner turmoil and intense self-consciousness.

There are no doubt periods of transition and crisis in the lives of most of us that are comparable with those which the immigrant experiences when he leaves home to seek his fortunes in a strange country. But in the case of the marginal man the period of crisis is relatively permanent. The result is that he tends to become a personality type. Ordinarily the marginal man is a mixed blood, like the Mulatto in the United States or the Eurasian in Asia, but that is apparently because the man of mixed blood is one who lives in two worlds, in both of which he is more or less of a stranger. The Christian convert in Asia or in Africa exhibits many if not most of the characteristics of the marginal man—the same spiritual instability, intensified self-consciousness, restlessness, and *malaise*.

It is in the mind of the marginal man that the moral turmoil which new cultural contacts occasion manifests itself in the most obvious forms. It is in the mind of the marginal man—where the changes and fusions of culture are going on—that we can best study the processes of civilization and of progress.

# V. Collective Behavior

**14**

# SOCIAL CONTROL

## I. *Social Control Defined*

SOCIAL CONTROL has been studied, but, in the wide extension that sociology has given to the term, it has not been defined.
All social problems turn out finally to be problems of social control.
In the introductory chapter to this volume social problems were
divided into three classes: Problems (*a*) of administration, (*b*)
of policy and polity, (*c*) of social forces and human nature. Social
control may be studied in each one of these categories. It is with
social forces and human nature that sociology is mainly concerned.
Therefore it is from this point of view that social control will be
considered in this chapter.

In the four preceding chapters the process of interaction, in
its four typical forms, competition, conflict, accommodation, and
assimilation, has been analyzed and described. The community and
the natural order within the limits of the community, it appeared,
are an effect of competition. Social control and the mutual subordination of individual members to the community have their
origin in conflict, assume definite organized forms in the process
of accommodation, and are consolidated and fixed in assimilation.

Through the medium of these processes, a community assumes
the form of a society. Incidentally, however, certain definite and
quite spontaneous forms of social control are developed. These
forms are familiar under various titles: tradition, custom, folkways, mores, ceremonial, myth, religious and political beliefs,

---

Chapter 12, reprinted in part from Robert E. Park and Ernest W. Burgess,
*Introduction to the Science of Sociology* (Chicago: University of Chicago
Press, 2d ed., 1924), pp. 785–99.

dogmas and creeds, and finally public opinion and law. In this chapter it is proposed to define a little more accurately certain of these typical mechanisms through which social groups are enabled to act. In the chapter on "Collective Behavior" which follows, materials will be presented to exhibit the group in action.

It is in action that the mechanisms of control are created, and the materials under the title "Collective Behavior" are intended to illustrate the stages, (a) social unrest, (b) mass movements, (c) institutions in which society is formed and reformed. Finally, in the chapter on "Progress," the relation of social change to social control will be discussed and the role of science and collective representations in the direction of social changes indicated.

The most obvious fact about social control is the machinery by which laws are made and enforced, that is, the legislature, the courts, and the police. When we think of social control, therefore, these are the images in which we see it embodied and these are the terms in which we seek to define it.

It is not quite so obvious that legislation and the police must, in the long run, have the support of public opinion. Hume's statement that governments, even the most despotic, have nothing but opinion to support them, cannot be accepted without some definition of terms, but it is essentially correct. Hume included under opinion what we would distinguish from it, namely, the mores. He might have added, using opinion in this broad sense, that the governed, no matter how numerous, are helpless unless they too are united by "opinion."

A king or a political "boss," having an army or a political "machine" at his command, can do much. It is possible, also, to confuse or mislead public opinion, but neither the king nor the boss will, if he be wise, challenge the mores and the common sense of the community.

Public opinion and the mores, however, representing as they do the responses of the community to changing situations, are themselves subject to change and variation. They are based, however, upon what we have called fundamental human nature, that is, certain traits which in some form or other are reproduced in every form of society.

During the past seventy years the various tribes, races, and nationalities of mankind have been examined in detail by the students of
ethnology, and a comparison of the results shows that the fundamental
patterns of life and behavior are everywhere the same, whether among
the ancient Greeks, the modern Italians, the Asiatic Mongols, the Aus-
tralian blacks or the African Hottentots. All have a form of family
life, moral and legal regulations, a religious system, a form of government, artistic practices, and so forth. An examination of the moral code
of any given group, say the African Kaffirs, will disclose many identities with that of any other given group, say the Hebrews. All groups
have such "commandments" as "Honor thy father and mother," "Thou
shalt not kill," "Thou shalt not steal." Formerly it was assumed that
this similarity was the result of borrowing between groups. When
Bastian recorded a Hawaiian myth resembling the one of Orpheus and
Eurydice, there was speculation as to how this story had been carried
so far from Greece. But it is now recognized that similarities of culture
are due, in the main, not to imitation, but to parallel development. The
nature of man is everywhere essentially the same and tends to express
itself everywhere in similar sentiments and institutions.[1]

There are factors in social control more fundamental than the
mores. Herbert Spencer, in his chapter on "Ceremonial Government," has defined social control from this more fundamental point
of view. In that chapter he refers to "the modified forms of action
caused in men by the presence of their fellows" as a form of control
"out of which other more definite controls are evolved." The
spontaneous responses of one individual to the presence of another
which are finally fixed, conventionalized, and transmitted as social
ritual constitute that "primitive undifferentiated kind of government from which political and religious government are differen-
tiated, and in which they continue immersed."

In putting this emphasis upon ceremonial and upon those
forms of behavior which spring directly and spontaneously out of
the innate and instinctive responses of the individual to a social
situation, Spencer is basing government on the springs of action
which are fundamental, so far, at any rate, as sociology is concerned.

[1]    Robert E. Park and Herbert A. Miller, *Old World Traits Transplanted* (New York, 1921), pp. 1–2.

## II. *Classification of the Materials*

The selections on social control have been classified under three heads: (*a*) elementary forms of social control, (*b*) public opinion, and (*c*) institutions. This order of the readings indicates the development of control from its spontaneous forms in the crowd, in ceremony, prestige, and taboo; its more explicit expression in gossip, rumor, news, and public opinion; to its more formal organization in law, dogma, and in religious and political institutions. Ceremonial, public opinion, and law are characteristic forms in which social life finds expression as well as a means by which the actions of the individual are co-ordinated and collective impulses are organized so that they issue in behavior, that is, either (*a*) primarily expressive—play, for example—or (*b*) positive action.

A very much larger part of all human behavior than we ordinarily imagine is merely expressive. Art, play, religious exercises, and political activity are either wholly or almost wholly forms of expression, and have, therefore, that symbolic and ceremonial character which belongs especially to ritual and to art, but is characteristic of every activity carried on for its own sake. Only work, action which has some ulterior motive or is performed from a conscious sense of duty, falls wholly and without reservation into the second class.

*a) Elementary forms of social control.* Control in the crowd, where rapport is once established and every individual is immediately responsive to every other, is the most elementary form of control.

Something like this same direct and spontaneous response of the individual in the crowd to the crowd's dominant mood or impulse may be seen in the herd and the flock, the "animal crowd."

Under the influence of the vague sense of alarm, or merely as an effect of heat and thirst, cattle become restless and begin slowly moving about in circles, "milling." This milling is a sort of collective gesture, an expression of discomfort or of fear. But the very expression of the unrest tends to intensify its expression and so increases the tension in the herd. This continues up to the point where some sudden sound, the firing of a pistol or a flash of lightning, plunges the herd into a wild stampede.

Milling in the herd is a visible image of what goes on in subtler and less obvious ways in human societies. Alarms or discomforts frequently provoke social unrest. The very expression of this unrest tends to magnify it. The situation is a vicious circle. Every attempt to deal with it merely serves to aggravate it. Such a vicious circle we witnessed in our history from 1830 to 1861, when every attempt to deal with slavery served only to bring the inevitable conflict between the states nearer. Finally there transpired what had for twenty years been visibly preparing and the war broke.

Tolstoi in his great historical romance, *War and Peace*, describes, in a manner which no historian has equaled, the events that led up to the Franco-Russian War of 1812, and particularly the manner in which Napoleon, in spite of his efforts to avoid it, was driven by social forces over which he had no control to declare war on Russia, and so bring about his own downfall.

The condition under which France was forced by Bismarck to declare war on Prussia in 1870, and the circumstances under which Austria declared war on Serbia in 1914 and so brought on the world war, exhibit the same fatal circle. In both cases, given the situation, the preparations that had been made, the resolutions formed and the agreements entered into, it seems clear that after a certain point had been reached every move was forced.

This is the most fundamental and elementary form of control. It is the control exercised by the mere play of elemental forces. These forces may, to a certain extent, be manipulated, as is true of other natural forces; but within certain limits, human nature being what it is, the issue is fatally determined, just as, given the circumstances and the nature of cattle, a stampede is inevitable. Historical crises are invariably created by processes which, looked at abstractly, are very much like milling in a herd. The vicious circle is the so-called "psychological factor" in financial depressions and panics and is, indeed, a factor in all collective action.

The effect of this circular form of interaction is to increase the tensions in the group and, by creating a state of expectancy, to mobilize its members for collective action. It is like attention in the individual: it is the way in which the group prepares to act.

Back of every other form of control—ceremonial, public opinion, or law—there is always this interaction of the elementary social forces. What we ordinarily mean by social control, however, is the arbitrary intervention of some individual—official, functionary, or leader—in the social process. A policeman arrests a criminal, an attorney sways the jury with his eloquence, the judge passes sentence; these are the familiar formal acts in which social control manifests itself. What makes the control exercised in this way social, in the strict sense of that term, is the fact that these acts are supported by custom, law, and public opinion.

The distinction between control in the crowd and in other forms of society is that the crowd has no tradition. It has no point of reference in its own past to which its members can refer for guidance. It has therefore neither symbols, ceremonies, rites, nor ritual; it imposes no obligations and creates no loyalties.

Ceremonial is one method of reviving in the group a lively sense of the past. It is a method of reinstating the excitements and the sentiments which inspired an earlier collective action. The savage war dance is a dramatic representation of battle and as such serves to rouse and reawaken the warlike spirit. This is one way in which ceremonial becomes a means of control. By reviving the memories of an earlier war, it mobilizes the warriors for a new one.

Ernst Grosse, in *The Beginnings of Art*, has stated succinctly what has impressed all first-hand observers, namely, the important role which the dance plays in the lives of primitive peoples.

The dances of the hunting peoples are, as a rule, mass dances. Generally the men of the tribe, not rarely the members of several tribes, join in the exercises, and the whole assemblage then moves according to one law in one time. All who have described the dances have referred again and again to this "wonderful" unison of the movements. In the heat of the dance the several participants are fused together as into a single being, which is stirred and moved as by one feeling. During the dance they are in a condition of complete social unification, and the dancing group feels and acts like a single organism. *The social significance of the primitive dance lies precisely in this effect of social uni-*

*fication.* It brings and accustoms a number of men who, in their loose and precarious conditions of life, are driven irregularly hither and thither by different individual needs and desires, to act under one impulse with one feeling for one object. It introduces order and connection, at least occasionally, into the rambling, fluctuating life of the hunting tribes. It is, besides wars, perhaps the only factor that makes their solidarity vitally perceptible to the adherents of a primitive tribe, and it is at the same time one of the best preparations for war, for the gymnastic dances correspond in more than one respect to our military exercises. It would be hard to overestimate the importance of the primitive dance in the culture development of mankind. All higher civilization is conditioned upon the uniformly ordered co-operation of individual social elements, and primitive men are trained to this co-operation by the dance.[2]

The dance, which is so characteristic and so universal a feature of the life of primitive man—at once a mode of collective expression and of collective representation—is but a conventionalized form of the circular reaction, which in its most primitive form is represented by the milling of the herd.

*b) Public opinion.* We ordinarily think of public opinion as a sort of social weather. At certain times, and under certain circumstances, we observe strong, steady currents of opinion, moving apparently in a definite direction and toward a definite goal. At other times, however, we note flurries and eddies and countercurrents in this movement. Every now and then there are storms, shifts, or dead calms. These sudden shifts in public opinion, when expressed in terms of votes, are referred to by the politicians as "landslides."

In all these movements, cross-currents and changes in direction which a closer observation of public opinion reveals, it is always possible to discern, but on a much grander scale, to be sure, that same type of circular reaction which we have found elsewhere, whenever the group was preparing to act. Always in the public, as in the crowd, there will be a circle, sometimes wider, sometimes narrower, within which individuals are mutually responsive to

[2]    Ernest Grosse, *The Beginning of Art* (New York, 1897), pp. 228–29.

motives and interests of one another, so that out of this interplay of social forces there may emerge at any time a common motive and a common purpose that will dominate the whole.

Within the circle of the mutual influence described, there will be no such complete rapport and no such complete domination of the individual by the group as exists in a herd or a crowd in a state of excitement, but there will be sufficient community of interest to insure a common understanding. A public is, in fact, organized on the basis of a universe of discourse, and within the limits of this universe of discourse, language, statements of fact, news will have, for all practical purposes, the same meanings. It is this circle of mutual influence within which there is a universe of discourse that defines the limits of the public.

A public, like a crowd, is not to be conceived as a formal organization like a parliament or even a public meeting. It is always the widest area over which there is conscious participation and consensus in the formation of public opinion. The public has not only a circumference, but it has a center. Within the area within which there is participation and consensus there is always a focus of attention around which the opinions of the individuals which compose the public seem to revolve. This focus of attention, under ordinary circumstances, is constantly shifting. The shifts of attention of the public constitute what is meant by the changes in public opinion. When these changes take a definite direction and have or seem to have a definite goal, we call the phenomenon a social movement. If it were possible to plot this movement in the form of maps and graphs, it would be possible to show movement in two dimensions. There would be, for example, a movement in space. The focus of public opinion, the point namely at where there is the greatest "intensity" of opinion, tends to move from one part of the country to another.[3] In America these movements, for reasons that could perhaps be explained historically, are likely to be along the meridians, east and west, rather than north and south. In the course of this geographical movement of public opinion, however,

3    See A. L. Lowell, *Public Opinion and Popular Government* (New York, 1913), pp. 12–13.

we are likely to observe changes in intensity and changes in direction (devagation).

Changes in intensity seem to be in direct proportion to the area over which opinion on a given issue may be said to exist. In minorities opinion is uniformly more intense than it is in majorities and this is what gives minorities so much greater influence in proportion to their numbers than majorities. While changes in intensity have a definite relation to the area over which public opinion on an issue may be said to exist, the devagations of public opinion, as distinguished from the trend, will probably turn out to have a direct relation to the character of the parties that participate. Area as applied to public opinion will have to be measured eventually in terms of social rather than geograhical distance, that is to say, in terms of isolation and contact. The factor of numbers is also involved in any such calculation. Geographical area, communication, and the number of persons involved are in general the factors that would determine the concept "area" as it is used here. If party spirit is strong the general direction or trend of public opinion will probably be intersected by shifts and sudden transient changes in direction, and these shifts will be in proportion to the intensity of the party spirit. Charles E. Merriam's recent study of political parties indicates that the minority parties formulate most of the legislation in the United States.[4] This is because there is not very great divergence in the policies of the two great parties and party struggles are fought out on irrelevant issues. So far as this is true it insures against any sudden change in policy. New legislation is adopted in response to the trend of public opinion, rather than in response to the devagations and sudden shifts brought about by the development of a radical party spirit.

All these phenomena may be observed, for example, in the Prohibition Movement. Dicey's study of *Law and Public Opinion in England* showed that while the direction of opinion in regard to specific issues had been very irregular, on the whole the movement had been in one general direction. The trend of public opinion is the name we give to this general movement. In defining the trend, shifts, cross-currents, and flurries are not considered. When we speak of the tendency or direction of public opinion we usually mean the trend over a definite period of time.

[4]    *The American Party System* (New York, 1922), chap. 8.

When the focus of public attention ceases to move and shift, when it is fixed, the circle which defines the limits of the public is narrowed. As the circle narrows, opinion itself becomes more intense and concentrated. This is the phenomenon of crisis. It is at this point that the herd stampedes.

The effect of crisis is invariably to increase the dangers of precipitate action. The most trivial incident, in such periods of tension, may plunge a community into irretrievable disaster. It is under conditions of crisis that dictatorships are at once possible and necessary, not merely to enable the community to act energetically, but in order to protect the community from the mere play of external forces. The manner in which Bismarck, by a slight modification of the famous telegram of Ems, provoked a crisis in France and compelled Napoleon III, against his judgment and that of his advisers, to declare war on Germany, is an illustration of this danger.[5]

[5]    "On the afternoon of July 13, Bismark, Roon, and Moltke were seated together in the Chancellor's Room at Berlin. They were depressed and moody; for Prince Leopold's renunciation had been trumpeted in Paris as a humiliation for Prussia. They were afraid, too, that King William's conciliatory temper might lead him to make further concessions, and that the careful preparations of Prussia for the inevitable war with France might he wasted, and a unique opportunity lost. A telegram arrived. It was from the king at Ems, and described his interview that morning with the French ambassador. The king had met Benedetti's request for the guarantee required by a firm but courteous refusal; and when the ambassador had sought to renew the interview, he had sent a polite message through his aide-de-camp informing him that the subject must be considered closed. The Chancellor at once saw his opportunity. In the royal despatch, though the main incidents were clear enough, there was still a note of doubt, of hesitancy, which suggested a possibility of further negotiation. The excision of a few lines would alter, not indeed the general sense, but certainly the whole tone of the message. Bismark, turning to Moltke, asked him if he were ready for a sudden risk of war; and on his answering in the affirmative, took a blue pencil and drew it quickly through several parts of the telegram. Without the alteration or addition of a single word, the message, instead of appearing a mere "fragment of a negotiation still pending," was thus made to appear decisive. In the actual temper of the French people there was no doubt that it would not only appear decisive, but insulting, and that its publication would mean war.

It is this narrowing of the area over which a definite public opinion may be said to exist that at once creates the possibility and defines the limits of arbitrary control, so far as it is created or determined by the existence of public opinion.

Thus far the public has been described almost wholly in terms that could be applied to a crowd. The public has been frequently described as if it were simply a great crowd, a crowd scattered as widely as news will circulate and still be news.[6] But there is this difference. In the heat and excitement of the crowd, as in the choral dances of primitive people, there is for the moment what may be described as complete fusion of the social forces. Rapport has, for the time being, made the crowd, in a peculiarly intimate way, a social unit.

No such unity exists in the public. The sentiment and tendencies which we call public opinion are never unqualified expressions of emotion. The difference is that public opinion is determined by conflict and discussion, and made up of the opinions of individuals not wholly at one. In any conflict situation, where party spirit is aroused, the spectators, who constitute the public, are bound to take sides. The impulse to take sides is, in fact, in direct proportion to the excitement and party spirit displayed. The result is, however, that both sides of an issue get considered. Certain contentions are rejected because they will not stand criticism. Public opinion formed in this way has the character of a judgment, rather than a mere unmeditated expression of emotion, as in the crowd. The public is never ecstatic. It is always more or less rational. It is this fact of conflict, in the form of discussion, that introduces into the

---

"On July 14 the publication of the 'Ems telegram' became known in Paris, with the result that Bismark had expected. The majority of the Cabinet, hitherto in favour of peace, were swept away by the popular tide; and Napoleon himself reluctantly yielded to the importunity of his ministers and of the Empress, who saw in a successful war the best, if not the only, chance of preserving the throne for her son. On the evening of the same day, July 14, the declaration of war was signed" (W. Alison Phillips, *Modern Europe, 1815–1899* [London, 1903], pp. 465–66).

[6]      G. Tarde, *L'opinion et la foule* (Paris, 1901).

control exercised by public opinion the elements of rationality and of fact.

In the final judgment of the public upon a conflict or an issue, we expect, to be sure, some sort of unanimity of judgment, but in the general consensus there will be some individual differences of opinion still unmediated, or only partially so, and final agreement of the public will be more or less qualified by all the different opinions that co-operate to form its judgment.

In the materials which follow a distinction is made between public opinion and the mores, and this distinction is important. Custom and the folkways, like habit in the individual, may be regarded as a mere residuum of past practices. When folkways assume the character of mores, they are no longer merely matters of fact and common sense, they are judgments upon matters which were probably once live issues and as such they may be regarded as the products of public opinion.

Ritual, religious or social, is probably the crystallization of forms of behavior which, like the choral dance, are the direct expression of the emotions and the instincts. The mores, on the other hand, in so far as they contain a rational element, are the accumulation, the residuum, not only of past practices, but of judgments such as find expression in public opinion. The mores, as thus conceived, are the judgments of public opinion in regard to issues that have been settled and forgotten.

L. T. Hobhouse, in his volume, *Morals in Evolution*, has described, in a convincing way, the process by which, as he conceives it, custom is modified and grows under the influence of the personal judgments of individuals and of the public. Public opinion, as he defines it, is simply the combined and sublimated judgments of individuals.

Most of these judgments are, to be sure, merely the repetition of old formulas. But occasionally, when the subject of discussion touches us more deeply, when it touches upon some matter in which we have had a deeper and more intimate experience, the ordinary patter that passes as public opinion is dissipated and we originate a moral judgment that not only differs from, but is in conflict with, the prevailing opinion. In that case "we become, as it were, centers from which judgments of one kind or another radiate and from which they pass forth to fill the atmosphere of opinion and take their place among the influences that mould the judgments of men."

The manner in which public opinion issues from the interaction of individuals, and moral judgments are formed that eventually become the basis of law, may be gathered from the way in which the process goes on in the daily life about us.

No sooner has the judgment escaped us—a winged word from our own lips—than it impinges on the judgment similarly flying forth to do its work from our next-door neighbor, and if the subject is an exciting one the air is soon full of the winged forces clashing, deflecting or reinforcing one another as the case may be, and generally settling down toward some preponderating opinion which is society's judgment on the case. But in the course of the conflict many of the original judgments are modified. Discussion, further consideration, above all, the mere influence of our neighbour's opinion reacts on each of us, with a stress that is proportioned to various mental and moral characteristics of our own, our clearness of vision, our firmness, or, perhaps, obstinacy of character, our self-confidence, and so forth. Thus, the controversy will tend to leave its mark, small or great, on those who took part in it. It will tend to modify their modes of judgment, confirming one, perhaps, in his former ways, shaping the confidence of another, opening the eyes of a third. Similarly, it will tend to set a precedent for future judgments. It will affect what men say and think on the next question that turns up. It adds its weight, of one grain it may be, to some force that is turning the scale of opinion and preparing society for some new departure. In any case, we have here in miniature at work every day before our eyes the essential process by which moral judgments arise and grow.[7]

*c) Institutions.* An institution, according to Sumner, consists of a concept and a structure. The concept defines the purpose, interest, or function of the institution. The structure embodies the idea of the institution and furnishes the instrumentalities through which the idea is put into action. The process by which purposes, whether they are individual or collective, are embodied in struc-

[7]    L. T. Hobhouse, *Morals in Evolution: A Study in Comparative Ethics* (New York, 1915), pp. 13–14.

tures is a continuous one. But the structures thus formed are not physical, at least not entirely so. Structure, in the sense that Sumner uses the term, belongs, as he says, to a category of its own. "It is a category in which custom produces continuity, coherence, and consistency, so that the word 'structure' may properly be applied to the fabric of relations and prescribed positions with which functions are permanently connected." Just as every individual member of a community participates in the process by which custom and public opinion are made, so also he participates in the creation of the structure, that "cake of custom" which, when it embodies a definite social function, we call an institution.

Institutions may be created just as laws are enacted, but only when a social situation exists to which they correspond will they become operative and effective. Institutions, like laws, rest upon the mores and are supported by public opinion. Otherwise they remain mere paper projects or artefacts that perform no real function. History records the efforts of conquering peoples to impose upon the conquered their own laws and institutions. The efforts are instructive, but not encouraging. The most striking modern instance is the effort of King Leopold of Belgium to introduce civilization into the Congo Free State.[8]

Law, like public opinion, owes its rational and secular character to the fact that it arose out of an effort to compromise conflict and to interpret matters which were in dispute.

To seek vengeance for a wrong committed was a natural impulse, and the recognition of this fact in custom established it not merely as a right but as a duty. War, the modern form of trial by battle, the vendetta, and the duel are examples that have survived down to modern times of this natural and primitive method of settling disputes.

In all these forms of conflict custom and the mores have tended to limit the issues and define the conditions under which disputes might be settled by force. At the same time public opinion, in passing judgment on the issues, exercised a positive influence on the outcome of the struggle.

Gradually, as men realized the losses which conflicts incurred, the community has intervened to prevent them. At a time when the

8    E. D. Morel, *King Leopold's Rule in Africa* (London, 1904).

blood feud was still sanctioned by the mores, cities of refuge and sanctuaries were established to which one who had incurred a blood feud might flee until his case could be investigated. If it then appeared that the wrong committed had been unintentional or if there were other mitigating circumstances, he might find in the sanctuary protection. Otherwise, if a crime had been committed in cold blood, "lying in wait," or "in enmity," as the ancient Jewish law books called it, he might be put to death by the avenger of blood, "when he meeteth him."[9]

Thus, gradually, the principle became established that the community might intervene, not merely to insure that vengeance was executed in due form, but to determine the facts, and thus courts which determined by legal process the guilt or innocence of the accused were established.

It does not appear that courts of justice were ever set up within the kinship group for the trial of offenses, although efforts were made there first of all, by the elders and the headmen, to compromise quarrels and compose differences.

Courts first came into existence, the evidence indicates, when society was organized over wider areas and after some authority had been established outside of the local community. As society was organized over a wider territory, control was extended to ever wider areas of human life until we have at present a program for international courts with power to intervene between nations to prevent wars.[10]

Society, like the individual man, moves and acts under the influence of a multitude of minor impulses and tendencies which mutually interact to produce a more general tendency which then dominates all the individuals of the group. This explains the fact that a group, even a mere casual collection of individuals like a crowd, is enabled to act more or less as a unit. The crowd acts under the influence of such a dominant tendency, unreflectively, without definite reference to a past or a future. The crowd has no past and no future. The public introduces into this vortex

9    L. T. Hobhouse, p. 85.
10    The whole process of evolution by which a moral order has been established over ever wider areas of social life has been sketched in a masterly manner by Hobhouse in his chapter, "Law and Justice," pp. 72–158.

of impulses the factor of reflection. The public presupposes the existence of a common impulse such as manifests itself in the crowd, but it presupposes, also, the existence of individuals and groups of individuals representing divergent tendencies. These individuals interact upon one another *critically*. The public is, what the crowd is not, a discussion group. The very existence of discussion presupposes objective standards of truth and of fact. The action of the public is based on a universe of discourse in which things, although they may and do have for every individual somewhat different value, are describable at any rate in terms that mean the same to all individuals. The public, in other words, moves in an objective and intelligible world.

Law is based on custom. Custom is group habit. As the group acts it creates custom. There is implicit in custom a conception and a rule of action, which is regarded as right and proper in the circumstances. Law makes this rule of action explicit. Law grows up, however, out of a distinction between this rule of action and the facts. Custom is bound up with the facts under which the custom grew up. Law is the result of an effort to frame the rule of action implicit in custom in such general terms that it can be made to apply to new situations, involving new sets of facts. The distinction between the law and the facts did not exist in primitive society. The evolution of law and jurisprudence has been in the direction of an increasingly clearer recognition of this distinction between law and the facts. This has meant in practice an increasing recognition by the courts of the facts, and a disposition to act in accordance with them. The present disposition of courts, as, for example, the juvenile courts, to call to their assistance experts to examine the mental condition of children who are brought before them and to secure the assistance of juvenile-court officers to advise and assist them in the enforcement of the law, is an illustration of an increasing disposition to take account of the facts.

The increasing interest in the natural history of the law and of legal institutions, and the increasing disposition to interpret it in sociological terms, from the point of view of its function, is another instance of the same tendency.

# 15

# COLLECTIVE BEHAVIOR

## I. *Collective Behavior Defined*

A COLLECTION of individuals is not always, and by the mere fact of its collectivity, a society. On the other hand, when people come together anywhere, in the most casual way, on the street corner or at a railway station, no matter how great the social distances between them, the mere fact that they are aware of one another's presence sets up a lively exchange of influences, and the behavior that ensues is both social and collective. It is social, at the very least, in the sense that the train of thought and action in each individual is influenced more or less by the action of every other. It is collective in so far as each individual acts under the influence of a mood or a state of mind in which each shares, and in accordance with conventions which all quite unconsciously accept, and which the presence of each enforces upon the others.

The amount of individual eccentricity or deviation from normal and accepted modes of behavior which a community will endure without comment and without protest will vary naturally enough with the character of the community. A cosmopolitan community like New York City can and does endure a great deal in the way of individual eccentricity that a smaller city like Boston would not tolerate. In any case, and this is the point of these observations, even in the most casual relations of life, people do not behave in the presence of others as if they were living alone like Robinson Crusoe, each on his individual island. The very

---

Chapter 13, reprinted in part from Robert E. Park and Ernest W. Burgess, *Introduction to the Science of Sociology* (Chicago: University of Chicago Press, 2d ed., 1924), pp. 865–78.

fact of their consciousness of each other tends to maintain and enforce a great body of convention and usage which otherwise falls into abeyance and is forgotten. Collective behavior, then, is the behavior of individuals under the influence of an impulse that is common and collective, an impulse, in other words, that is the result of social interaction.

## II.  *Social Unrest and Collective Behavior*

The most elementary form of collective behavior seems to be what is ordinarily referred to as "social unrest." Unrest in the individual becomes social when it is, or seems to be, transmitted from one individual to another, but more particularly when it produces something akin to the milling process in the herd, so that the manifestations of discontent in A communicated to B, and from B reflected back to A, produce the circular reaction described in the preceding chapter.

The significance of social unrest is that it represents at once a breaking up of the established routine and a preparation for new collective action. Social unrest is not of course a new phenomenon; it is possibly true, however, that it is peculiarly characteristic, as has been said, of modern life. The contrast between the conditions of modern life and of primitive society suggests why this may be true.

The conception which we ought to form of primitive society, says Sumner, is that of small groups scattered over a territory. The size of the group will be determined by the conditions of the struggle for existence and the internal organization of each group will correspond (1) to the size of the group, and (2) to the nature and intensity of the struggle with its neighbors.

Thus war and peace have reacted on each other and developed each other, one within the group, the other in the intergroup relation. The closer the neighbors, and the stronger they are, the intenser is the warfare, and then the intenser is the internal organization and discipline of each. Sentiments are produced to correspond. Loyalty to the group, sacrifice for it, hatred and contempt for outsiders, brotherhood within, warlikeness without—all grow together, common products of the same situation. These relations and sentiments constitute a social philosophy. It is sanctified by connection with religion. Men of an others-group are outsiders with whose ancestors the ancestors of the we-group waged war. The ghosts of the latter will see with pleasure their descendants keep up the fight, and will help them. Virtue consists in killing, plundering, and enslaving outsiders.[1]

The isolation, territorial and cultural, under which alone it is possible to maintain an organization which corresponds to Sumner's description, has disappeared within comparatively recent times from all the more inhabitable portions of the earth. In place of it there has come, and with increasing rapidity is coming, into existence a society which includes within its limits the total population of the earth and is so intimately bound together that the speculation of a grain merchant in Chicago may increase the price of bread in Bombay, while the act of an assassin in a provincial town in the Balkans has been sufficient to plunge the world into a war which changed the political map of three continents and cost the lives, in Europe alone, of 8,500,000 combatants.

The first effect of modern conditions of life has been to increase and vastly complicate the economic interdependence of strange and distant peoples, i.e., to destroy distances and make the world, as far as national relations are concerned, small and tight.

The second effect has been to break down family, local, and national ties, and emancipate the individual man.

When the family ceases, as it does in the city, to be an economic unit, when parents and children have vocations that not only intercept the traditional relations of family life, but make them well nigh impossible, the family ceases to function as an organ of social control. When the different nationalities, with their different national cultures, have so far interpenetrated one another that each has permanent colonies within the territorial limits of the other, it is inevitable that the old solidarities, the common loyalties and the common hatreds that formerly bound men together in primitive kinship and local groups should be undermined.

A survey of the world today shows that vast changes are every-

---

[1]     W. G. Sumner, *Folkways*. (Boston, 1906), pp. 12–13.

where in progress. Not only in Europe but in Asia and in Africa new cultural contacts have undermined and broken down the old cultures. The effect has been to loosen all the social bonds and reduce society to its individual atoms. The energies thus freed have produced a world-wide ferment. Individuals released from old associations enter all the more readily into new ones. Out of this confusion new and strange political and religious movements arise, which represent the groping of men for a new social order.

## III. *The Crowd and the Public*

Gustave Le Bon, who was the first writer to call attention to the significance of the crowd as a social phenomenon,[2] said that mass movements mark the end of an old régime and the beginning of a new.

"When the structure of a civilization is rotten, it is always the masses that bring about its downfall."[3] On the other hand, "all founders of religious or political creeds have established them solely because they were successful in inspiring crowds with those fanatical sentiments which have as result that men find their happiness in worship and obedience and are ready to lay down their lives for their idol."[4]

The crowd was, for Le Bon, not merely any group brought together by the accident of some chance excitement, but it was above all the emancipated masses whose bonds of loyalty to the old order had been broken by "the destruction of those religious,

---

[2]  Scipio Sighele, in a note to the French edition of his *Psychology of Sects*, claims that his volume, *La Folla delinquente*, of which the second edition was published at Turin in 1895, and his article "Physiologie du succès," in the *Revue des Revues*, October 1, 1894, were the first attempts to describe the crowd from the point of view of collective psychology. Le Bon published two articles, "Psychologie des foules" in the *Revue scientifique*, April 6 and 20, 1895. These were later gathered together in his volume *Psychologie des foules*, Paris, 1895. See Sighele *Psychologie des sectes*, pp. 25, 39.

[3]  Gustave Le Bon, *The Crowd: A study of the popular mind.* (New York, 1900), p. 19.

[4]  *Ibid.*, p. 83.

political, and social beliefs in which all the elements of our civilization are rooted." The crowd, in other words, typified for Le Bon the existing social order. Ours is an age of crowds, he said, an age in which men, massed and herded together in great cities without real convictions or fundamental faiths, are likely to be stampeded in any direction for any chance purpose under the influence of any passing excitement.

Le Bon did not attempt to distinguish between the crowd and the public. This distinction was first made by Tarde in a paper entitled "Le Public et la foule," published first in *La Revue de Paris* in 1898, and included with several others on the same general theme under the title *L'Opinion et la foule* which appeared in 1901. The public, according to Tarde, was a product of the printing press. The limits of the crowd are determined by the length to which a voice will carry or the distance that the eye can survey. But the public presupposes a higher stage of social development in which suggestions are transmitted in the form of ideas and there is "contagion without contact."[5]

The fundamental distinction between the crowd and the public, however, is not to be measured by numbers nor by means of communication, but by the form and effects of the interactions. In the public, interaction takes the form of discussion. Individuals tend to act upon one another critically; issues are raised and parties form. Opinions clash and thus modify and moderate one another.

The crowd does not discuss and hence it does not reflect. It simply "mills." Out of this milling process a collective impluse is formed which dominates all members of the crowd. Crowds, when they act, do so impulsively. The crowd, says Le Bon, "is the slave of its impulses."

"The varying impulses which crowds obey may be, according to their exciting causes, generous or cruel, heroic or cowardly, but they will always be so imperious that the interest of the individual, even the interest of self-preservation, will not dominate them."[6]

When the crowd acts it becomes a mob. What happens when two mobs meet? We have in the literature no definite record. The

5    *L'Opinion et la foule* (Paris, 1901), pp. 6–7.
6    *The Crowd*, p. 41.

nearest approach to it are the occasional accounts we find in the stories of travelers of the contacts and conflicts of armies of primitive peoples. These undisciplined hordes are, as compared with the armies of civilized peoples, little more than armed mobs. Captain S. L. Hinde in his story of the Belgian conquest of the Congo describes several such battles. From the descriptions of battles carried on almost wholly between savage and undisciplined troops it is evident that the morale of an army of savages is a precarious thing. A very large part of the warfare consists in alarms and excursions interspersed with wordy duels to keep up the courage on one side and cause a corresponding depression on the other.[7]

Gangs are conflict groups. Their organization is usually quite informal and is determined by the nature and imminence of the conflicts with other groups. When one crowd encounters another it either goes to pieces or it changes its character and becomes a conflict group. When negotiations and palavers take place as they eventually do between conflict groups, these two groups, together with the neutrals who have participated vicariously in the conflict, constitute a public. It is possible that the two opposing savage hordes which seek, by threats and boastings and beatings of drums, to play upon each other's fears and so destroy each other's morale, may be said to constitute a very primitive type of public.

Discussion, as might be expected, takes curious and interesting forms among primitive peoples. In a volume, *Iz Derevni: 12 Pisem* ("From the Country: 12 Letters"), A. N. Engelgardt describes the way in which the Slavic peasants reach their decisions in the village council.

---

[7]     Sidney L. Hinde, *The Fall of the Congo Arabs* (London, 1897), p. 147. Describing a characteristic incident in one of the strange confused battles Hinde says: "Wordy war, which also raged, had even more effect than our rifles. Mahomedi and Sefu led the Arabs, who were jeering and taunting Lutete's people, saying that they were in a bad case, and had better desert the white man, who was ignorant of the fact that Mohara with all the forces of Nyange was camped in his rear. Lutete's people replied: 'Oh, we know all about Mohara; we ate him the day before yesterday.' " This news became all the more depressing when it turned out to be true. See also Hirn, *The Origins of Art*, p. 269, for an explanation of the role of threats and boastings in savage warfare.

In the discussion of some questions by the *mir* [organization of neighbors] there are no speeches, no debates, no votes. They shout, they abuse one another—they seem on the point of coming to blows; apparently they riot in the most senseless manner. Some one preserves silence, and then suddenly puts in a word, one word, or an ejaculation, and by this word, this ejaculation, he turns the whole thing upside down. In the end, you look into it and find that an admirable decision has been formed and, what is most important, a unanimous decision. . . . (In the division of land) the cries, the noise, the hubbub do not subside until everyone is satisfied and no doubter is left.[8]

## IV. *Crowds and Sects*

Reference has been made to the crowds that act, but crowds do not always act. Sometimes they merely dance or, at least, make expressive motions which relieve their feelings. "The purest and most typical expression of simple feeling," as Hirn remarks, "is that which consists of mere random movements."[9] When these motions assume, as they so easily do, the character of a fixed sequence in time, that is to say when they are rhythmical, they can be and inevitably are, as by a sort of inner compulsion, imitated by onlookers. "As soon as the expression is fixed in rhythmical form its contagious power is incalculably increased."[10]

This explains at once the function and social importance of the dance among primitive people. It is the form in which they prepare for battle and celebrate their victories. It gives the form at once to their religious ritual and to their art. Under the influence of the memories and the emotions which these dances stimulate the primitive group achieves a sense of corporate unity, which makes corporate action possible outside of the fixed and sacred routine of ordinary daily life.

If it is true, as has been suggested, that art and religion had their origin in the choral dance, it is also true that in modern

---

[8]     Robert E. Park and Herbert A. Miller, *Old World Traits Transplanted* (New York, 1921), Document 23, pp. 32–33.

[9]     Yrjö Hirn, *The Origins of Art* (London, 1900), p. 87. A psychological and sociological inquiry.

[10]     *Ibid.*, p. 80.

times religious sects and social movements have had their origin in crowd excitements and spontaneous mass movements. The very names which have been commonly applied to them—Quakers, Shakers, Convulsionaires, Holy Rollers—suggest not merely the derision with which they were at one time regarded, but indicate likewise their origin in ecstatic or expressive crowds, the crowds that *do not act*.

All great mass movements tend to display, to a greater or less extent, the characteristics that Le Bon attributes to crowds. Speaking of the convictions of crowds, Le Bon says:

When these convictions are closely examined, whether at epochs marked by fervent religious faith, or by great political upheavals such as those of the last century, it is apparent that they always assume a peculiar form which I cannot better define than by giving it the name of a religious sentiment.[11]

Le Bon's definition of religion and religious sentiment will hardly find general acceptance but it indicates at any rate his conception of the extent to which individual personalities are involved in the excitements that accompany mass movements.

A person is not religious solely when he worships a divinity, but when he puts all the resources of his mind, the complete submission of his will, and the whole-souled ardour of fanaticism at the service of a cause or an individual who becomes the goal and guide of his thoughts and actions.[12]

Just as the gang may be regarded as the perpetuation and permanent form of "the crowd that acts," so the sect, religious or political, may be regarded as a perpetuation and permanent form of the orgiastic (ecstatic) or expressive crowd.

"The sect," says Sighele, "is a crowd *triée*, selected, and permanent; the crowd is a transient sect, which does not select its members. The sect is the *chronic* form of the crowd; the crowd is the *acute* form of the sect."[13] It is Sighele's conception that the crowd is an elementary organism, from which the sect issues, like

11   Le Lon, p. 82.
12   *Ibid.*, p. 83.
13   Scipio Sighele, *Psychologie des sectes* (Paris, 1898), p. 46.

the chick from the egg, and that all other types of social groups "may, in this same manner, be deduced from this primitive social protoplasm." This is a simplification which the facts hardly justify. It is true that, implicit in the practices and the doctrines of a religious sect, there is the kernel of a new independent culture.

## V.  *Sects and Institutions*

A sect is a religious organization that is at war with the existing mores. It seeks to cultivate a state of mind and establish a code of morals different from that of the world about it and for this it claims divine authority. In order to accomplish this end it invariably seeks to set itself off in contrast with the rest of the world. The simplest and most effective way to achieve this is to adopt a peculiar form of dress and speech. This, however, invariably makes its members objects of scorn and derision, and eventually of persecution. It would probably do this even if there was no assumption of moral superiority to the rest of the world in this adoption of a peculiar manner and dress.

Persecution tends to dignify and sanctify all the external marks of the sect, and it becomes a cardinal principle of the sect to maintain them. Any neglect of them is regarded as disloyalty and is punished as heresy. Persecution may eventually, as was the case with the Puritans, the Quakers, the Mormons, compel the sect to seek refuge in some part of the world where it may practice its way of life in peace.

Once the sect has achieved territorial isolation and territorial solidarity, so that it is the dominant power within the region that it occupies, it is able to control the civil organization, establish schools and a press, and so put the impress of a peculiar culture upon all the civil and political institutions that it controls. In this case it tends to assume the form of a state, and become a nationality. Something approaching this was achieved by the Mormons in Utah. The most striking illustration of the evolution of a nationality from a sect is Ulster, which now has a position not quite that of a nation within the English empire.

This sketch suggests that the sect, like most other social institutions, originates under conditions that are typical for all institutions of the same species; then it develops in definite and predictable ways, in accordance with a form or entelechy that is predetermined by characteristic internal process and mechanisms, and that has, in short, a nature and natural history which can be described and explained in sociological terms. Sects have their origin in social unrest to which they give a direction and expression in forms and practices that are largely determined by historical circumstances; movements which were at first inchoate impulses and aspirations gradually take form; policies are defined, doctrine and dogmas formulated; and eventually an administrative machinery and efficiencies are developed to carry into effect policies and purposes. The Salvation Army, of which we have a more adequate history than of most other religious movements, is an example.

A sect in its final form may be described, then, as a movement of social reform and regeneration that has become institutionalized. Eventually, when it has succeeded in accommodating itself to the other rival organizations, when it has become tolerant and is tolerated, it tends to assume the form of a denomination. Denominations tend and are perhaps destined to unite in the form of religious federations—a thing which is inconceivable of a sect.

What is true of the sect, we may assume, and must assume if social movements are to become subjects for sociological investigation, is true of other social institutions. Existing institutions represent social movements that survived the conflict of cultures and the struggle for existence.

Sects, and that is what characterizes and distinguishes them from secular institutions, at least, have had their origin in movements that aimed to reform the mores—movements that sought to renovate and renew the inner life of the community. They have wrought upon society from within outwardly. Revolutionary and reform movements, on the contrary, have been directed against the outward fabric and formal structure of society. Revolutionary movements in particular have assumed that if the existing structure could be destroyed it would then be possible to erect a new moral order upon the ruins of the old social structures.

A cursory survey of the history of revolutions suggests that the most radical and the most successful of them have been religious. Of this type of revolution Christianity is the most conspicuous example.

## VI. *Classification of the Materials*

The materials in this chapter have been arranged under the headings: (*a*) social contagion, (*b*) the crowd, and (*c*) types of mass movements. The order of materials follows, in a general way, the order of institutional evolution. Social unrest is first communicated, then takes form in crowd and mass movements, and finally crystallizes in institutions. The history of almost any single social movement—woman's suffrage, prohibition, protestantism—exhibits in a general way, if not in detail, this progressive change in character. There is at first a vague general discontent and distress. Then a violent, confused, and disorderly, but enthusiastic and popular movement arises. Finally the movement takes form; develops leadership, organization; formulates doctrines and dogmas. Eventually it is accepted, established, legalized. The movement dies, but the institution remains.

*a) Social contagion.* The ease and the rapidity with which a cultural trait originating in one cultural group finds its way to other distant groups is familiar to students of folklore and ethnology. The manner in which fashions are initiated in some metropolitan community, and thence make their way, with more or less rapidity, to the provinces is an illustration of the same phenomenon in a different context.

Fashion plays a much larger role in social life than most of us imagine. Fashion dominates our manners and dress but it influences also our sentiments and our modes of thought. Everything in literature, art or philosophy that was characteristic of the middle of the nineteenth century, the "mid-Victorian period," is now quite out of date and no one who is intelligent now-a-days practices the pruderies, defends the doctrines, nor shares the enthusiasms of that period. Philosophy, also, changes with the fashion and Sumner says that even mathematics and science do the same. Lecky in his history of Rationalism in Europe describes in great detail how the belief in witches, so characteristic of the Middle Ages, gradually disappeared with the period of enlightenment and progress.[14] But the enlightenment of the eighteenth century was itself a fashion and is now quite out of date. In the meantime a new popular and scientific interest is growing up in obscure mental phenomena which no man with scientific training would have paid any attention to a few years ago because he did not believe in such things. It was not good form to do so.

But the changes of fashion are so pervasive, so familiar, and, indeed, universal phenomena that we do not regard the changes which they bring, no matter how fantastic, as quite out of the usual and expected order. Gabriel Tarde, however, regards the "social contagion" represented in fashion (imitation) as the fundamental social phenomenon.[15]

The term social epidemic, which is, like fashion, a form of social contagion, has a different origin and a different connotation. J. F. C. Hecker, whose study of the Dancing Mania of the Middle Ages, published in 1832, was an incident of his investigation of the Black Death, was perhaps the first to give currency to the term.[16] Both the Black Death and the Dancing Mania assumed the form of epidemics and the latter, the Dancing Mania, was in his estimation the sequel of the former, the Black Death. It was perhaps this similarity in the manner in which they spread—the one by physical and the other by psychical infection—that led him to speak of the spread of a popular delusion in terms of a physical science. Furthermore, the hysteria was directly traceable, as he believed, to the prevailing conditions of the time, and this seemed to put the manifestations in the world of intelligible and controllable phenomena, where they could be investigated.

It is this notion, then, that unrest which manifests itself in social epidemics is an indication of pathological social condi-

---

[14]    W. E. H. Lecky, *History of the Rise and Influence of the Spirit of Rationalism in Europe* (New York, 1866), vol. I.
[15]    See Gabriel Tarde, *Laws of Imitation.*
[16]    J. F. C. Hecker, *Die Tanzwuth, eine Volkskrankheit im Mittelater.* (Berlin, 1832.) See Introduction of *The Black Death and the Dancing Mania.* Translated from the German by B. G. Babington. Cassell's National Library. (New York, 1888.)

tions, and the further, the more general, conception that unrest does not become social and hence contagious except when there are contributing causes in the environment—it is this that gives its special significance to the term and the facts. Unrest in the social organism with the social ferments that it induces is like fever in the individual organism, a highly important diagnostic symptom.

*b) The crowd.* Neither Le Bon nor any of the other writers upon the subject of mass psychology has succeeded in distinguishing clearly between the organized or "psychological" crowd, as Le Bon calls it, and other similar types of social groups. These distinctions, if they are to be made objectively, must be made on the basis of case studies. It is the purpose of the materials under the general heading of "The 'Animal' Crowd," not so much to furnish a definition, as to indicate the nature and sources of materials from which a definition can be formulated. It is apparent that the different animal groups behave in ways that are distinctive and characteristic, ways which are predetermined in the organism to an extent that is not true of human beings.

One other distinction may possibly be made between the so-called "animal" and the human crowd. The organized crowd is controlled by *a common purpose* and acts to achieve, no matter how vaguely it is defined, a common end. The herd, on the other hand, has apparently no common purpose. Every sheep in the flock, at least as the behavior of the flock is ordinarily interpreted, behaves like every other. Action in a stampede, for example, is collective but it is not concerted. It is very difficult to understand how there can be concerted action in the herd or the flock unless it is on an instinctive basis. The crowd, however, responds to collective representations. The crowd does not imitate or follow its leader as sheep do a bellwether. On the contrary, the crowd *carries out the suggestions of the leader*, and even though there be no division of labor each individual acts more or less in his own way to achieve a common end.

In the case of a panic or a stampede, however, where there is no common end, the crowd acts like a flock of sheep. But a stampede or a panic is not a crowd in Le Bon's sense. It is not a psychological unity, nor a "single being," subject to "the mental unity of crowds.[17] The panic is the crowd in dissolution. All effective methods for dispersing crowds involve some method of distracting attention, breaking up the tension, and dissolving the mob into its individual units.

*c) Types of mass movements.* The most elementary form of mass movement is a mass migration. Such a mass movement displays, in fact, many of the characteristics of the "animal" crowd. It is the "human" herd. The migration of a people, either as individuals or in organized groups, may be compared to the swarming of the hive. Peoples migrate in search of better living conditions, or merely in search of new experience. It is usually the younger generation, the more restless, active, and adaptable, who go out from the security of the old home to seek their fortunes in the new. Once settled on the new land, however, immigrants inevitably remember and idealize the home they have left. Their first disposition is to reproduce as far as possible in the new world the institutions and the social order of the old. Just as the spider spins his web out of his own body, so the immigrant tends to spin out of his experience and traditions, a social organization which reproduces, as far as circumstances will permit, the organization and the life of the ancestral community. In this way the older culture is transplanted and renews itself, under somewhat altered circumstances, in the new home. That explains, in part, at any rate, the fact that migration tends to follow the isotherms, since all the more fundamental cultural devices and experience are likely to be accommodations to geographical and climatic conditions.

In contrast with migrations are movements which are sometimes referred to as crusades, partly because of the religious fervor and fanaticism with which they are usually conducted and partly because they are an appeal to the masses of the people for direct action and depend for their success upon their ability to appeal to some universal human interest or to common experiences and interests that are keenly comprehended by the common man.

The Woman's Christian Temperance Crusade, referred to in

[17]    Le Bon, p. 26.

the materials, may be regarded, if we are permitted to compare great things with small, as an illustration of collective behavior not unlike the crusades of the eleventh and twelfth centuries.

Crusades are reformatory and religious. This was true at any rate of the early crusades, inspired by Peter the Hermit, whatever may have been the political purposes of the popes who encouraged them. It was the same motive that led the people of the Middle Ages to make pilgrimages which led them to join the crusades. At bottom it was an inner restlessness, that sought peace in great hardship and inspiring action, which moved the masses.

Somewhat the same widespread contagious restlessness is the source of most of our revolutions. It is not, however, hardships and actual distress that inspire revolutions but hopes and dreams, dreams which find expression in those myths and "vital lies," as Vernon Lee calls them,[18] which according to Sorel are the only means of moving the masses.

The distinction between crusades, like the Woman's Temperance Crusade, and revolutions, like the French Revolution, is that one is a radical attempt to correct a recognized evil and the other is a radical attempt to reform an existing social order.

[18]   Vernon Lee [pseud.], *Vital Lies* (London, 1912). Studies of some varieties of recent obscurantism.

**16**

# CHARACTERISTICS OF THE
# SECT

SOME FIFTY-SIX years ago Charles Nordhoff, who had been in his day a sailor, a newspaper correspondent, and a writer for the magazines, wrote a book entitled, *The Communistic Societies of the United States.* The volume which records the author's personal observations of the societies he visited is written with no apparent preconceptions or doctrinaire notions with regard to the peoples and the institutions it describes, but manifests, rather, the uncommitted and wide-ranging curiosity of a man who had observed the world broadly and who was interested in these somewhat quaint and curious manifestations of human nature and collective life mainly for their own sake.

In the early part of the nineteenth century, while America still regarded itself as a refuge for the persecuted and the oppressed of Europe, the United States became what Russia at an earlier date had been, a haven for queer sects, religious and political. At the time Nordhoff wrote, most of these societies had already passed through the first period of exaltation and had reached the point in their life-cycle where they had settled down to a struggle with the prosaic realities of a free and secular society. Either the experiments had failed and the societies were in the process of dissolution, or they had, at any rate, lost the sense of high enterprise with which they had begun. This probably seemed to Nordhoff an appropriate time to report upon the actual achieve-

Introduction to *The Pilgrims of Russian-Town,* by Pauline V. Young (Chicago: University of Chicago Press, 1932), pp. xi–xx.

ments of these Utopias and to learn from the peoples themselves how far their hopes and anticipations had been realized.

Most, if not all, of the communities Nordhoff visited were sectarian in character, although not all of them were what one would ordinarily describe as "religious." All were founded, at any rate, in order that the societies which supported them might have the security and the isolation necessary to enable them to establish and maintain a life-policy, or "way of life"—to use the language of religious discourse—that was more in accordance with their convictions as to what life should be than they had been able to achieve in the competitive, pecuniary, and individualistic society about them.

Anyone who has read Nordhoff's volume and has found himself interested in the questions which his observations raise, will find Dr. Young's more detailed and systematic study of a single sect interesting and instructive. *The Pilgrims of Russian-Town* may be regarded, in some sense, as a sequel to *The Communistic Societies of the United States.*

The Molokans are, to be sure, not precisely communistic, certainly not professedly so. On the other hand, they are not a competitive society, since life in the community is modeled on the familial pattern and all members regard themselves as brothers and sisters. The main point is, however, that the Molokans have "a way of life," and, as they believe, "a better way of life" than the people about them. This way of life prescribes for every member, in most of the more intimate and personal affairs of life, what each should or should not do. These prescriptions are, furthermore, relatively absolute and inalterable. They are not subject to revision by individual initiative or by any sort of referendum.

The ideal of such a society is unanimity in all things. It is of the nature of sects, not only religious but political, to be this way. It is this which distinguishes them from other forms and types of collective life.

This volume is concerned, first of all, with the Molokans themselves—not with the type of which they are so interesting an example. In substance it is a case history, an account at the same time of the varying fortunes of a primitive religious sect, transplanted from the isolation of a rural community in the Russian Caucasus to the seething and bustling activity of one of America's most rapidly changing cities.

In view of this fact, it seems appropriate to say something by way of introduction of a more general nature in regard to the character of sects, so far as that general character is known. As a matter of fact, very little that may be regarded as characteristic of sects is known. Until Sighele published his little volume on the subject, I do not suppose that sects were supposed to have any characteristics that were general and typical, although Le Bon classified them in his epoch-making volume on *The Crowd* as a type of homogeneous crowd.

Sighele, as his discussion of the subject indicates, was mainly concerned with political, rather than religious, sects and did not refer specifically to the differences between them. He did not, perhaps, regard these differences as particularly significant of fundamentals. A sect, as he described it, is a group of "individuals differing in birth, in education, in profession, in social status; but united and, indeed, voluntarily cemented by an extremely strong bond, a common faith and ideal."

Two things are peculiarly characteristic of sects as here defined: (1) the heterogeneity of its component elements and (2) the solidarity in which these divergent elements are bound together, once they are animated by a common ideal and a common faith. Sighele still thinks of a sect as in some sense a crowd, but "a crowd picked out and permanent. The crowd is a transitory sect which has not chosen its members. The sect is a chronic kind of crowd. The crowd is an acute kind of sect. The crowd is composed of a multitude of grains of sand without cohesion; the sect is a block of marble which resists every effort."[1]

It is a spontaneous and informal character of the sect—at least in its origins—that apparently leads writers in the field of collective psychology to identify it with crowds. The crowd is conceived

[1]    Translated from S. Sighele, *Psychologie des sects*, pp. 42–51. Quoted in R. E. Park and E. W. Burgess, *Introduction to the Science of Sociology*, p. 24.

as the most elementary form in which collective action takes place. Institutions have their origin, more often than is generally realized, in crowd movements.

Any faith, whether it be Islamism, Buddhism, Christianity, patriotism, socialism, anarchy, cannot but pass through this sectarian phase. It is the first step, the point where the human group, in leaving the twilight zone of the anonymous and mobile crowd, raises itself to a definition and to an integration which may then lead up to the highest and most perfect human group, the nation.[2]

Institutions grow up, as Hughes has pointed out, because social movements never quite accomplish all they undertake to do. There is always "unfinished business"—something still to be done which is eventually turned over to a committee or to a secretariat, and eventually to a corps of permanent functionaires. This, at any rate, is one way in which institutionalization takes place in a secular society.[3]

Le Bon says that all mass movements have a religious character. That would mean that all institutions which grow out of mass movements have a religious origin. Le Bon's definition of religion and of the nature of the religious sentiment needs, perhaps, some qualification. It is, however, interesting and suggestive. He says:

A person is not religious solely when he worships a divinity, but when he puts all the resources of his mind, the complete submission of his will, and the whole-souled ardour of fanaticism at the service of a cause or an individual who becomes the goal and guide of his thoughts and actions.[4]

With respect to the whole-souled devotion which individuals sometimes exhibit to a political faith which they profess, and with respect to the fanaticism with which they sometimes give them-

[2]    Sighele, *ibid.*
[3]    Everett Cherrington Hughes, *The Growth of an Institution: The Chicago Real Estate Board* (Chicago: published by the Society for Social Research by the University of Chicago Press, 1931).
[4]    Le Bon, *The Crowd* (London, 1897), p. 82.

selves to a secular cause, there seems to be no difference between the members of a religious and political sect.

In any case, the distinctions between religious and political sects, though they are not always easy to make in particular instances, are not as fundamental as they seem. The essential difference between the two seems to be that religious sects, in describing their program as "a way of life," almost always project their life-policies and the Utopias they hope to achieve beyond the limits of human experience and control. This makes life in this world merely a preparation for a world that is to come. Political sects, on the other hand, are determined that such heavens as they hope for will be achieved presently, on this earth, and, as far as possible, here and now. In the long run this distinction involves a profound difference. The political sects—i.e., the anarchists, socialists, communists, etc.—have a program of action—radical action. The religious groups—like the Quakers, Shakers, Holy Rollers, and others—are just as radical but, as far as political action is concerned, they are passive and resigned.

It is characteristic, at any rate, of those religious societies with which we are most familiar, that they, like Margaret Fuller, "accept the universe." They accept the universe and make no great effort to change existing political and social conditions. They are, however, profoundly conscious of their responsibilities for themselves. They are meticulous in conforming to the sectarian tabus and in maintaining the sectarian ritual. In short, they are concerned about their souls rather more than they are about politics. Political sects, on the other hand, are inclined to accept nothing and are prepared to assume—in a world where nothing is impossible—responsibility for all of us and everything.

The difference between the sects begins at the source, in the types of crowds in which they have their origins. The political crowd is the crowd that acts. It may be a mob. It may take the form of a strike. It is very frequently, at a time and place, an expression of what Bancroft calls "popular justice." This includes such manifestations as lynch law and such summary forms of justice as were administered by the vigilantes on the Pacific Coast. The political crowd is an extroverted group. The religious crowd, as typified in our religious revivals, is an expressive, sometimes an orgiastic crowd. Above all, it is introverted, turned inward, absorbed in its mystical experiences, and eventuates, finally, in what may be described as an introverted society—the religious sect.

The religious sect not only does not act in the sense that this is true of the political sect; rather it is disposed to withdraw from this world in order to preserve its faith in the next. Its energies find expression in ritual, sometimes in holy dances, as in the case of the Shakers and of the early Christians. What it seeks through these exercises and ecstasies is something approching a collective trance, in which each individual has a sense of personal complete-ness, of mystic solidarity, and of community with every other indi-vidual in the group. It is in this way that the faith of the faithful is continuously renewed and the integrity of the organization and of its heritage is preserved.

Religious sects have in common with political, at least in the early stages of their evolution, a certain intransigency and, as I have already said, a radicalism. They are both in origin conflict groups, and in both cases this conflict tends to assume a funda-mental and revolutionary character.

Every revolution, that is at all thoroughgoing—that is, in fact, anything more than a reform of existing abuses—seems likely to have its origin in a sect, ordinarily a political sect. It is in the ferment and fervor of sectarian life that new ideas and new ideals of life take form and make themselves articulate. The sect is radical, just because it seeks to formulate, not a new political program, but a new life-policy; and it is in the light of this new life-policy that every other more transient interest is viewed.

Political parties are characteristically accommodating and compromising, but the sect is intransigent and irreconcilable. Political parties formulate policies and seek to give consistency to their actions by making them conform to party doctrines. How-ever, political doctrines and the practical inferences to be drawn from them are at least discussible. Not so in the case of the sect. Its rules of conduct are absolute. A political society in which but one party is recognized and but one party rules inevitably assumes, in the long run, the form of a theocracy, in which the ruling party is merely the ruling sect.

It is in some such frame of reference and from such a point of view as here indicated that one needs to view the case of the Molokans if that case is to contribute to an understanding of sects in general and of the particular type of sect of which the Molokans are a specific instance.

Any attempt to look at religious sects or any other form and type of collective behavior in the formal, objective, and comparative way here suggested inevitably leaves out of consideration the intense, vivid, and often tumultuous subjective life of the sect— the internal tensions, conflicts, repressions, and sublimations incident to the effort of the sect to maintain the integrity of its collective life and to act consistently in accordance with the prescriptions of its self-enforced discipline.

It is quite probable that if one were permitted, in the first instance, to dig deep enough into the memories and experiences of individual sectarians, he would find somewhere in their histories the record of incidents and accidents which would account for much of their ritual, belief, and sectarian behavior generally that now seems quite unintelligible. Most of the behavior of individuals, and of societies, that strikes us as eccentric is undoubtedly subjectively, rather than objectively, conditioned. Tabus, ritual, and creeds have certainly arisen at different times in the efforts of societies to act, and, above all, to act consistently, that is to say, in accordance with some program, moral code, or rule of conduct. Most of these codes, rules of conduct, usages, and ceremonies which have now become traditional might be explained, if their whole early history was known, as an expression or organ of some normal or perverted social function.

In any case, the effort to act consistently in accordance with a program involves the necessity of maintaining tension at a high level and over a considerable period of time. The necessity of relaxation after such a period of tension, and of new integration and concentration after a period of relaxation, accounts for a good many of our holy days and a good many of our holidays.

There are days when we go into retreat, to gather ourselves together, to redefine our life-purposes and reform our life-programs. There are other days, however, when we relax and permit ourselves all sorts of extravagances and absurdities. Most every historical society will be found to have its periods of revivals and renewal of faith as well as its saturnalia and periods of license. This is just as likely to be true of religious sects as of other societies.

What seems to be peculiar about these introverted societies we classify as "sects" is that either individually or collectively they have at some time or times in their history been balked in their efforts to act. We may express it by saying that they have suffered some sort of psychic trauma, from the consequences of which they have never fully recovered.

In society, inhibitions take the form of socially sanctioned tabus. A mildly compulsive idea may take the form in the sect—or other form of society, for that matter—of ritual. Creeds seem frequently to have their origin in the conflicts of religious societies with other religious societies. Creeds are frequently rationalizations of practices and of rites which may have arisen historically out of conditions to which there are no references in the formulated creeds.

The author of this volume has not attempted anything like a Freudian interpretation of the practices of the Molokan sect. For the purposes of this volume no such interpretation is called for. What the story of *The Pilgrims of Russian-Town* offers the student of human nature, and particularly the student of religious sects, is, however, if not a psychoanalytic analysis, at least a sympathetic account of the customs, the attitudes, and, in general, of the *inner life* of the sect at a critical period of its history.

This study, which is the fruit of five years of patient investigation, was made possible in the first instance, not only because the author had the good fortune to possess a fluent reading and speaking knowledge of the Russian language, but also because she was able to penetrate into the inner sanctum of Molokanism. This has enabled her to perform, for the Russian sectarians themselves and for the American public, a task that neither could well perform for themselves. Through her interpretations of their experience, the

Molokans have been enabled to achieve a more adequate conception of themselves and of their perculiar problems in America than they would otherwise have done. This study has assisted in orienting the Colony to its social environment. It has served, at the same time, to interpret these interesting folk both to their neighbors and to the American public in a way to make their intercourse in the future less difficult and more fruitful than it has been in the past.

# 17

# MORALE AND THE NEWS

## I. *Propaganda*

SINCE WAR has invaded the realm of the spirit, morale has assumed a new importance in both war and peace. Total war is now an enterprise so colossal that belligerent nations find it necessary not only to mobilize all their resources, material and moral, but to make present peace little more than a preparation for future war. Under these conditions so-called psychic warfare, which can be carried on in the between states of actual belligerency, has assumed an importance and achieved a technical efficiency which, if it has not changed the essential nature of war, has profoundly altered the character of peace, making it much harder to bear.

The object of attack in psychic warfare is morale, and less that of the men in arms than of the civil population back of the lines. For the "strategy of terror" is directed rather more at noncombatants and against those who must wait and endure than against those who have some way of striking back.[1] Incidentally, this is one way in which total warfare, in so far as it is a war of nerves, fails to achieve its ends. It fails because it gives everyone something to do; something also which, since it involves participation, if only symbolically, in a great collective enterprise, is at once a source of inspiration and release. It tends thus finally to increase the solidarity and improve the morale not only of the civil population but of the army as well. It seems at any rate to have done this and more in England, where it has, apparently, created a national spirit and

---

Reprinted from *American Journal of Sociology*, 47 (November, 1941): 360–77.

[1]    Edmond Taylor, *Strategy of Terror* (Boston: Houghton Mifflin Co., 1940).

a national solidarity such as has not existed there since the date of the Spanish Armada.

The will to join with others in collective action is one of the elementary motives that move mankind. The consciousness and the excitement of participation in great events constitutes one of the most exhiliarating and satisfying of human experiences. In the reverberation which such participation invariably arouses in other minds the action of every individual participant acquires a new dignity and a new glory as well as an added moral support.

It is in and through these vast collective enterprises—wars, revolutions or social movements, like the labor movement—that new institutions come into existence and old ones are sometimes rejuvenated. No one seems to have understood this better than José Ortega y Gasset, the author of *Invertebrate Spain*. No one, at the time that this volume was published in 1937, had more reason to understand it, for these essays are devoted to an analysis of the processes by which the integration and the disintegration of the Spanish empire and the Spanish national unity came about. What he says about Spain is peculiarly pertinent today to conditions in the rest of the world and to the subject of this paper. The first of these essays is entitled "How To Make and Break a Nation."

"It is not yesterday, tradition, the past," he says, "which is the decisive, the determining force in a nation. Nations are made and go on living by having a program for the future." It is neither important nor necessary to unity and solidarity, he adds, "that the component parts of a society coincide in their ideas and their desires; the important, the essential thing is that each should know and to a certain extent incorporate into his own life the ideas and the desires of the others."[2]

There is probably no other social process, no form of interaction, by which the individual components of a society are so effectively or so completely integrated, if not fused, as they are by participation in some form of collective action. In fact, as it is conceived by some writers, society exists and is "in being," to

[2]    José Ortega y Gasset, *Invertebrate Spain* (New York: Norton, 1937), pp. 19–45.

use a nautical term, only when it is capable of concerted and consistent action.[3]

The so-called "we" group is typically the group that acts. Particularly is this true if one includes under this term every form of society in which ethnocentrism or group self-consciousness ordinarily manifests itself. It is true that a crowd or a mob does not think of itself as "we"; not at least until it comes in contact and in conflict with some other crowd or mob. In the latter case it presently assumes the character of a gang, gives itself a name, and perhaps assumes some vague sort of exclusive possession over the territory which is its peculiar habitat. This is characteristic of some of the lower animals—birds in particular. If I venture to mention this very lowly type of society in this connection, it is to emphasize the fact that not only armies and nations have need of some sort of morale but every other type of social group as well which must act effectively in order to survive in conflict with other societies.

The arts and devices by which a morale of a people can be raised and a national spirit revived if not created, as well as the methods by which national solidarity of an enemy people can be undermined and eventually destroyed, have been convincingly demonstrated in the recent history of Europe and are abundantly illustrated in the current news. There is, in the firsthand reports of observers and participants of the present conflict in Europe, material for a more realistic political science, such as has been historically attributed to Machiavelli but has been more recently and more systematically exemplified in the writings of the Italian sociologist, Pareto. For such a realistic political science, firsthand accounts of political events like William Shirer's *Berlin Diary* are a kind of source book. His account of one of the earlier Nuremberg "pep-meetings" of the Nazi party is a contribution not merely to history but to sociology. "Pep-meeting" is not the right word for the Nuremberg ceremonies. Something less secular and more suggestive of a religious revival would better describe it. Here is an

[3]     J. A. Thomson, "Animal Sociology," *Encyclopaedia Britannica* (14th ed.), I, 971.

excerpt from that diary under the date of Nuremberg, September 5, 1934.

I'm beginning to comprehend, I think, some of the reasons for Hitler's astounding success. Borrowing a chapter from the Roman church, he is restoring pageantry and colour and mysticism to the drab lives of twentieth-century Germans. This morning's opening meeting in the Luitpold Hall on the outskirts of Nuremberg was more than a gorgeous show; it also had something of the mysticism and religious fervour of an Easter or Christmas Mass in a great Gothic cathedral. The hall was a sea of brightly coloured flags. Even Hitler's arrival was made dramatic. The band stopped playing. There was a hush over the thirty thousand people packed in the hall. Then the band struck up the *Badenweiler March,* a very catchy tune, and used only, I'm told, when Hitler makes his big entries. Hitler appeared in the back of the auditorium, and followed by his aides, Göring, Goebbels, Hess, Himmler, and the others, he strode slowly down the long centre aisle while thirty thousand hands were raised in salute. It is a ritual, the old-timers say, which is always followed. Then an immense symphony orchestra played Beethoven's *Egmont Overture.* Great Klieg lights played on the stage, where Hitler sat surrounded by a hundred party officials and officers of the army and navy. Behind them the "blood flag," the one carried down the streets of Munich in the ill-fated Putsch. Behind this, four or five hundred S.A. standards. When the music was over, Rudolf Hess, Hitler's closest confidant, rose and slowly read the names of the Nazi "martyrs"—brown-shirts who had been killed in the struggle for power—a roll-call of the dead, and the thirty thousand seemed very moved.

In such an atmosphere no wonder, then, that every word dropped by Hitler seemed like an inspired Word from on high. Man's—or at least the German's—critical faculty is swept away at such moments, and every lie pronounced is accepted as high truth itself.

The arts and devices of spiritual warfare are many and various and more subtle no doubt than any analysis has thus far disclosed. But one of the weapons of psychic warfare, both of offense and of defense, is propaganda.[4] Harold Lasswell, who has made propaganda the subject of an extended investigation and who writes

4    See Kimball Young and R. D. Lawrence, *Bibliography on Censorship and Propaganda* ("University of Oregon Journalism Series," No. 1 [Eugene, Ore.: University of Oregon, 1928]).

more shrewdly about the subject than most others with whose writings I am familiar, has sought to distinguish between education and propaganda. His distinction is based on the difference between two elements or two aspects of culture which he describes as "technique" and "value." He says: "The inculcation of traditional value attitudes is generally called education, while the term propaganda is reserved for the spreading of the subversive, debatable or merely novel attitudes."[5]

The distinction is substantially that between news and propaganda or, better still, between news and editorial. The editorial page seeks to inculcate not merely attitudes but opinions; and editorial opinions may be either "subversive, debatable, or merely novel," and are, for most newspaper readers in the United States, since they do not read them, neither one nor the other.

The difference between news and editorial is one thing that every newspaperman knows, when he needs to, even if he is not always able to formulate a definition that makes the distinction clear for all cases. The essence, or intrinsic quality, of news is hard to come at, but news is not propaganda, and it is not editorial. In a general way one may say that news states the fact, editorial, the truth. The facts may call for reflection, for deliberation, and sometimes for more facts. The truth, however, has the character of finality. Having it, i.e., having the whole truth, one stops investigation, ceases to reflect, and is either silent like a plant or acts like a human being. Propaganda is likely to be a little more imperative than the ordinary editorial. Since it seeks action, it aims to dispel doubt and it pretends sometimes to the finality of truth even if it is only a half-truth or a downright lie.

News may be and often is, when the facts are such as to serve the purpose of the propagandist, the best kind of propaganda, but news and facts are always capable of more than one interpretation, and that would be fatal—reflection is always fatal—to propaganda.

It is because events are capable of more than one interpretation that we discuss them. It is out of these discussions that public opinion emerges. Discussions not only make public opinion, they

[5]   Harold D. Lasswell, "Propaganda," *Encyclopedia of the Social Sciences* (New York, 1934), XII, 522.

sometimes make war. But as far as my observation goes, they rarely ever make peace. That does not seem to be their function. When discussion is carried on in the orderly, academic fashion, which Socrates first introduced and philosophers have kept up ever since, it is called dialectic. The function of dialectic, if it also can be regarded as a social process, seems to be to test opinions. One tests opinions by finding out if they are consistent in their different expressions. The outcome of discussion is usually to lay bare the submerged hypotheses, not to say submerged complexes, on which divergent opinions are based. This sometimes leads to an agreement, but it sometimes reveals differences so profound and so charged with emotion and sentiment that further discussion appears unprofitable, if not impossible. When that happens to individuals there seems to be no way of carrying on the controversy except by fighting. When it happens to nations, as it has happened recently in the case of England and Germany, it leads to war.

From this point of view war, whether physical or psychic, presents itself as an instance of the dialectic process. When a discussion ceases to be academic, when it takes finally the form of an armed conflict, it does not cease, to use the language of a recent writer, to be a "battle of minds where ideas, ideologies, propaganda, and emotions clash in ordered ranks, disciplined like soldiers."[6] In this battle of minds and wills, in which the purpose of each belligerent is to maintain, and if possible enhance, its own morale and at the same time undermine and weaken that of the enemy, propaganda, whether it seeks merely to interpret events or to indoctrinate and defend the assumptions and the ideology in accordance with which events are interpreted, is a principal weapon of offense and defense.

## II. *Morale*

There seems to be some uncertainty as to just what morale is and where it is located. Is it in the individual or in the group or

[6]    Taylor, p. 1.

in both? Whether its locus is in the group or in the individual, there is no doubt of its importance. It counts much in battle but how much? No one knows precisely. It is one of those imponderables with which one must reckon but which one cannot weigh.

Morale in an army is a "will to fight"; in the civil population it is the ability to endure hardships at home and bad news from the front. This will to fight and to endure seems to be a compound of several other imponderable components: courage, confidence, and the Christian virtues faith, hope, and charity, provided by "charity" one means understanding—the kind of understanding one expects to find in small fighting units or in a well-organized family. It is the understanding that is the basis of *esprit de corps.* The charity which notoriously begins at home does not include the enemy, and charity in the abstract is not a qualification of a fighting man.

Morale, though it is dependent upon the qualities we call virtues, is not to be identified with morals or with mores. Morals are habits, and, like conscience, are rooted in tradition. When they encounter new conditions they are likely to be confused and involved in conflict, compromise, and casuistry. This is the case of the conscientious objector. Morale, on the other hand, is prospective; it rests on such discipline and solidarity as anywhere exists, but its outlook is forward. It is will, the tendencies of the organism to act, organized about a faith in the future rather than about an interest in or a pious concern for the past. Morale, whether in war or in peace, is will; the will to act and to persevere in a course of acting until the hopes which inspired it have been realized. While we ordinarily limit the term "morale" to action, we also apply it to situations in which activity is routine and does not seem to be either controlled or directed.

When President Roosevelt addressed the American people on March 12, 1933, most of the banks in the United States were closed, and most of the people in the United States were in a state of panic. In the course of his remarks he said: "After all, there is an element in the readjustment of our financial system more important than currency, more important than gold, and that is the confidence of the people." The effect of this address has been described as magical. Bronislaw Malinowski, whose studies among the Trobriand Islanders has made him an authority on the subject of magic, would say, I suspect, that the President's speech was magic. The effects brought about by words and symbols, as I understand him, are the essence of magic.[7] One of the functions of the magician in primitive society, he tells us, is to restore morale when fear in the presence of some unforeseen or unprecedented event, like the recent invasion from Mars as reported by Orson Welles, has shaken it.[8]

This seems to demonstrate again, what has often been demonstrated before, that words and symbols which create and maintain the morale of an army are equally necessary to maintain the morale of a civil society. It seems, therefore, that we must recognize morale as a factor in all our collective enterprises. It is a factor in the operation of the stock exchange, quite as much as it is in the activities of the Communist party.

It is interesting to note that upon the same date that President Roosevelt made his historic radio address to the people of the United States the press announced the triumph of the Nazi party, or perhaps one might better say of the Nazi sect, in the elections in Prussia. Commenting on this election, the *New York Times* correspondent said: "Through the election history of the National Socialists and the Nationalists, Germany for the first time since the days of the Old Empire, has been unified." Incidentally, some two hundred persons were killed in the course of the campaign, but the New York correspondent believed at this time that "violence was spent."[9]

Morale has not only its spiritual but its physical, more specifically its physiological, aspect. From the point of view of physiology, and perhaps of sociology, morale seems to be the ability of an individual or of a society to maintain tension over a period of time; to carry on an action or an enterprise to completion. The action, with interruptions, may continue, it seems, indefinitely

7    *Argonauts of the Western Pacific* (London, 1932).
8    See Hadley Cantril, *The Invasion from Mars* (Princeton, N.J.: Princeton University Press, 1940).
9    F. T. Birchell, *New York Times*, March 12, 1933.

as is the case of one who acts consistently to achieve a career or to carry out a project to which he has devoted a lifetime. What tension, in its most elementary phase, involves, one may gather from watching a cat waiting for a mouse, or a predatory animal stalking its prey.

Early in the present century sociological speculation and research were given a new orientation mainly by the writings of two men: Scipio Sighele in Italy and Gustav le Bon in France. Le Bon, whose little treatise on *The Crowd* (*Le Foule*) has done much to popularize the new point of view, discovered that, under certain specific conditions, a casual gathering of individuals, drawn together by no common purpose and having apparently no common interests, could, and if the necessary conditions were present would, in response to what he called "the mental unity of crowds" be suddenly, not to say miraculously, transformed, becoming, as he expressed it, no longer an agglomeration of individuals but "a single being."

All this, as he states it, sounds portentous. What he is describing, however, is a familiar experience. It is the fact that a crowd, when excited, becomes a mob and becomes, what a mere agglomeration could not, a very effective agency for carrying on very elementary forms of collective action—a lynching, for example. One may observe much the same phenomenon in a herd of cattle or a flock of sheep. Mary Austin, in her little volume entitled *The Flock*, has described the way in which, under the influence of some distress or sudden terror, a flock of sheep will sometimes mill about in an ever narrowing circle "until they perish by suffocation."[10]

What happens under such circumstances is what happens in a crowd when the attention of every individual is, by chance, focused upon some more than usually exciting object or incident. By a psychological process, not unlike the milling of the flock or herd, the interest and the excitement of every individual is intensified by the response each unconsciously makes to the manifest

[10]    Mary Austin, *The Flock*, quoted in Park and Burgess, *Introduction to the Science of Sociology*, 2d ed. (Chicago: University of Chicago Press, 1924), pp. 881–82.

interest of every other individual. The crowd assumes under these circumstances the character of a closed circuit, each individual responding to his own excitement as he sees it reflected in the attitudes and emotions of his neighbor. The effect of this circular reaction is to produce a steady reinstatement of the original stimulus as well as a corresponding increase in the suggestibility, excitement, and tension in every individual until the crowd is a collective unit, psychologically integrated and completely mobilized for whatever action is expected or by chance suggests itself. In any case the impending action, if it takes place at all, will be sudden, impetuous, and, unless manipulated by some outsider, quite unpremeditated and unplanned.

Since its actions are unpremeditated, unplanned, and without perspective, one would probably not, in the sense in which that term is usually used, speak of morale in the crowd. When, however, an action as projected and planned requires not merely readiness to act but the will to act consistently amid all the accidents, incidents, and changes of fortunes of a long campaign, morale acquires the meaning we give it when we speak, as we do so frequently nowadays, of morale in the army and morale in the civilian population. Nevertheless, in the broader sense in which that term is sometimes employed, as when one refers to the prevailing state of mind in France before and since the German conquest, one may, it seems, speak of the morale of any society or of any group in which some sort of concert is maintained by some sort of communication. In such a society there will be changes in tension in response to changes in life-conditions; changes in orientation in response to events as they occur. In human society there are always fashions. As fashions come in and go out, social tensions rise and fall, and society, which inevitably faces in the direction from which the news comes, alters its attitude to its world in response to these changes reported in the press.

One of the most pervasive forms in which tension and will manifest themselves in individuals and in society is in moods. Every occasion, be it a funeral or a wedding, has its characteristic atmosphere. Every gathering, even if it is no more than a crowd on the street, is dominated by some sentiment. One is more likely to notice this mood, perhaps, when one cannot share it. In that case, whether it be a sad or a happy occasion, one is repelled and inevitably seeks more congenial company.

I was constantly impressed, in reading William Shirer's *Berlin Diary*, with the fact that he seemed to note every change in the spiritual weather in a world that was for him every day a little less congenial than the day before. This moral atmosphere seems to be a very faithful index as well as a condition of morale in a civil community—even in a smaller community like that of the diplomatic circle in a foreign country. At any rate it has been a constant concern of Hitler and of his propaganda bureau to preserve in Germany an atmosphere in the civilian population that would support the morale of the army in the field and the program of the government at home. It is this that gives significance to the Nuremberg ceremonies that Shirer describes. It is obviously the purpose of all the ceremony and the ritual associated with the Nazi movement to create an atmosphere, a tension, and an expectancy which, in focusing attention upon the things hoped for, will effectively inhibit any consideration that runs counter to those hopes.

To maintain this atmosphere and protect the German population from the "poison," as Goebbels called it, of foreign propaganda has been the purpose of the censorship. To interpret and mediate the effect of such reports of events as reached them are the functions of the propaganda bureau.

It is obvious that the impulse, the will to act, expresses itself in characteristically different ways in different types of societies; different, that is to say, in the crowd, in the gang, in the political party, and in the sect. In fact, it may express itself in all these different ways in the successive phases of the evolution of a collective action. This collective impulse assumes in the course of its evolution most of the characteristics of a mind—that is, of a collective mind. Thus, Mary Austin speaks of the "flock mind," Le Bon describes the idiosyncracies of the "crowd mind." We are familiar with the phrase "public mind." The question as to where this so-called mind or will is located, whether it is a phase or an aspect, like class consciousness, of the individual consciousness or has some sort of independent existence, seems to lose most of its importance if we mean by "collective mind" no more than the unity and intimate interdependence which makes it possible for individuals to act concertedly and consistently. The capacity to act collectively is apparently created by that interpenetration of mind involved in communication.

In the gang or other intimate group, where association is based on familiar and personal relation, morale takes the form of *esprit de corps*. In a political party which is a conflict or discussion group it is represented by a policy, supported by a formal principle of some sort. In a religious sect morale is supported by the authority of a creed or by dogmas which cannot be questioned. It seems that the Nazi party, in the course of its history, has passed through all the phases represented by the four types of society I have mentioned. Its first appearance was in a *Putsch* or coup d'état that was carried out by a group almost as little organized as a mob. From that point it fought its way up in a kind of gang warfare with the communists. It became later a political party and as such gained a new status when its supporters gained representation in the Reichstag. Meanwhile it had taken on, at least in the case of its leaders, the character of a more or less fanatical political, if not religious, sect. It now includes among its spiritual possessions not only a ritual and a creed but, in the volume *Mein Kampf*, a Bible. Finally, it has in Hitler its prophet, if not its God. As a political sect it has attempted to suppress every form of dissent with all the fervor and fanatical vigor of a newborn religion. Under its direction the German people are now apparently engaged in a holy war to reorganize the social life of the planet in all its fundamental aspects —economic, political, and religious.

If this statement is a little too summary to do justice to the historical facts, it at least suggests what morale can be under a totalitarian government such as exists today in Germany and what it cannot be in a more secular society like our own.

## III. *News*

The distinction between activity and action, as I conceive it, is that action has perspective, has a beginning and an end, and, in the process of transition from the first impulse in which it has its origin to its final consumation in a final overt act, it is likely to encounter events that sometimes make that consummation precarious. Action, in short, is activity that is controlled and directed. That is the reason, when and if action is prolonged and difficult, it requires, to insure success, "will" in the individual and, in the group, morale. These actions and their perspectives give the dimensions of the world in which, one might say, life actually goes on, as distinguished from the academic world where not life but thought, a preparation for action, goes on.

Each and all of us live in a world of which we are the center, and the dimensions of this world are defined by the direction and the distances from which the news comes to us. For news is not something new merely, it is something important; and it comes to us with an urgency that requires action, even if no more than a change of attitude or the reaffirmation of an opinion.

All this is of no importance except in so far as it suggests the relativity of worlds in which men are actively alive and for whose orderly existence they are in some way personally responsible. What comes to us in the way of a record of events from elsewhere, that is, outside of or on the outer limits of our world, is mainly myth, legend, or literature; something that is perhaps intrinsically interesting but not so immediately important that something needs to be done about it. It is because the world in which we live is like this that we discover it visibly expanding about us as the perspective of our practical interests and actions lengthen.

How profoundly these perspectives have been changed during the process of the present war! Suddenly, after the fall of France, it seemed as if the planet had grown smaller and our world larger. The isolationists among us are those who for various reasons not wholly articulate, I suspect, are unwilling or unable to accept this change. It is in a realm defined by the circulation of news rather than by the world with which we are in immediate contact that all our great collective enterprises—war, revolution, and national government—are carried on.

The task of organizing, of energizing, and, above all, of animating with a common will and a common purpose vast armies and whole peoples is an incredibly complicated but, with modern means of communication, not impossible task. At any rate, the German government, with the assistance of the censorship and the propaganda bureau, seems, as far as is humanly possible, to have succeeded, from time to time, in imbuing its armies and, to a less extent, its civil population with something of the unanimity of Le Bon's psychological crowd. This has helped to maintain the morale of the nation in the successive crises through which it has passed.

The German army, one hears, has been greatly democratized in the course of its rejuvenation. There has come into existence a comradeship between the officers and men that did not exist in the Prussian army before the National-Socialist revolution. This has created in the army, and particularly in the navy, an *esprit de corps* that did not exist during the first World War.

German political technicians, with the aid of German scholars in the several social sciences, history, anthropology, and the new German science, *Geopolitik,* have developed, as their contribution to the national morale, a political philosophy which is designed to justify the German people's claim to the position of the dominant race in Europe. They have at the same time formulated a political program which promises, if successful, to make this claim good. Since Europe has held, perhaps still holds, a dominant position in the modern world, German domination of Europe would imply domination of the world.

Finally, Herr Hitler and his associates seem to have inspired the army, if not the people, with an invincible faith in their mission and destiny—a faith such as would ordinarily exist only in a religious sect. Hitler and his junto have sought to support that faith by ritual, by myth, and, above all, by ceremonies that revive from time to time the atmosphere and the mood of exaltation in which it was originally conceived. This faith in their mission and destiny has been transmitted to Germans abroad, living in what one might describe as the Diaspora of this latest of the "Chosen People." From that source other peoples, who, according to Nazi doctrines, can never hope to be identified with the master-race have nevertheless been infected by its doctrine.

Morale and discipline, as Hermann Rauschning, the author of *Revolution of Nihilism,* says, is now a religion in Germany and has achieved in that nation an unprecedented high level of intensity and effectiveness. It has nevertheless been created and sustained by essentially the same means as social solidarity and discipline have been created and maintained wherever men have been associated to form societies and to act collectively.

A nation includes within its wide embrace all ordinary forms of association with which we are familiar, i.e., local, familial, economic, political, religious, and racial. It is the problem of national morale to co-ordinate these groups so that they co-operate rather than clash. In the language of the Nazi party's political technicians, it is the problem of *Gleichschaltung.* It has been achieved by co-ordinating, subordinating and eventually fusing every local and minor loyalty into a totalitarian loyalty to the national state. Where that has not been actually achieved, as in the case of the Lutherans and Catholics, it has nevertheless been attempted. There is already considerable literature, psychological and pedagogical, which shows what was attempted and what has been achieved in the army, the schools, and the press.[11]

The relation of news to morale is not so obvious as is that of the other page of the newspaper, the editorial. News comes to us and to the newspaper we read from every part of the world in which we and its other readers are interested. It comes ordinarily, provided it is not written up so that our interest in it is symbolic and literary rather than factual, in the form of disconnected items. Newspapermen have discovered that, other things being equal, news items are read in inverse ratio to their length. The national weekly newspapers like *Time* and *Newsweek* have discovered that they can give a new news interest to these items (1) by classifying them and (2) by digging up so-called background materials which enable us to see them in their relation to other events widely dispersed in time and space. To put a news item in a setting of historical or otherwise related facts gives it a character which is sometimes historical and sometimes sociological. Such an item becomes history in so

---

[11]    See *German Psychological Warfare: Survey and Bibliography* (New York: Committee for National Morale, 1940).

far as it finds a place in the historical sequence. It becomes sociological in so far as, when classified, it throws light upon social process irrespective of the place or time in which the process takes
place.

As here described, news has no influence upon political action
or morale. Its tendency is to disperse and distract attention and
thus decrease rather than increase tension. The ordinary function
of news is to keep individuals and societies oriented and in touch
with their world and with reality by minor adjustments. It is not
its function ordinarily to initiate secular social movements which,
when they move too rapidly, bring about catastrophic consequences. On the other hand, when some important or disturbing
event occurs that "makes the front page" and captures the headlines, it may also capture and hold attention for days and weeks,
like the story of the abduction of the Lindbergh baby and the
subsequent trial and execution of the alleged abductor.

The story of such an event or series of events is not an item, it
is a "story"—a continued story, in fact; one that may grow more
absorbing as each day and each issue of the press brings forth some
new development. In this way it may become so absorbing as to
dwarf interest in every other lesser incident in local or current
history. As a story it becomes more enthralling just because it is
published in instalments which give opportunity for readers to
reflect, speculate, or brood over the significance of each successive instalment. Under the circumstances readers of the news interpret these incidents and all the details in terms of memories of
their own experiences and of similar tragic episodes with which
they are familiar. In this way the news ceases to be mere news and
acquires the significance of literature, but of realistic literature
like the "true stories" of the popular magazines and of the earlier
ballads that preceded them in the history of the newspaper.[12]
What fixes and holds the interest of the reader tends to disorient
him; tends to possess him.

It is the same with wars in which we seem to see history in the
making; wars in which the fate of nations and of civilization is in-

12    Helen Hughes, *The Human Interest Story* (Chicago: University of
Chicago Press, 1940).

volved. It is when attention is focused on these events which are not items but chapters from the current history that we who are spectators eventually get sympathetically involved. Under these circumstances it is inevitable that we should, in accordance with the differences of our personal experiences and our personal prejudices, interpret events and history differently. It is inevitable that we should take sides, since discussion tends to emphasize and bring out differences as well as obscure, temporarily at least, more fundamental points of view upon which we are united. This is unfortunate, perhaps, for national morale requires above everything else that in a crisis we should act as a nation and be united as a people.

Public opinion is therefore not a good index of morale because, being the fruit of discussion, it intensifies differences. Public opinion is on the surface of things and does not reflect the attitudes and points of view on which the community is united. The very existence of public opinion is itself evidence that we are not at the moment as one in regard to what as a nation or a people we should do. However, as things get discussed and drop out of discussion, the direction which public opinion takes in the course of time indicates the direction in which collective will, in the process of formation, is taking. This is what the Gallup polls show.

Public discussion of public policy during periods of crisis, when discussion tends to become embittered, invariably brings to the surface not only divergent points of view but the memories and original experiences upon which these interpretations of events are based. One has but to read the exasperated and often outrageous views expressed in letters to the editor to recognize that these letters are the reflections of personal frustrations and of deep emotional experiences whose sources are often so obscure that it would require the skill of a psychoanalyst to discover them. But in so far as freedom of discussion gets to the source of this emotional violence and so brings it into the open, discussion to that extent contributes something indirectly to the national morale. These controversial letters serve as a purge to the minds of those who wrote them and give comfort to those who would like to have written them if they could.

In a recent copy of the *Detroit Free Press* I ran across a very clever and not ill-natured indictment of Harold Ickes. He was described as the kind of a man who writes exasperating and exasperated letters to the editor. Well, probably Harold Ickes is that kind of a man, but he has been a great comfort to me and I am sure to others. He exaggerates, to be sure, as an exasperated man will; but he says things that someone should say, and I am certain through my own experience that he is improving the morale of the country. I recall what he has said about Lindbergh, whom I admire. I wish I could hear him on Senator Gerald Nye. I suppose he has at some time landed on the senator from North Dakota, but if so I have missed it.

Getting this stuff off our chest is, as I have suggested, good for the country. It improves morale, and, besides that, one can be certain that no one who comes out with the bitterness that is in him is going to be a fifth columnist. These letters to the press are not public opinion, however. They are merely personal opinions. If they could be accompanied by a confession "sudden, complete, and bitter" which would reveal the context in which they were formed, they would throw a great light on the sources of discontent which make it difficult in a country like ours, composed of people who have come to us from the ends of the earth, to unite wholeheartedly, except in a great national emergency, on an all-out totalitarian policy, such as a great national emergency requires that we should.

I said at the outset of this paper that war tended to assume the character of a dialectic process in which ideas rather than force play the leading role. As events make the issues as originally conceived and stated obsolete, belligerents find it necessary from time to time to redefine their aims and discover more fundamental and more resonable grounds to justify the course they have chosen to pursue. In the long run, particularly if conflict is prolonged, it becomes necessary not merely to satisfy the questions which reflection has raised at home but to justify the aims and conduct of the war to the public abroad which may not be wholly committed to either side. In this case war ceases to have the character of an international *coup d'état*, aiming by means of a *Blitzkrieg* to present the world with a *fait accompli,* and becomes more and more a war of ideas and ideologies. Such wars inevitably come to have the character of revolutions. They end in that case by bringing about not merely changes in material possessions but in institutions and the fundamental conceptions of life. It is, in fact, why in so far as they do this that war can be said to function in the historical process.

Under these circumstances, morale supported by a principle of reason ceases to be a matter of either hope or fear and becomes a morale force. In the long run it is these morale forces that determine the issues for which wars are carried on.

# The Sociological Writings of Robert E. Park

*The Man Farthest Down: A Record of Observation and Study in Europe,* by Booker T. Washington with the collaboration of Robert E. Park, Garden City: Doubleday, Page & Co., 1918.

"Racial Assimilation in Secondary Groups with Particular Reference to the Negro," *Publication of the American Sociological Society,* 8 (1913): 66–83; also *American Journal of Sociology,* 19 (March, 1914): 606–23. *Race and Culture,* pp. 204–20.

"The City: Suggestions for the Investigation of Human Behavior in the City Environment," *American Journal of Sociology,* 20 (March, 1915): 577–612; revised in *The City,* by Park *et al.* (1925), pp. 1–46. *Human Communities,* pp. 13–51.

Introduction to *The Japanese Invasion* by Jesse F. Steiner, Chicago: A. C. McClurg & Co., 1917, pp. vii–xvii. *Race and Culture,* pp. 223–29.

"Methods of Forming Public Opinion Applicable to Social Welfare Publicity," *Proceedings of the National Conference of Social Work,* 1918, pp. 615–22. *Society,* pp. 143–51.

"Education in Its Relation to the Conflict and Fusion of Cultures: With Special Reference to the Problems of the Immigrant, the Negro, and Missions," *Publications of the American Sociological Society,* 13 (1918): 38–63. *Race and Culture,* pp. 261–83.

---

Abbreviated reference to the appropriate volume of *Collected Papers* appears after each reprinted selection. Full citations are given at the end of the bibliography.

"Foreign Language Press and Social Progress," *Proceedings of the National Conference of Social Work*, Forty-seventh annual session, April 14–20, 1920, pp. 493–500. *Society*, pp. 165–75.

*Introduction to the Science of Sociology*, by Robert E. Park and Ernest W. Burgess. Chicago: University of Chicago Press, 1921. 2d ed. 1924.

"Sociology and the Social Sciences," *American Journal of Sociology*, 26 (January, 1921): 401–24; 27 (July, 1921): 1–21; 27 (September, 1921): 169–83; also as chapter 1 in *Introduction to the Science of Sociology. Society*, pp. 187–242.

*The Immigrant Press and Its Control*. New York: Harper, 1922.

"Negro Race Consciousness as Reflected in Race Literature," *American Review*, 1 (September, 1923): 505–17. *Race and Culture*, pp. 284–300.

"The Mind of the Rover," *World Tomorrow*, 6 (September, 1923): 269–70; retitled "The Mind of the Hobo: Reflections upon the Relation between Mentality and Locomotion," in *The City* (1925), pp. 156–60. *Human Communities*, pp. 91–95.

"The Natural History of the Newspaper," *American Journal of Sociology*, 29 (November, 1923): 273–89; also in *The City* (1925), pp. 80–98. *Society*, pp. 89–104.

"A Race Relations Survey: Suggestions for a Study of the Oriental Population of the Pacific Coast," *Journal of Applied Sociology*, 8 (March, 1924): 195–205. *Race and Culture*, pp. 158–65.

"The Concept of Social Distance: As Applied to the Study of Racial Attitudes and Racial Relations," *Journal of Applied Sociology*, 8 (July, 1924): 339–44. *Race and Culture*, pp. 256–60.

"Experience and Race Relations: Opinion, Attitudes, and Experience as Types of Human Behavior," *Journal of Applied Sociology*, 9 (September, 1924): 18–24. *Race and Culture*, pp. 152–57.

"The Concept of Position in Sociology," *Publications of the American Sociological Society*, 20 (1925): 1–14; retitled "The Urban Community as a Spatial Pattern and a Moral Order," in *The Urban Community*, ed. Ernest W. Burgess. Chicago: University of Chicago Press, 1926, pp. 3–18. *Human Communities*, pp. 165–77.

*The City*, by Robert E. Park, Ernest W. Burgess, and Roderick D. McKenzie, with a bibliography by Louis Wirth. Chicago: University of Chicago Press, 1925; reissued 1966.

"Community Organization and Juvenile Delinquency," in *The City* (1925), pp. 99–112. *Human Communities*, pp. 52–63.

"Magic, Mentality, and City Life," in *The City* (1925), pp. 123–41. *Human Communities*, pp. 102–17.

"Culture and Cultural Trends," *Publications of the American Sociological Society*, 19 (1925): 24–36. *Race and Culture*, pp. 24–35.

"Immigrant Community and Immigrant Press,' *American Review*, 3 (March, 1925): 143–52. *Society*, pp. 152–64.

"Community Organization and the Romantic Temper," *Social Forces*, 3 (May, 1925): 673–77; also in *The City* (1925), pp. 113–22. *Human Communities*, pp. 64–72.

"Behind our Masks," *Survey Graphic*, May 1, 1926, pp. 135–39. *Race and Culture*, pp. 244–55.

"Our Racial Frontier on the Pacific," *Survey Graphic*, May 1, 1926, pp. 192–96. *Race and Culture*, pp. 138–151.

Introduction to *The Natural History of Revolution* by Lyford P. Edwards. Chicago: University of Chicago Press, 1927, pp. ix–xiii. *Society*, pp. 34–37.

Editor's Preface to *The Gang: A Study of 1,313 Gangs in Chicago* by Frederick M. Thrasher. Chicago: University of Chicago Press, 1927, pp. ix–xii. *Human Communities*, pp. 96–98.

"Human Nature and Collective Behavior," *American Journal of Sociology*, 32 (March, 1927): 733–41. *Society*, pp. 13–21.

"Topical Summaries of Current Literature: The American Newspaper," *American Journal of Sociology*, 32 (March, 1927): 806–13. *Society*, pp. 176–84.

Introduction to *The Strike* by Ernest T. Hiller. Chicago: University of Chicago Press, 1928, pp. vii–x. *Society*, pp. 30–33.

Foreward to *The Ghetto* by Louis Wirth. Chicago: University of Chicago Press, 1928, pp. ix–xi. *Human Communities*, pp. 99–101.

"Human Migration and the Marginal Man," *American Journal of Sociology*, 33 (May, 1928): 881–93. *Race and Culture*, pp. 345–56.

"The Bases of Race Prejudice," *Annals of the American Academy of Political and Social Science*, 140 (November, 1928): 11–20. *Race and Culture*, pp. 230–43.

"Sociology," in *Research in the Social Sciences*, ed. Wilson Gee. New York: Macmillan, 1929, pp. 3–49. *Human Commuunities*, pp. 178–209.

"The City as a Social Laboratory," in *Chicago: An Experiment in Social Science Research*, ed. T. V. Smith and Leonard D. White. Chicago:

University of Chicago Press, 1929, pp. 1–19. *Human Communities*, pp. 73–87.

Introduction to *The Gold Coast and the Slum* by Harvey W. Zorbaugh. Chicago: University of Chicago Press, 1929, pp. vii–x. *Human Communities*, pp. 88–90.

"Urbanization as Measured by Newspaper Circulation,' *American Journal of Sociology*, 35 (July, 1929) : 60–79.

"Murder and the Case Study Method," *American Journal of Sociology*, 36 (November, 1930) : 447–54.

"The Sociological Methods of William Graham Sumner, and of William I. Thomas and Florian Znaniecki," in *Methods in Social Science: A Case Book*, ed. Stewart A. Rice. Chicago: University of Chicago Press, 1931, pp. 154–75. *Society*, pp. 243–66.

"Human Nature, Attitudes, and the Mores," in *Social Attitudes*, ed. Kimball Young. New York: Henry Holt, 1931, pp. 17–45. *Society*, pp. 267–92.

"Mentality of Racial Hybrids," *American Journal of Sociology*, 36 (January, 1931) : 534–51. *Race and Culture*, pp. 377–92.

"Personality and Cultural Conflict," *Publications of the American Sociological Society*, 25 (May, 1931) : 95–110. *Race and Culture*, pp. 357–71.

Introduction to *The Pilgrims of Russian-Town*, by Pauline V. Young. Chicago: University of Chicago Press, 1932, pp. xi–xx. *Society*, pp. 22–29.

"Newspaper Circulation and Metropolitan Regions," by Robert E. Park and Charles Newcomb, in *The Metropolitan Community*, ed. Roderick D. McKenzie. New York: McGraw-Hill, 1933, pp. 98–110. *Human Communities*, pp. 210–22.

"Dominance: The Concept, Its Origin and Natural History," in *Readings in Human Ecology*, ed. Roderick D. McKenzie. Ann Arbor, Mich.: George Wahr, 1934, pp. 381–85. *Human Communities*, pp. 159–64.

"Race Relations and Certain Frontiers," *Race and Culture Contacts*, ed. Edwin B. Reuter. New York: McGraw-Hill, 1934, pp. 57–85. *Race and Culture*, pp. 117–37.

Introduction to *Shadow of the Plantation* by Charles S. Johnson. Chicago: University of Chicago Press, 1934, pp. xi–xxiv; reissued 1966. *Race and Culture*, pp. 66–78.

"Industrial Fatigue and Group Morale," *American Journal of Sociology*, 40 (November, 1934) : 349–56. *Society*, pp. 293–300.

Introduction to *Negro Politicians* by Harold F. Gosnell. Chicago: University of Chicago Press, 1935, pp. xiii–xxv. *Race and Culture*, pp. 166–76.

"Social Planning and Human Nature," *Publications of the American Sociological Society*, 29 (August, 1935): 19–28. *Society*, pp. 38–49.

"The City and Civilization," *Syllabus and Selected Readings*, Social Science II. University of Chicago Press, 1936, pp. 204–20. *Human Communities*, pp. 128–41.

"Succession: An Ecological Concept," *American Sociological Review*, 1 (April, 1936): 171–79. *Human Communities*, pp. 223–32.

"Human Ecology," *American Journal of Sociology*, 42 (July, 1936): 1–15. *Human Communities*, pp. 145–58.

Introduction to *Interracial Marriage in Hawaii* by Romanzo Adams. New York: Macmillan, 1937, pp. vii–xiv. *Race and Culture*, pp. 189–95.

Introduction to *The Etiquette of Race Relations in the South* by Bertram W. Doyle. Chicago: University of Chicago Press, 1937, pp. xi–xxiv. *Race and Culture*, pp. 177–88.

Introduction to *The Marginal Man* by Everett V. Stonequist. New York: Charles Scribner's Sons, 1937, pp. xiii–xviii. *Race and Culture*, pp. 372–76.

"A Memorandum on Rote Learning," *American Journal of Sociology*, 43 (July, 1937): 23–36. *Race and Culture*, pp. 53–65.

Introduction to *An Island Community* by Andrew W. Lind. Chicago: University of Chicago Press, 1938, pp. ix–xvi. *Human Communities*, pp. 233–39.

"Reflections on Communication and Culture," *American Journal of Sociology*, 44 (September, 1938): 187–205. *Race and Culture*, pp. 36–52.

*An Outline of the Principles of Sociology*, ed. Robert E. Park. New York: Barnes & Noble, Inc., 1939.

"The Nature of Race Relations," in *Race Relations and the Race Problem*, ed. Edgar T. Thompson, Durham, N.C.: Duke University Press, 1939, pp. 3–45. *Race and Culture*, pp. 81–116.

"Symbiosis and Socialization: A Frame of Reference for the Study of Society," *American Journal of Sociology*, 45 (July, 1939): 1–25. *Human Communities*, pp. 240–62.

Introduction to *News and the Human Interest Story* by Helen MacGill Hughes. Chicago: University of Chicago Press, 1940, pp. xi–xxiii. *Society*, pp. 105–14.

"News as a Form of Knowledge: A Chapter in the Sociology of Knowledge," *American Journal of Sociology*, 45 (March, 1940): 669–86. *Society*, pp. 71–88.

"Physics and Society," *Canadian Journal of Economics and Political Science*, 6 (May, 1940): 135–52; also in *Essays in Sociology*, ed. Clyde W. M. Hart. Toronto: University of Toronto Press, 1940, pp. 1–18. *Society*, pp. 301–21.

"The Social Function of War: Observations and Notes," *American Journal of Sociology*, 46 (January, 1941): 551–70. *Society*, pp. 50–68.

"News and the Power of the Press," *American Journal of Sociology*, 47 (July, 1941): 1–11. *Society*, pp. 115–25.

"Morale and the News," *American Journal of Sociology*, 47 (November, 1941): 360–77. *Society*, pp. 126–42.

"Modern Society," *Biological Symposia*, 8 (1942): 217–40. *Society*, pp. 322–41.

Introduction to *Negroes in Brazil* by Donald Pierson. Chicago: University of Chicago Press, 1942, pp. xi–xxi. *Race and Culture*, pp. 196–203.

"Racial Ideologies," in *American Society in Wartime*, ed. William F. Ogburn. Chicago: University of Chicago Press, 1943, pp. 165–84. *Race and Culture*, pp. 301–15.

"Education and the Cultural Crisis," *American Journal of Sociology*, 48 (May, 1943): 728–36. *Race and Culture*, pp. 316–30.

"Missions and the Modern World," *American Journal of Sociology*, 50 (November, 1944): 177–83. *Race and Culture*, pp. 331–41.

*The Collected Papers of Robert Ezra Park*, ed. Everett C. Hughes, Charles S. Johnson, Jitsuichi Masuoka, Robert Redfield, and Louis Wirth. 3 vols. Glencoe, Ill.: Free Press, 1950–55. Vol. I, *Race and Culture*, 1950; Vol. II, *Human Communities: The City and Human Ecology*, 1952; Vol. III, *Society: Collective Behavior, News and Opinion, Sociology and Modern Society*, 1955.